FOOTBINDING AS FASHION

FOOTBINDING
AS FASHION

ETHNICITY, LABOR, AND STATUS
IN TRADITIONAL CHINA

JOHN ROBERT
SHEPHERD

UNIVERSITY OF WASHINGTON PRESS
Seattle

UNIVERSITY OF WASHINGTON PRESS
www.washington.edu/uwpress

LIBRARY OF CONGRESS CATALOGING-IN-PUBLICATION DATA
Names: Shepherd, John Robert author.
Title: Footbinding as fashion : ethnicity, labor, and status in traditional China / John Robert
     Shepherd.
Description: First edition. | Seattle, Washington : University of Washington Press, [2018] |
     Includes bibliographical references and index. |
Identifiers: LCCN 2018012491 (print) | LCCN 2018027211 (ebook) | ISBN 9780295744421 (ebook)
     | ISBN 9780295744414 (hardcover : acid free paper) | ISBN 9780295744407 (paperback :
     acid free paper)
Subjects: LCSH: Footbinding—China—History. | Women—Employment—China. | Women—
     China—Social conditions.
Classification: LCC GT498.F66 (ebook) | LCC GT498.F66 S45 2018 (print) | DDC 391.4/
     130951—dc23
LC record available at https://lccn.loc.gov/2018012491

COVER ILLUSTRATION: *Women and Children*, courtesy of Sidney D. Gamble Photographs,
Archive of Documentary Arts, David M. Rubenstein Rare Book and Manuscript Library,
Duke University.

FOR THREE MENTORS:
Arthur P. Wolf, 1932–2015
Ramon H. Myers, 1929–2015
G. William Skinner, 1925–2008

When Adam delved and Eve span, who was then the gentleman?

—JOHN BALL, 1381

Contents

Illustrations

Acknowledgments

Over the many years during which the material for this book has taken shape I have incurred many scholarly debts, which I am pleased to acknowledge here.

My research in the historical demography of Taiwan has benefited from my participation in the Population and Society in Taiwan and the Netherlands research group, organized by the late Arthur P. Wolf, Theo Engelen, and Chuang Ying-chang, in conjunction with the Program for Historical Demography of the Research Center for Humanities and Social Sciences, Academia Sinica, Taipei. At the Program for Historical Demography, Yang Wen-shan, Chen Shu-juo, Huang Yu-lin, and others have provided much valuable assistance, as has Fan I-chun at the Center for Geographic Information Science, Academia Sinica. I have benefited in many ways from my association with colleagues at Academia Sinica, particularly in the Institute of Taiwan History and the Institute of Ethnology, who have generously shared their deep knowledge of Taiwan and its peoples.

The work from which this project sprang received generous support from many sources. A Fulbright-Hays Faculty Research Abroad Fellowship and a Chiang Ching-kuo Foundation for International Scholarly Exchange Scholar Grant made possible a year in Taiwan in 2006–7 at the Program for Historical Demography, Academia Sinica. A University of Virginia sesquicentennial research leave and a grant from the School of Historical Studies made possible a year at the Institute for Advanced Study, Princeton, New Jersey, in 2003–4. A Mellon Postdoctoral Fellowship in Anthropological Demography, spent in the Department of Demography, University of California, Berkeley, in 1997–98, provided invaluable training. Grants from the Weedon Fund of the University of Virginia's East Asia Center are gratefully acknowledged.

For opportunities to present my ongoing research on footbinding, I thank the Hong Kong Institute for the Humanities and Social Sciences at the

University of Hong Kong, 2011; the Department of Anthropology and the East Asia Center at the University of Virginia, 2012; and the Program for Historical Demography and the Institute for Taiwan History, Academia Sinica, 2013.

I thank my colleagues in the East Asia Center and the Department of Anthropology at the University of Virginia for their help and encouragement. I am especially grateful to the Library Express On-Grounds service and the Scholars' Lab of Alderman Library for their assistance. I owe special thanks to Calvin Hsu, formerly East Asia librarian, for help in locating documents, and to Chris Gist for preparing maps.

I would like to express my gratitude to the several colleagues who offered criticism and encouragement in response to earlier drafts of the chapter on footbinding during the Qing conquest, including Sue Naquin, Matt Sommer, Nicola Di Cosmo, Lynn Struve, Pamela Crossley, anonymous reviewers, Hu Minghui, and the editors of *Frontiers of History in China*.

Louise Edwards and Bill Lavely read the manuscript in full for the University of Washington Press and offered invaluable critiques and suggestions that greatly improved the final product. I very much appreciate the expert editorial help of Lorri Hagman and the staff of the University of Washington Press. Of course, none of these individuals bears responsibility for the deficiencies that remain.

Friends and colleagues who have provided help and support of many kinds include Chen Yung-fa, Myron Cohen, Stevan Harrell, Chis Isett, Maria and Phil Morgan, David and Ceceile Strand, and Janice Stockard. I have learned much (she would say too little) from my favorite sparring partner on all things footbinding, Hill Gates. Arthur Wolf, who followed the development of this project over many years, is greatly missed. And last but not least, I express my thanks to the Shepherd, Link, and Train families, whose company I always enjoy.

Abbreviations

When necessary to distinguish among languages, the following abbreviations precede romanized terms:

C   Chinese
H   Hokkien
J   Japanese
K   Korean
M   Manchu

Chronologies

Xianfeng. 1851–1861
Tongzhi 1862–1874
Guangxu 1875–1908
Xuantong 1909–1911

RULERS OF TAIWAN

Dutch East India Company 1624–1661
Zhengs. 1661–1683
Qing 1683–1895
Japan. 1895–1945
Republic of China 1945–

JAPANESE REIGN PERIODS

Meiji 1868–1912
Taishō 1912–1926
Shōwa 1926–1989

Notes on Usage

Chinese terms and names are romanized in accordance with the pinyin system. Chinese and Japanese names are provided with the family name first; authors who publish in English are cited by the name pattern they customarily use. Postal spellings have been employed in some place names. In two cases where the names of cities and prefectures are the same, postal spellings refer to the cities (Taipei, Taichung) and pinyin spellings refer to the prefectures (Taibei, Taizhong).

FOOTBINDING AS FASHION

Introduction

Seeking Status, Avoiding Shame

In the northern provinces I noticed that nearly all the women
had contracted feet; and the same may be said of the island of
Formosa. In some other parts of the empire the custom does not
prevail to the same extent.

—JOHN HENRY GRAY, *China: A History of the
Laws, Manners, and Customs of the People*

CHINESE footbinding has long been an object of curiosity to both Chinese and Western observers. Historians have traced its origin to the courtesan culture of the Song (960–1279) and earlier dynasties, when the footbinding fashion became associated with notions of female beauty and the erotic overtones of small feet. To achieve the most pleasing small shape, a young girl's feet were tightly wrapped in binding cloths until, after a few years of excruciating pain, her toes were bent under the sole and her arch was broken, leaving her hobbled for life. Considered fashionable by the court elite, the practice soon spread to the provinces. The few Confucian moralists who discussed the fashion condemned it, and none rose to its defense. Yet, despite its mean origins, its questionable morality, its impracticality, and the suffering it caused young girls, the practice seems only to have gained in popularity in the Ming (1368–1644) and Qing (1644–1911) periods, when it spread into the lower ranks of society and grew entrenched in Chinese custom. What accounts for its popularity? Analysts have emphasized footbinding's role as a mark of prestige, a display of conspicuous consumption, a prerequisite to

3

a good marriage, and even a practice that safeguarded women from outdoor labor. Social critics have emphasized the role of footbinding as an instrument of patriarchal oppression of wives and daughters and a disciplinary technique used to exploit the labor of young girls. Cultural anthropologists have noted footbinding's affinity to modes of body deformation practices in other cultures (wasp waists, tattoos, piercings, neck rings, etc.).[1]

All of these perspectives on footbinding contain grains of truth, but not all are of equal weight or can be accepted without scrutiny. Many view footbinding as a means to an end (beauty, prestige, marriageability, patriarchal dominance, or labor discipline), but the custom cannot be reduced to the purposes it sometimes serves (whether explicitly and consciously in the minds of actors or not) or the interests it may benefit. Such functional interpretations cannot explain why footbinding rather than some other practice was used to achieve the designated ends. A nonrational and arbitrary cultural convention, footbinding became a societal norm, enforced by the pressure to conform.[2] Where it gained hegemonic status, footbinding promised not just prestige for the bound-footed, but contempt for the natural-footed. Where its hold on minds went unchallenged, footbinding acquired force sufficient to overcome both compassion for the suffering of young girls and reasoned objections to their crippling (whether based on economic, health, or moral grounds). To study footbinding is to study the power of an arbitrary fashion to shape the experience of millions of women over hundreds of years.

Yet footbinding did not prevail everywhere in China. How and where did footbinding achieve its hegemonic power? How did the fashions adopted by social elites penetrate the lower orders? Did economic conditions determine where footbinding might take root? Did ethnic rivalries stimulate its spread when one group adopted footbinding as a badge of identity? Did non-binding groups reject the practice, escape its influence, or find it too burdensome to adopt? What forces could undermine footbinding's power? What consequences did footbinding have for women's lives and those of their male kin?

HISTORICAL OVERVIEW

Footbinding is thought to have originated as a fashion among dancers and courtesans in court circles of dynasties predating the Song. During the Song, the practice, having gained cachet as a sign of beauty and high status, was adopted by the concubines, wives, and daughters of the national elite.[3] It is generally supposed that the fashion then trickled down to provincial elites and commoners by a process of status emulation.[4] Song historian Patricia Ebrey considers the practice to have become "entrenched" by the end of the Song, and she cites Tao Zongyi, writing in the fourteenth century, reporting that "people were ashamed not to practice it."[5] Footbinding spread further with the flourishing of an urban mercantile culture in the sixteenth century. As a form of conspicuous consumption, footbinding appealed to upwardly mobile merchant and literati families competing for status.[6] According to historian Dorothy Ko, the speed of footbinding's spread bewildered the South China scholar Hu Yinglin, who, writing at the end of the sixteenth century, noted that "people would make fun" of those who did not conform to the fashion.[7] So at least in some sectors of society, and in some locales, the fashion had taken hold.

Scholars have little concrete idea of where the process of diffusion (which places or what social classes?) stood by the end of the Ming dynasty. Clearly footbinding had penetrated deeply enough, at least in late-Ming North China, to have been seen as a threat to Manchu martial culture and to cause the founders of the Qing to ban the practice among the banners (populations owing hereditary military service).[8] Although the Qing historian Zhao Yi's claim that footbinding was practiced "all over the empire" might suggest that it had become customary for the average woman by the eighteenth century, the picture of regional variation that emerges in the nineteenth and early twentieth centuries provides evidence of nearly universal binding in some regions but not in others, of binding widespread in North China but not in South China.[9] Had this pattern appeared by the end of the Ming, or was it the product of developments that took place only after the Qing rose to power? The sources fail to provide definitive answers.

The numbers of the bound-footed undoubtedly grew along with the increase in population during the Qing, but there is no systematic and detailed information that documents whether footbinding spread into new regions and classes (increasing the proportion of women bound-footed) or remained confined to areas and strata where it had gained prominence by the late Ming. Two hypotheses to be examined suggest that footbinding did continue to spread during the Qing.[10] One commonly accepted view claims that footbinding spread in reaction to Qing attempts to suppress the practice and was adopted to express Han ethnic pride and anti-Manchu sentiment. The second hypothesis suggests that footbinding became feasible for women of the working classes when the spread of cotton textile handicrafts provided gainful but sedentary employment that was compatible with bound feet. What is not in doubt is that the popular culture that defined bound feet as beautiful, status conferring, and the key to good marriages survived uninterrupted in the transition from Ming to Qing.

Only in the first decades of the twentieth century were ethnographic reports, economic surveys, and censuses documenting footbinding produced that could provide the range and depth of information sufficient for detailed studies of footbinding in selected locales. Measures of the proportions of women bound-footed at the district level, along with historical, ethnographic, and economic sources, make possible the mapping of the spatial distribution of footbinding in Taiwan, Hebei, Beijing, and Liaoning. These studies capture the state of footbinding at the end point of processes long at work in the previous centuries and before anti-footbinding campaigns brought the practice to an end. The analysis of these cases provides insight into the processes (ethnic, economic, status) that strengthened or weakened the practice of footbinding in Qing localities.

SOURCES AND METHODS

Since 1990 there has been an outpouring of literature on the culture of footbinding in Chinese society. Three genres characterize much of this literature: studies rooted in literary and historical writings; studies of the material culture of footbinding represented in footwear, painting, and photography; and works based on ethnographic accounts, surveys, and demographic materials.[11] This study combines the first and last of these genres. As a work of historical anthropology, it includes both historiographic study and social scientific inquiries. The case studies of footbinding in Taiwan, Hebei, Beijing, and Liaoning combine historical and ethnographic reports with quantitative measures.

Most discussions of the practice of footbinding in late imperial Chinese society have relied on qualitative evidence from Chinese- and Western-language sources, often anecdotal in nature, referring to situations and experiences scattered in time and space, and providing little context. Usually the information comes from casual comments culled from works devoted to other topics rather than from observations gathered systematically. Anecdotal accounts reporting what people said about footbinding are a rich source of hypotheses about the motivations of Chinese actors who bound girls' feet, but they provide much less reliable evidence about what such actors actually did with respect to binding in their own families and on the extent to which the practice of footbinding varied among social groups and localities.

Contemporaneous ethnographic works devoting whole sections to footbinding provide a fuller background and richer context for the custom.[12] Recent studies based on retrospective interviews of elderly women from village communities in several provinces take an important step forward by attending to both the family and the work lives of women whose feet were bound.[13]

Studies of footbinding all acknowledge that binding was not uniformly practiced and that wide variations existed with respect to the proportion of girls binding, the ages binding began, and the degrees of deformation binding caused. They also acknowledge that assessing such variation, along with other characteristics of the population, is fundamental to understanding the social and cultural pressures that encouraged binding in some circumstances and discouraged it in others.[14] Most of these studies have mistakenly assumed that census evidence on footbinding for whole populations does not exist.[15] They have overlooked the extraordinary early twentieth-century censuses of Taiwan and the less detailed surveys of North China, including Hebei and Liaoning in 1928.

Using measures of proportions bound and economic and ethnic data, this study analyzes spatial variation in the practice of footbinding across entire provinces. Early twentieth-century censuses of footbinding, because they survey whole populations, rather than small samples in scattered localities of unknown representativeness, add appreciably to understanding the contours of the practice across selected regions. The Taiwan censuses of 1905 and 1915, the most detailed and comprehensive accounting of the practice before it declined, provide measures of footbinding disaggregated to prefectures and townships varying in ethnic composition and economic regime. The much simpler 1928 surveys of footbinding in Hebei and Liaoning provide evidence of county-level spatial variation in the practice in a period when the campaigns against footbinding were beginning to have an impact. Correlating ethnic and economic indicators with the census measures of footbinding makes it possible to test hypotheses against the evidence of variation across whole provinces. The ethnographic accounts of footbinding customs preserved in the writings of authors who valued the opinions and lives of ordinary women provide insight into the human meanings behind the spatial patterns. A rich and diverse set of materials makes it possible to cross-check a variety of source types, rather than become entrapped in any single source or perspective. The case studies of Taiwan, Hebei, Beijing, and Liaoning presented here examine in detail the patterns of footbinding in historical periods and regions of China where uniquely rich sources can shed light on the nature of the social formations that supported and undermined the fashion of footbinding in its heyday.

The case studies illustrate the diversity of settlement histories and ethnic mixtures within Chinese dominions and the varying fates of the footbinding fashion in these different environments. In contrast to the long history of continuous settlement in Hebei, Taiwan and Liaoning were frontiers of settlement in the Qing.[16] Taiwan, off the southeast coast of China, was settled in the seventeenth and eighteenth centuries by Chinese immigrants from southern Fujian (Hoklo) and northeast Guangdong (Hakka). The northeastern territory of Liaoning, set aside by the Qing as a reserve for banner and imperial household estates, saw large numbers of land-hungry Han migrants from Hebei and Shandong settle there in the nineteenth century. The studies of Taiwan and Liaoning illustrate the processes by which footbinding customs were and were not reproduced, depending on the ethnic patterns and status hierarchies that emerged in the course of settlement.

There are also sharp economic differences between the cases. Taiwan enjoys a southern climate with plentiful rainfall and a long growing season, which enabled its farmers to produce tea, rice, and sugarcane for export. Farmers in the northern climates of Hebei and Liaoning, with drier conditions and a shorter growing season, produced wheat, sorghum, and soybeans and, in some areas of Hebei, commercial crops of cotton and cotton textile handicrafts. The studies of Taiwan, Liaoning, and Hebei explore the impact of these economic differences on female labor and its compatibility with footbinding. Despite the contrasts in settlement histories and economies, Hebei and Taiwan shared cultural traditions strongly influenced by literati elites. Qing historian Ho Ping-ti's calculation of the numbers earning the highest examination degree (*jinshi*) per million population shows Fujian (the home of Taiwan's Hoklo) and Hebei ranking in the top three provinces in both the Ming and Qing periods.[17] Notwithstanding their many differences in history and economies, footbinding was widely practiced in both Taiwan and Hebei. Assessing how the many points of difference among the case study locales operated to strengthen or weaken the hold of the footbinding fashion is the task this study undertakes.

The case studies included here cast doubt on ethnic identity and labor compatibility theories about the spread of footbinding and demonstrate the independent power of status hierarchies and social pressure to shape the lives of women. The cases treating the Qing conquest, Hakka-influenced Hoklo, and banner-influenced North Chinese contradict assumptions that footbinding intensified as a way to mark ethnic differences between footbinding and non-binding groups. Notions that footbinding was most intense where it was compatible with the work women did in agriculture or handicrafts are contradicted by the findings from Taiwan and Hebei that reveal no connection between footbinding and cropping patterns and textile handicrafts. Instead, footbinding was nearly universal in solidly Hoklo Taiwan communities and in counties of Hebei, whatever their economies.

Where the footbinding fashion gained hegemonic power, and binding became nearly universal, women bound their feet more out of fear of ridicule, and a desire to avoid the stigma attached to natural feet, than in the vain hope that binding would elevate their status. Status emulation may have spread the practice into the lower orders in earlier centuries, but when the process reached a point where binding was nearly universal, the footbinding convention was less a means to raise one's status than a social pressure that punished with ridicule and disrespect those who failed to conform. Footbinding had acquired hegemonic power in areas of North China and among the Hoklo, where it was nearly universal among all strata of society at the beginning of the twentieth century. But when Hakka influenced Hoklo in Taiwan and in Chaozhou Prefecture, Guangdong, and banner fashions influenced North Chinese in Beijing and Liaoning, footbinding's hold was broken and natural feet advanced.

CHAPTER 1

The Qing Conquest
and Footbinding

I N the early decades of the seventeenth century a new center of power
emerged in China's northeast, led by a non-Han Manchu dynasty. In 1644,
China was wracked by internal rebellion, rebels seized the capital at Beijing,
and the Ming emperor committed suicide. Seizing the opportunity created
by the collapse of the Ming court, Manchu armies entered Beijing and proclaimed a new Qing dynasty. In the ensuing years, Qing forces succeeded in
defeating remnant Ming supporters and asserting dominion over the empire.

Did the triumph of a non-Han conquest dynasty spur a proto-nationalist
reaction among Chinese that led to the spread of footbinding?[1] Students of
Qing history regularly learn that although at the beginning of the dynasty
the Manchu conquerors prohibited footbinding throughout the empire, they
were forced to rescind the prohibition when women resisted.[2] Qing attempts
to ban footbinding made binding into a politically charged ethnic marker
that embodied for Han anti-Qing sentiments and caused the bans to backfire
and footbinding to spread further.[3] Evaluating these claims requires a close
scrutiny of the sources documenting Qing policies toward footbinding and
the subsequent distortions of that record perpetuated by nineteenth- and
twentieth-century historians.

THE PRE-CONQUEST BANS OF 1636 AND 1638

Hair and dress regulations were an early feature of the rising Manchu state's
policies governing its multiethnic population. When in the early 1620s

Manchu forces wrested Liaodong from Ming control, the regime faced the challenge of incorporating large numbers of Chinese into the subject population. As a mark of submission and test of loyalty, surrendering males were required to shave their heads and adopt the Manchu hairstyle, or queue.[4] The Manchu rulers also discouraged sartorial distinctions, which hindered integrating the newly subjugated population into the Manchu polity on an equal and uniform basis.[5] These policies were not always successful, and an expanding Chinese population presented continuing challenges to the maintenance of Manchu cultural dominance.

In 1636, Hong Taiji, Nurhaci's successor as the leader of the rising Manchu state, became concerned that exposure to Han lifestyles had weakened Manchu military skills.[6] In 1636 and 1637, he warned his followers that the adoption of Han (M: Nikan) attire, customs, and language and the decline of horse-riding and archery skills had led to the fall of the Jurchen Jin dynasty (1115–1234), from which the Manchus claimed descent. To prevent a similar fate for his newly named Qing state, Hong Taiji demanded that his followers maintain Manchu cultural traditions and attire. These decrees stress the incompatibility of the free-flowing robes and wide sleeves worn by Han men and Manchu martial skills of horse-riding and mounted archery, which required belted waists and tight-fitting sleeves.[7] A separate 1636 decree preserved in the draft Veritable Records cautioned Manchus against the influence of degenerate Han customs (*Hanren zhi louxi*) and for the first time explicitly extended the dress regulations to females. This decree took the further step of ordering all Han officials and commoners, males and females (*fan Hanren guanmin nannü*), to adopt Manchu apparel (*Manzhou shiyang*) and threatened severe punishment for those who did not comply. The new regulations specify that Han men were in addition not to wear broad collars, wide sleeves, and Ming-style hats and were required to belt the waist (*nanren buxu chuan daling daxiu, dai rongmao, ge yao shuyao*). The 1636 regulations also make the earliest explicit mention of women's footbinding: they forbid Han women to wear certain hairstyles and to bind feet (*nüren buxu shutou, chanjiao*).[8] These decrees make clear that all Manchu subjects, including Han males and females, were expected to conform to Manchu cultural traditions in attire.

In 1638, Hong Taiji again instituted harsh punishments for "those who adopted the hats and clothing of a foreign country [i.e., Ming China] and caused women to tie up their hair and bind their feet [*shufa guozu*]; such persons, although subjects of our dynasty, have their hearts elsewhere." This phrasing makes the failure by either men or women to conform to Manchu traditions of attire a sign of disloyalty.[9] A Manchu version of the 1638 decree (but not the version in the Chinese Veritable Records) specifies that those found binding their feet should suffer death by having the feet chopped off.[10] A condensed and reworded version of the 1638 decree, calling for the severe punishment of those who imitated foreign clothing, hairstyle, and bound feet, but making no reference to "causing" women to bind (and dropping the reference to "hearts elsewhere"), is given in *Records from within the Eastern Gate* (Donghua lu).[11] All later Qing commentators cite this truncated version of the 1638 decree when they trace prohibitions on footbinding to the pre-1644 era.

By this series of decrees Hong Taiji mandated Manchu attire, including both the queue and the ban on footbinding, among the banner populations (the hereditary military caste that drew members from the Manchus, Mongols, Han, and others) as well as any civilian Han population under Manchu control.[12] The decrees served multiple purposes: removing distinctions between Han and other Manchu subjects and making them all equally subject to the same state regulations; eliminating practices that undermined the martial traditions of the Manchus; and creating visible signs of loyalty. The hair and dress regulations expressed pride in Manchu traditions and preserved them against the encroachment of Han fashions. The decrees also made women's natural feet an "ethnic" marker of Qing identity for Manchu and other bannerwomen and for all female subjects of the early Manchu state.

THE TONSURE EDICT AND ANTI-QING SENTIMENT

Prominent scholars have claimed that the early Manchu prohibitions on footbinding (1636, 1638, 1645?, 1664–68) failed among the Han majority because they were "defied" by women and that "resistance" caused the fashion to spread further.[13] But evidence does not support the widely repeated assertion that Manchu prohibitions on footbinding were extended to the civilian Han population of China proper after the conquest, although the Qing court early in the Kangxi reign (1662–1722) did briefly consider a proposal to ban footbinding among the general population in China. Nor does Qing politicization of a cultural trait as a badge of identity (natural feet among bannerwomen) automatically convert what was already a long-standing practice of footbinding among Han into a marker either of Han opposition or of ethnic identity. An ethnic marker and boundary maintenance hypothesis has thus been invoked to explain the continued spread of footbinding in the

Han population.[14] But no evidence has been produced to demonstrate that resistance or identity ever motivated binding and could explain its unabated popularity in the Qing period.

Proponents of the notion that the Qing enforced bans on footbinding in the post-1644 context rely on sources that discuss prohibitions dated to 1645 and 1664–68, as well as the 1636 and 1638 bans. These sources and their interpretation by modern scholars have rarely been subjected to scrutiny.[15] The 1636 and 1638 edicts, issued before the Manchus entered Beijing in 1644, applied at the time they were issued only to the multiethnic population of the Liao basin under Manchu control, where they were successful among the banners, and as the nineteenth-century ethnographic evidence suggests, more generally. In need of clarification is whether the 1636 and 1638 bans were extended to the civilian population of China proper in 1645 or in any year of the Shunzhi reign (1644–61) and whether women's footbinding was also included in the hair and dress regulations that the Qing imposed on Chinese men.

In June 1644, Qing forces entering Beijing initially imposed but twenty-one days later suspended the requirement that civilian men (ministers and commoners, *chen min*) adopt the queue as a sign of loyalty.[16] A year later, in July 1645, after defeating southern Ming forces and extending Qing control to Nanjing, a tonsure command (*tifa ling*) was promulgated, rescinding the suspension. Arguing that differences in customs would lead to divided loyalties (*erxin*), the decree made adopting the queue a test of loyalty to the new regime. The tonsure decree set a ten-day limit on adopting the queue, but set no time limit for officeholders to adopt Manchu-style male dress.[17] In response to the sudden forced imposition of the queue, serious rebellions broke out in several Jiangnan localities, which the Manchus suppressed, brutally.[18] The history of the tonsure edict makes clear that there was no automatic extension of the 1636 and 1638 dress regulations to the civilian population of China proper during the conquest, but only a selective and strategically timed enforcement.

None of the orders suspending or reimposing the queue and recorded in the Qing Veritable Records make any reference to footbinding. The earliest sources referring to a ban on footbinding in 1645 appear nearly two hundred years later, in the early nineteenth-century works of Yu Zhengxie (1775–1840) and Qian Yong (1759–1844).[19] Neither Yu nor Qian cites a source for a 1645 ban, nor does any other later author. In fact, a 1668 memorial retracting a ban on footbinding proposed in an edict of 1664 explicitly contradicts any claim that there was a 1645 ban on footbinding.[20]

The edict of 1664, which prohibits footbinding among civilians, was published in 1951 but has never before been cited by any modern student of footbinding (nor was it cited by any Qing-period scholar). The edict, dated the third year, fourth month, and third day of the Kangxi reign (1664), does not appear in the Veritable Records, and the only published copy is of a draft preserved in the archives of the Grand Secretariat (*Neige daku dang'an*) in Taipei.[21] The edict endorsed a recommendation of the Manchu-dominated Assembly of Deliberative Princes, Ministers, and Censors to ban footbinding among civilians.[22] Addressed to the Board of Rites, the edict begins by declaring that within the empire, differences of custom should not be tolerated (*tianxia yijia, neiwai fengsu buke youyi*), yet civilian females (*minjian funü*) continue to bind their feet and harm their bodies (*juxing guozu huishang quanti*), following a vile custom passed down unchanged from the former dynasty (*wangguo louxi*). The edict affirmed that a compassionate monarch in a prosperous age could not tolerate practices that violate nature and destroy bodies (*shang benzhi hui quanti*). Moreover, Taizu (Nurhaci, r. 1616–26) and Taizong (Hong Taiji, r. 1627–43) left strict orders mandating head shaving and banning footbinding, and to stop shaving and continue footbinding would violate the precedents set by these imperial forefathers. Exempting those who had already bound their feet, the assembly recommended that footbinding should cease for all women born from the first year of the present Kangxi reign, 1662 (*zi Kangxi yuannian yilai suosheng nüzi yingting qi guozu zhe*).

The rationale for the prohibition on footbinding given by the edict of 1664 makes some interesting rhetorical shifts. In the 1636 and 1638 edicts, the key concerns of Hong Taiji were preservation of Manchu martial skills and the expression of loyalty in the subject population by conformity to Manchu hair and dress customs, but these themes are downplayed here. The 1664 edict stresses respect for the precedents set by the dynastic founders, the need to reform degenerate Ming practices, and the importance of creating a uniformity of custom in the new empire, which is also a prominent theme of the tonsure command. The expression of compassion for those injuring themselves by binding, whose loyalty is not questioned, introduces a new theme.[23] The edict thus adopts an approach milder than the punitive one of Hong Taiji's decrees. Note also that the precedents cited for the prohibition refer to the imperial predecessors Taizu and Taizong and make no mention of any precedent from the more recent reign of the Shunzhi emperor, who ruled during the conquest of China proper (Shizu, r. 1644–61). The edict implies that although in Hong Taiji's time both the tonsure and the ban on footbinding had been enforced, the latter had not been enforced in the more recent reign. Unlike the tonsure command, the draft edict does not call for its transmission to the provinces, nor does it specify sanctions for violation of the ban, an issue the 1668 memorial reports had been referred to the Board of Rites for deliberation; thus it is unlikely the proposed ban came into effect at this time.

The story of the short life of this proposed ban on footbinding is continued in the 1668 memorial preserved in *Trivial Thoughts in Yin An* (Yin'an suoyu) by Wang Bu, a native of Jiaxing, Zhejiang. Wang was a low-ranking scholar and minor official who served in grain transport at the end of the Ming and died some time following 1670, the date of the last event he recorded, and prior to 1684, when his son published his manuscript.[24] Wang Bu transcribes a memorial dated the seventh month of 1668 (Kangxi 7) that is the earliest and fullest source documenting the repeal of the 1664 ban cited by any later Qing commentator. The 1668 memorial sets the context, quotes the earlier 1664 (Kangxi 3) edict that proposed the ban on footbinding, discusses the punishments that would enforce the ban, and then recommends that the proposed ban be withdrawn.[25]

The memorial of 1668 begins by stating it is submitted pursuant to a policy review by the Board of Rites aimed at restoring old precedents (*zhuofu jiuzhang*). As part of this review the senior president of the Censorate, Wang Xi (1628–1703, *jinshi* 1647), has reported that prior to 1661 civilian women were not forbidden to bind their feet (*Shunzhi shiba nian yiqian minjian zhi nü wei jin guozu*), thereby establishing that there was no Shunzhi-era (1644–61) precedent for a ban on footbinding. Yet in 1664, an edict, issued on the recommendation of the Assembly of Deliberative Princes, Ministers, and Censors, forbade binding the feet of women born in and after the first year of the Kangxi reign (1662) and instructed the Board of Rites to determine how to implement the ban. In the first month of the current year (1668), the board recommended that the fathers of women who violate the ban should be punished by forty strokes of the bamboo and exile. Punishments were also set for household heads and officials who failed to detect violations among women under their jurisdiction. Because these punishments are too severe, and the prohibition an opportunity for false accusations (by claiming women with bound feet but born before 1662 had in fact been born after 1662 and were subject to the prohibition), Wang Xi recommended that the prohibition should be voided (*xiangying mian jinzhi ke ye*). At the end of the memorial a rescript is appended that adopts this recommendation (and another, to be discussed shortly).[26]

Note that women born in or after 1662 would have been six years old or younger in 1668, and only a minority could have started binding (and none could have completed the process) before the prohibition was rescinded. Moreover, the punishments, if they were ever implemented, could have been in force for only a few months (from the first to the seventh month of 1668) when the ban was repealed. So there could have been only a few cases (if any) brought under the ban and little opportunity for women to express "resistance." Thus the Kangxi ban on footbinding of 1664–68 was effectively aborted.

Immediately following the recommendation to rescind the ban on footbinding, the 1668 memorial continues on a second topic: whether the rigid eight-legged essay format should be used in the civil service examinations. The memorial first establishes the old precedent by noting that examinations prior to 1662 (Kangxi 1) required the eight-legged essay. It then quotes an edict of the eighth month of 1663 (Kangxi 2.8) that characterized the essay as a superfluous and empty form bearing no relation to government affairs, ordered an end to its use, and provided that only questions of policy be included in the exams. The memorialist notes that the format had been excised from the exams held in 1664 and 1667 and recommends restoring the eight-legged essay according to the precedent established prior to 1662. The recommendation was adopted.[27]

What connection between these two disparate practices, footbinding and the eight-legged essay, could bring them together in the same memorial? Relevant here is an excerpt written by the well-known official and poet Wang Shizhen (1634–1711, *jinshi* 1658), which is the next earliest source documenting the repeal of the 1664 ban on footbinding. In 1665–68, Wang was in his early thirties and serving in the Board of Rites. Wang noted in his self-compiled biography that when he first took up office, Wang Xi and Huang Ji (1612–1686, *jinshi* 1647) were vice presidents of the board.[28] In 1668, Wang Shizhen was promoted to be an assistant director in the Department of Ceremonies of the Board of Rites, and Wang notes this was when the eight-legged essay was restored.[29] In his *Casual Talks by the North Side of the Pond* (Chibei outan, 1691) he mentions the easing of the footbinding ban (*kuan minjian nüzi guozu zhi jin*) only in passing, as part of a longer discussion of the restoration of the eight-legged essay to the civil service examinations.[30] He gives no details regarding the earlier 1664 ban on footbinding, nor does he date its rescission or the restoration of the eight-legged essay. Wang Shizhen does note that at this time

Wang Xi, now president of the Censorate, called for discussion of a return to old precedents, and in response he advocated restoring the eight-legged essay and the old exam format, a proposal that Huang Ji, now the minister of rites, supported.[31] With respect to the ban on footbinding, Wang merely notes that the restoration of the eight-legged essay and the lifting of the prohibition on footbinding by civilian women were both approved at the same time.[32] In his biography, Wang Shizhen's entry for 1668 focuses on the changes in the examination system and does not mention the repeal of the footbinding prohibition. Wang talks expansively about the importance of the return to old precedents, the reform of misgovernment, and the restoration of enlightened government "as in the Shunzhi reign" and takes pride in his own role in these events.[33]

Although Wang Shizhen's brief mention of the rescission of the footbinding ban at the time the eight-legged essay was restored has prompted claims that footbinding, like the examinations, had an especial association with Confucian culture, Wang Xi's preface to his memorial of 1668 makes clear that it is the program to restore old precedents that connects the two issues.[34] The rescinding of the 1664 ban on footbinding in 1668 must be understood as part of the general pullback from the ambitious reform policies that had been pursued in the early years of the Kangxi reign. These policies had been adopted by the "Oboi regents" controlling the government on behalf of the Kangxi emperor, who was only seven years old on his accession in 1661.[35] Following on the Jiangnan tax and the Ming history cases of 1661–63, which they saw as evidence of continued Chinese incorrigibility, the Oboi regents adopted unprecedented reforms, including the elimination of the eight-legged essay from the civil service examinations and the banning of footbinding. Oboi and his fellow regents have been seen as Manchu nativists suspicious of both Chinese loyalty and Chinese "refinements." They were determined to correct the course of policy followed by the Shunzhi emperor, whom they saw as overly sympathetic to the Chinese.[36] An alternative interpretation downplays the significance of Manchu nativism motivating these policies and stresses the advocacy by reformist Chinese scholar-officials, who had been long-standing critics of the use of the eight-legged essay in the examinations.[37] Footbinding, too, had long been the subject of literati critique.[38] Note that the rhetorical shift in the 1664 edict, which did not question the loyalty of those who bound and expressed compassion for those harmed by binding, accords with the reformist rather than the nativist interpretation of the motives for its issuance. Whatever their source, the regents' reform policies antagonized Chinese literati still attached to Ming precedents.

Censor Wang Xi, who plays a key role in the rescinding of the footbinding ban, is also identified by Wang Shizhen as instrumental in the restoration of the eight-legged essay. Both the 1668 memorial and Wang Shizhen connect Wang Xi to the program of "restoring old precedents" (*zhuofu jiuzhang*). This program is described in the memorial carrying that name that takes pride of place in Wang Xi's collected works, is discussed in the entry for 1668 in his chronological biography (*nianpu*), and is mentioned in the account of his life in the draft Qing history.[39] As the Kangxi emperor's party moved to push the regents aside in 1667–69, policy changes such as those that reinstated the eight-legged essay, and rescinded the ban on footbinding, were adopted to mollify the literati and solidify support for the young emperor among his non-banner Chinese officials. This program included the refurbishing of the Shunzhi emperor's memory and his reign's more conciliatory policies toward Chinese subjects. With regard to footbinding, the precedents to be restored were those of the Shunzhi reign, not the reign of Hong Taiji. Wang Xi and Huang Ji (mentioned by Wang Shizhen) played important roles as members of the emperor's party in these contests for control.[40] Thus footbinding and the eight-legged essay are linked through the politics of the Oboi regency, not through some Confucian cultural aura connecting the examination system and the footbinding fashion. The Kangxi ban on footbinding was aborted, not because it was defied by bound-footed women (or their menfolk), but because it was a casualty of a power struggle at court between groups advocating very different visions for Qing rule.

Although both the elimination and the restoration of the eight-legged essay to the examinations are well documented in the Qing Veritable Records and other standard sources, there is no discussion there of the abortive Kangxi proposal to ban footbinding or of any 1645 ban during the conquest era.[41] Wang Bu's transcription of Wang Xi's memorial remains the sole source providing detailed information on the fate of the regents' proposed ban on footbinding. The broader historical context is lost in the multiple references to the repeal made in the later literary sources on footbinding.

WAS THERE A 1645 BAN ON FOOTBINDING?

The 1664 edict, Wang Xi's 1668 memorial discussing in detail the repeal of the 1664 edict, Wang Shizhen's brief notice of the repeal (but without precise dating), and a notation by the Shanghai scholar Ye Mengzhu are the only seventeenth-century sources recording any post-1644 ban on footbinding.[42]

None of them mention, let alone document, a 1645 prohibition, and the 1668 memorial states expressly that there was no Shunzhi-era ban. The history of footbinding the well-known poet and historian Zhao Yi (1727–1814) included in his *Miscellaneous Investigations during Retirement* (Gaiyu congkao, ca. 1790) is the sole eighteenth-century source cited by any later author. Zhao's brief history concludes with two lines concerning Qing policy toward footbinding. Zhao notes that in 1664 (Kangxi 3) footbinding was banned for women born after the beginning of the Kangxi reign, lists in brief the punishments prescribed, and cites as his source Wang Bu's *Trivial Thoughts in Yin An*. Zhao then notes that the ban of 1664 was lifted in 1668 and cites as his source Wang Shizhen's *Casual Talks by the North Side of the Pond*. Zhao makes no mention of any other ban, either pre- or post-1644.[43]

The absence of official notices in the Veritable Records documenting footbinding policies in the early Qing (and the failure to note the 1951 printing of the 1664 edict) has resulted in modern scholars of footbinding having to rely on a variety of nineteenth- and early twentieth-century prose writings, as evidence for multiple post-1644 bans on footbinding among civilian Han.[44] Many of these accounts are, like Wang Shizhen's, highly truncated and lacking in citations, and several introduce distortions and ambiguities. Two early nineteenth-century sources, written by Yu Zhengxie and Qian Yong, are drawn on, whether directly or indirectly, by every subsequent author claiming that a ban on footbinding by civilian women was promulgated in 1645.

Yu Zhengxie's long essay on the history of clothing and footbinding, "Postscript to the Book of Costumes of the Old Tang History," is included in his *Classified Drafts of the Thirtieth Year* (Guisi leigao) of 1833. Yu's brief note discussing Qing prohibitions on binding comes near the end of his essay, just before he concludes by stating his well-known objections to footbinding.[45] Yu is the first source to mention the decree promulgated by Hong Taiji in the seventh month of 1638 prescribing punishments for those following foreign (i.e., Han) customs such as footbinding. Yu's transcription corresponds to the decree as reproduced in *Records from within the Eastern Gate*, but edits the passage to refer only to footbinding by leaving out references to hair and dress. Yu then concludes his comments by stating, "Later it was decreed that women born after 1645 were forbidden to bind their feet, and in 1667 the prohibition was relaxed" (Hou you ding Shunzhi ernian yihou suosheng nüzi jin guozu, Kangxi liunian chi qi jin).[46] Unlike Zhao Yi, who is careful to cite his sources, Yu cites none.

Two details in Yu's account are at variance with the earlier sources. First, although Yu's account agrees with those of Wang Bu and Zhao Yi that the ban on footbinding is to apply prospectively (rather than to women whose feet are already bound), he dates the onset of the prohibition in 1645 (Shunzhi 2, in the middle of the troubles over the forced adoption of the queue), rather than in 1662 (Kangxi 1), as stated in the 1664 draft edict and by Wang Bu and Zhao Yi. Second, he also dates the lifting of the ban to 1667 rather than 1668. This leaves the ban on footbinding in effect for twenty-two years rather than six. Yu Zhengxie has muddled the dates reported in detail by Wang Bu and confirmed by Zhao Yi. But the effect of Yu's error is great, in that it leaves the ban in force over a much longer period, which would have affected the many women born after 1645 and completing the binding of their feet before 1667. If Yu Zhengxie's account were correct, and a prohibition was enforced over a twenty-two-year period, modern scholars maintaining a 1645 ban existed could be expected to have supported their claims by citing many references to reactions to the policy made in collections of random notes (biji) and other sources.

The next earliest nineteenth-century source, Collected Works from Lüyuan (Lüyuan conghua) by Qian Yong, dates from circa 1838 and contains a substantial essay on footbinding. Near the end of his account, Qian notes approvingly that the women of the Eight Banners do not bind their feet and advocates that officials ban footbinding by enlisting local elites to set an example and lead the way.[47] Qian then takes up the history of the Qing prohibitions. First, he cites the 1638 ban by transcribing the passage included in Records from within the Eastern Gate, which he edits to refer only to footbinding; the text differs only in minor ways from that of Yu Zhengxie. He then states without qualification that footbinding was prohibited in 1645 (Shunzhi ernian jin guozu); there is no hint that the prohibition might apply only to women born from that year, nor is there reference to a source. He next states that footbinding was prohibited again in 1664. Qian Yong repeats largely verbatim the detailed account provided by Wang Bu: he cites the return to old precedents in the seventh month of 1668 and censor Wang Xi's statement that there was no ban on footbinding for civilian women before 1661 (Shunzhi 18), that the decree of 1664 had banned footbinding for women born after 1662, that punishments (listed in detail) were proposed in 1668 for those in violation of the ban, that the punishments had been found to be too severe and an occasion for incriminating the innocent, and that therefore the ban was repealed. Qian Yong concludes by saying, "From that time the ban on footbinding was relaxed" (Guozu zi ci chi jin), and cites as his sources Wang Bu's Trivial Thoughts in Yin An (Yin'an suoyu) and Wang Shizhen's Casual Talks by the North Side of the Pond (Chibei outan).[48]

Qian makes no attempt to reconcile the statement that footbinding was banned in 1645 (for which no source is cited) with the statement he cites from Wang Bu that there was no ban on footbinding for civilian women born before 1661, nor does he explain why, if footbinding was banned in 1645, it had to be banned again in 1664. Although Qian treats in detail the 1638 decree and the 1664–68 episode, he provides no details and no source for any 1645 prohibition. Qian's account of the 1645 prohibition differs from that of Yu Zhengxie, who added the qualification that it applied only to women born after that year. Note that the authors of the two earliest nineteenth-century sources, Yu Zhengxie and Qian Yong, are both opponents of footbinding and favor its prohibition. The muddled chronology they introduce serves no apparent political agenda.

All later nineteenth- and early twentieth-century accounts claiming there were multiple bans on footbinding among civilian women in the post-conquest era draw on these two works by Yu Zhengxie and Qian Yong.[49] A summary listing of the sources relied on by each of these early authors to document the bans is in Table 1.1, along with a listing of mid- to late twentieth-century authors who cite them.

All sources stating that a ban on footbinding was imposed in 1645 thus date from the nineteenth century and after. No reference to 1645 is made by the seventeenth-century sources (the 1664 edict, the 1668 memorial transcribed by Wang Bu, Wang Shizhen, and Ye Mengzhu), which were written by men who lived through the Qing conquest and the early years of the Kangxi reign. Nor is any mention of a 1645 ban made by the sole eighteenth-century source, Zhao Yi.

The nineteenth-century sources provide no citations of any earlier source when they refer to a 1645 ban, are devoid of details about such a ban, and contradict one another as to whether the ban applied only to women born from that year or to all bound-footed women with no exceptions (as had the 1638 prohibition). Telling details (e.g., asserting the 1645 ban applied to women born on or after that date, inserting variant dates such as 1667) suggest many later authors copied from earlier authors and did no original research. In contrast to references to the 1638 and Kangxi-era prohibitions, which quote language from original sources (whether cited to a source or not), no quoted material is provided in the case of the 1645 ban.

The nineteenth-century sources are the first to take note of the 1638 ban; in doing so they copy the language of *Records from within the Eastern Gate*, compiled by Jiang Liangqi (1723–1789), which had only recently become available.[50] Perhaps the authors assumed that the policy of 1638 had been automatically

TABLE 1.1. Sources documenting Qing bans on footbinding among civilian women

Source	1638 ban?	1645 ban?	1664 ban?	1668 repeal?	Sources cited for post-1644 bans	Cited by modern author
Edict of 1664, *Ming Qing shiliao, ding bian*, published 1951	X	O	X	—	—	O
Memorial of 1668, Wang Bu, *Yin'an suoyu*, before 1684	O	No	X, detailed, females born from 1662	X, detailed	Transcribed memorial	O
Ye Mengzhu, *Yue shi bian*, late seventeenth century	O	O	X, early Kangxi	X, 1669	Personal knowledge	O
Wang Shizhen, *Chibei outan*, 1691	O	O	O	X	Personal experience	Nagao 1942, Levy 1967, Ko 1997, Feng and Chang 2002
Zhao Yi, *Gaiyu congkao*, ca. 1790	O	O	X, females born from 1662	X	Wang Bu, Wang Shizhen	Ko 1994, 1997
Yu Zhengxie, *Guisi leigao*, 1833	X	X, females born from 1645	O	X, 1667	O	Ko 1997
Qian Yong, *Lüyuan conghua*, ca. 1838	X	X, but also No	X, "again," females born from 1662	X	Wang Bu, Wang Shizhen	Feng Erkang 1986, Feng and Chang 2002, Leong 1997

Note: X = mentioned; O = not mentioned

extended into the post-1644 period, along with the command to adopt the queue in 1645? However, the policy imposing the queue had been rescinded for officials and civilians in 1644, leaving it applicable only to surrendering armed forces, and only later in 1645 was it reinstated to apply to all male subjects. Policies adopted in the post-1644 context were not automatic extensions of 1638 precedents but were adjusted to circumstances. Nor do any of the post-1644 Qing policy discussions dealing with the queue mention footbinding. Writing at a distance of two centuries, the nineteenth-century authors may have assumed Qing policy was simpler and more uniform than it was.

Evidence is thus strong that there never was a 1645 ban on footbinding. The tonsure order had already inflamed the populace to an unanticipated degree, and aggravating the situation by attempting to enforce an intrusive ban on footbinding would have been foolhardy. Even more damaging to the case for a 1645 ban is the absence of any record or memoir reporting attempts to implement such a ban. The evidence supporting the existence of a 1645 ban on footbinding is both inconsistent in its details and thin and appears to be a nineteenth-century invention. The notion of a 1645 ban is expressly contradicted by Wang Xi's statement in his 1668 memorial that there was no post-1644 ban on footbinding among civilian women before 1661. That leaves the abortive 1664 edict as the sole ban on footbinding in the post-conquest era directed at civilian women. The nonexistence of a 1645 ban and the repeal of the 1664 ban in 1668, before it could have affected girls born in 1662, deprive defiance and resistance by women any opportunity to have played a part in the 1668 repeal.

BOUND FEET AS SYMBOL?

In the absence of evidence for a 1645 ban, could other developments have caused footbinding to emerge as an important symbol of Ming loyalism in the transition period? Indirect connections between the tonsure edict and footbinding have been made by linking the rescission of the more lenient tonsure policy in favor of immediate imposition of the queue in July 1645 to the twice-serving official Sun Zhixie (d. 1647), who is reported advocating that the new dynasty should adopt its own dress regulations. The connection to footbinding comes solely from the report that Sun had curried favor with the Manchus not only by voluntarily shaving his head but by having the women in his family unbind their feet (if true, an extraordinary gesture).[51] In 1647, Sun and several members of his family fell victim to the rebel bandit Xie Qian at their home in Shandong's Zichuan County seat. Because of his role in the imposition of the tonsure, Ming loyalists disparaged Sun and celebrated his demise.[52] The story of Sun Zhixie has been used to support a theory elevating footbinding to the role of a politically charged ethnic marker on a par with the queue.[53]

It is not surprising that male loyalists disparaged Sun for trying to win favor by voluntarily adopting the queue and advocating the tonsure command, nor does it seem unusual that they would heap additional ridicule on him for going to the extreme of involving the women of his family in his political maneuvers.[54] But footbinding does not appear to have been at the center of the loyalists' critique of Sun. Modern authors relating this episode cite the same few seventeenth-century sources, which give varying accounts of what Sun and his family women did (Table 1.2).[55] Only one of the seventeenth-century sources, *Miscellaneous Sorrows* (Tongyu zaji) by Shi Dun (*jinshi* 1642), says that the Sun women unbound their feet (*fang jiao*).[56] *Records of Travel in the North* (Beiyou lu), a work by Tan Qian (1594–1657), says the Sun women braided their hair (*bian fa*).[57] The accounts of the Sun episode in other seventeenth-century sources, namely, *Miscellaneous Notes of Things Seen and Heard from the Hall of Studies* (Yantang jianwen zaji; attributed to Wang Jiazhen) and *Further Essays on Rumors* (Souwen xubi), do not mention the women at all.[58] The Veritable Records (and sources that derive from them) say that the Sun women adopted "Manchu dress" (*Man zhuang*).[59] "Zhuang" is a broad category that can include hairstyles, cosmetics, clothing, and jewelry and possibly footbinding.[60] As there were multiple differences in dress between Manchu and Han women, the term *Man zhuang* leaves unspecified which items may have been adopted by the Sun women.[61]

Modern sources weave the seventeenth-century accounts of the "shameless" Sun into single patriotic narratives, typical of late-Qing and early Republican nationalist historiography. Yet not all of these mention the release of bindings (see Table 1.2).[62] Modern versions of the story of Sun Zhixie have been used anachronistically to support a claim that for seventeenth-century loyalist literati footbinding became a symbol of Han, and especially Han male, identity and that Qing attempts to ban footbinding led to the spread of footbinding as an act of resistance.[63]

Legends of footbinding women as "loyal and heroic resisters," too, are used as evidence that footbinding became a marker of "political defiance and ethnic pride" in the context of the Ming loyalist resistance.[64] The "weak-kneed turncoat" and scholar-poet Qian Qianyi (1582–1664) has been contrasted with his brave wife, the bound-footed poet courtesan Liu Rushi (1618–1664).[65] During the conquest, Qian became a minister in the southern Ming government at Nanjing, and when it collapsed he quickly surrendered to the Qing. Liu reproached her husband for his disloyalty, and he later regretted his actions and joined her in supporting the loyalist resistance.[66] Qian's poems praised both Liu's beauty and bravery and immortalized her heroism.[67] Qian was one of a number of prominent seventeenth-century literati who romanticized courtesan culture, idealized love affairs with talented courtesans, and linked romantic love to moral courage.[68] But not all loyalist writers held Liu

TABLE 1.2. Sources documenting the story of Sun Zhixie

Source	Sun shaves and adopts Manchu dress	Sun advocates imposing the queue	Sun women change hair or dress	Sun women unbind their feet	Sun and family die a cruel death
OFFICIAL DOCUMENTARY SOURCES					
Shizu shilu, juan 20, Shunzhi 2.8 *bingshen* (1985, vol. 3: 177)	X	O	*Man zhuang*	O	O
Donghua lu, Shunzhi 2.8 *bingshen* (1968)	X	O	*Man zhuang*	O	O
Qingshi liezhuan, vol. 10, *juan* 79.25a–26b (*Er chen zhuan yi*) (1962)	X	O	O	O	X
Qing shi gao, juan 245, *liezhuan* 32 ([1927] 1977: 9631, 9633)	X	O	*Man zhuang*	O	X
UNOFFICIAL, SEVENTEENTH-CENTURY SOURCES CRITICAL OF SUN ZHIXIE					
Tan Qian, *Beiyou lu* (1960: 354)	X	*Guo su*	*Bian fa*	O	X
Souwen xubi (1974, *juan* 1:9b [p. 1554])	O	*Fu ti*	O	O	O
Yantang jianwen zaji (1968: 23–24)	X	*Cong bixia*	O	O	X
Shi Dun, *Tongyu zaji* (1959: 71–72)	O	O	O	*Fang jiao*	X
TWENTIETH-CENTURY ACCOUNTS					
Qingchao yeshi daguan (1921, vol. 3, *juan* 3: 6–7)	X	*Cong bixia*	O	O	X
Xu Ke, *Qingbai leichao* ([1928] 1966, sec. 91: 61)	X	*Cong bixia*	*Man zhuang*	O	X
Chen Shengxi, "Qingchu tifa ling" (1985: 76–77)	X	*Cong bixia*	*Man zhuang*	*Fang jiao*	X
Gu Cheng, *Nan Ming shi* (1997: 211)	X	O	O	*Fang zu*	O

Note: X = mentioned; O = not mentioned

and courtesan culture in high esteem. Others adopted the more orthodox Confucian view condemning courtesans, and one eighteenth-century playwright, Dong Rong (1711–1760), indicts Liu Rushi as "a symbol of sensual indulgence and dynastic decadence."[69]

When anti-Qing commentators did praise Liu Rushi, it was for her courageous loyalism and poetic talent, not because of her bound feet.[70] Nor is footbinding at the center of stories of other courtesans who achieved fame in the dynastic transition, often as victims, and who were later made into heroines of loyalism by Qing and early Republican writers.[71] Linking footbinding to Ming loyalism ignores the condemnation of the licentious behavior of (bound-footed) courtesans in literary representations of women's lives during the conquest.[72]

In sum, neither the case of Sun Zhixie nor that of Liu Rushi provides evidence that footbinding per se became a symbol of Ming loyalism or Han male identity in the transition period.

THE PHANTOM 1645 BAN ON FOOTBINDING

If indeed a ban on footbinding had been imposed in 1645 or at any time between then and 1664, one might expect that the ban would have aroused opposition, have added to the troubles ensuing on the tonsure edict, and be the subject of numerous memoirs and historical writings cited by students of the dynastic transition. However, a survey of the several recent works on late-imperial women's literature and literature produced during the dynastic transition reveals no documented reference to a Qing ban on footbinding by any author, male or female, let alone "resistance" to it.[73] Mention of footbinding in women's poetry is rare, in part because considerations of modesty limited women's willingness to write on the topic. In the few women's poems celebrating feminine beauty that mention footbinding, there is no mention of a ban.[74] Nor is a ban mentioned in the famous discussions of women's bound feet by the male authors Li Yu (1610–1680) and Yu Huai (1616–1696) in the seventeenth century and Yuan Mei (1716–1797) in the eighteenth century.[75]

When women during the transition do refer to their bound feet, they express discontent with female adornments and restrictive gender roles, coupled with woman warrior fantasies, not celebrations of footbinding.[76] Nowhere do contemporary writers (male or female) extol footbinding as a "cultured" practice that distinguishes Chinese women from "barbaric" Manchus (however subtly alluded to), worry that daughters will not benefit from beautifully bound feet because of a ban, or lament feet that have lost their beauty and have become misshapen by an order to unbind (as happened in reaction to bans in the twentieth century). Nor do writers celebrate the 1668 lifting of the abortive 1664 ban. If one *assumes* that repeated prohibitions made the topic too politically sensitive to risk addressing openly, then one can explain the rarity of references to footbinding, as in the case of Pu Songling's stories.[77] But fear of persecution does not explain why both male and female poets, such as Qian Qianyi and Wang Duanshu, risked commenting on men's shaved heads and Manchu costume but not on a ban on footbinding, surely a much less sensitive topic than the inflammatory tonsure command.[78]

The several reviews of anti-Manchu thought in the seventeenth century make no mention of footbinding or any Qing prohibition thereof.[79] A review of references to footbinding in literati writing finds no hint of Confucian approval of the practice and no reference in didactic texts for women.[80] Nor is there any reference to a ban or laments over the forced unbinding of feet in writings of two famous connoisseurs of footbinding, Yu Huai and Li Yu, who lived through the conquest and well into the Kangxi reign and wrote at length on women's beauty.[81] Nothing in these writings makes a case for footbinding as a practice intended to express covert anti-Qing sentiments or to assert Chinese civility in the face of barbarian onslaught. The corpus of seventeenth-century literature and historical writing is vast (and well beyond this anthropologist's field of competence), but the lack of references suggesting that footbinding expressed anti-Manchu sentiments is striking.

Is there any evidence in the regional distribution of footbinding for the claims that footbinding became associated with Han ethnicity or with resistance to the Qing conquest?[82] If Han women's feet were bound in order to express covert anti-Manchu or anti-Qing sentiments (their own or their mothers' and fathers'), then rates of binding should be highest in areas such as Jiangnan, where Ming loyalism and armed resistance to the Qing takeover and adoption of the queue was greatest.[83] Multiple surveys of the regional prevalence of footbinding confirm that this was not the case. These reviews report that it is the north of China (which more readily accepted the queue) that is reputed to have had the highest rates of binding and the smallest feet and that the rates of binding varied widely in the south and the central areas of China.[84] Zhao Yi and Qian Yong, writing in the late eighteenth and early nineteenth centuries, report that farm women rarely bound their feet in Suzhou, Songjiang, Hangzhou, and Jiaxing, in the heartland of Jiangnan.[85] The modern historian of footbinding, Gao Hongxing, reports that footbinding in Jiangnan was often done crudely, and the Jiangnan women who did bind did not have feet as small as the northerners.[86] The prevalence of binding in Yangzhou, despite the city's horrific experience of Qing atrocities during the conquest, is attributed to its wealthy merchant culture, not to anti-Qing sentiment, and even in Yangzhou, bound feet are reported as not especially small.[87] Thus the regional distribution of footbinding (highest rates of prevalence in the north and lower in Jiangnan) does not support the notion that Ming loyalism spurred the spread of footbinding. Conceivably, Ming loyalism could have motivated binding in elite families, if not the population at large, but it is the elite strata whose lives are best documented in contemporary writings, and their writings betray no evidence of such motivations.

If for the Han population footbinding was operating to maintain an ethnic boundary, one would expect to see evidence that ordinary Han women and men living in China proper were aware that the early Qing government had prohibited footbinding or even that Manchus did not practice footbinding. Could Han ethnic pride in footbinding have been stimulated by the presence of large-footed bannerwomen? The chances are small that the vast numbers of Han living outside banner garrison cities could have seen bannerwomen, let alone their large feet. In 1700, there were only thirteen banner garrisons in the provinces beyond Beijing, all stationed in separately walled banner quarters within strategically located Chinese cities. Banner populations were segregated from the Chinese population, and interaction with the surrounding Chinese population was limited, especially so for bannerwomen. If in 1700 the population of China is generously estimated at 200 million, and half of the banner population of the provincial garrisons (numbering four hundred thousand) is female, bannerwomen would account for only 0.1% of the Chinese population.[88] Given their small numbers and their segregated existence in only thirteen locales in China proper, the chances that millions of Han were ever exposed to bannerwomen were minuscule. Nor did exposure to the large banner population in the capital stimulate footbinding. In Beijing, footbinding among civilian Han was less frequent, showing Manchu influence, than in the surrounding province (which had also offered little resistance to the tonsure edict).[89]

When Qing-period Han women bound their own and their daughters' feet, they did so as members of a culture that had long defined bound feet as beautiful and promised rewards (e.g., better marriages) and admiration for those who bound. They likely bound their feet for the same reasons and in the same circumstances as earlier generations had under the Ming. Those who achieved the goal of small feet were proud of their accomplishment and looked down on those with bigger feet. No evidence has shown that the footbinding fashion depended on revulsion to a banner counterculture to maintain its hold on Han women's lives. Footbinding was not an attribute of Han identity in the way that not binding was for the identity of the banner population. Many working-class Han women never bound their feet, but that did not bring their status as Han into question.[90]

The notion that bound feet expressed anti-Manchu sentiment becomes even more untenable in the last years of the Qing. The greatest nineteenth-century threat to Qing dynastic rule came in mid-century from the Hakka-led Taipings. The Taiping revolutionaries sought to prohibit footbinding, demanded that women release their bindings, and threatened to execute those who did not comply; no report suggests the Taipings entertained the notion that footbinding expressed Han pride, Ming loyalism, or anti-Manchu sentiment.[91] Thus despite their virulent anti-Manchu stance, the Taipings were like the Manchus in rejecting footbinding. At the beginning of the new century came the anti-foreign uprising of the Boxers and Red Lanterns, who are reported targeting natural-footed women and women who had released their bindings. But they were pro- and not anti-Qing, and they did so not to root out Manchu influence, but because they saw unbound feet on Han women as signs of foreign missionary influence.[92] Neither the Taipings nor the Red Lanterns connected footbinding to anti-Manchu sentiment.

Some late-Qing and twentieth-century nationalist slogans reflect male humiliation felt on adopting the queue and women's persistence in binding their feet, as in the saying "Men surrendered, women did not" (Nan xiang nü bu xiang), but this appears to have been one of several parallel phrases that saw print only in the context of anti-Qing nationalism in the dynasty's final decades.[93] When interpreted to refer to footbinding and the queue (rather than female heroines and male collaborators), it is similar to a phrase found in Liang Qichao's 1896 essay "On Education for Women" (Lun nü xue). From a different political point of view, Liang laments the inability of the Qing to abolish footbinding and comments, "It was easier to change strong men's hair than weak women's feet" (Qiangnan zhi tou buru ruonü zhi zu).[94] Both formulations, reflecting the nineteenth-century works reviewed above, presume that the early Qing rulers did in fact ban footbinding. Participants in the very different struggles of the late Qing used these memorable catchphrases to provide retrospective views of the events of the seventeenth century. Republican historiography of the conquest period celebrated the romantic notion that women's footbinding embodied opposition to Manchu rule in contrast to men's submission embodied in the queue. Yet when Republican reformers paired bound feet with the queue, their goal was to abolish both; when caught up in anti-Manchu rhetoric, some even accused the Qing not of banning footbinding but of encouraging footbinding as a device to weaken the Han.[95] Indeed, interviews with men and women in Sichuan found they had been under the impression that footbinding was required by the government, not forbidden.[96] In the minds of ordinary Han women, footbinding was in accordance with Qing government dictates, not in defiance of them.

In late 1911, at the height of anti-Manchu revolutionary passions, violent clashes between revolutionary soldiers and Qing loyalist and banner forces broke out in several garrison cities. In Wuchang, Xi'an, and Nanjing, these clashes ended in massacres of banner people, including women whose identity as bannerwomen was betrayed by their unbound feet (if not by their hairstyles, dress, accent, or residence).[97] In these conflicts Han rebel soldiers saw bannerwomen's natural feet as a clear mark of Manchu identity and membership in a hated caste. But even in those polarized times, no evidence has been produced to show that the revolutionaries saw footbinding by Han as a patriotic act or that Han women bound their feet to express anti-Manchu sentiments.[98]

CONCLUSION

Evidence does not support the existence of a 1645 ban on footbinding. Modern scholars' frequent repetition of the notion of "repeated bans" in the post-1644 years that apply to footbinding by Han civilian women can all be traced back to the same few early nineteenth-century sources, primarily Yu Zhengxie's *Classified Drafts of the Thirtieth Year* and Qian Yong's *Collected Works from Lüyuan*. Yu and Qian mention the 1645 date but provide no background, documentation, or source for the reference, in contrast to their discussions of the 1638 ban and the 1664–68 episode. Qian Yong reports the explicit denial of any ban in the Shunzhi years included in Wang Xi's 1668 memorial, but fails to acknowledge that this contradicts his reference to a 1645 ban. Nor do any of these or the other nineteenth- and twentieth-century writers cite supporting evidence for a 1645 ban from literary or informal historical sources. No modern studies of footbinding have cited Wang Bu's transcription of Wang Xi's 1668 memorial since Qian Yong reported doing so circa 1838, nor have they cited the 1664 edict (published in 1951).

The historic context of the abortive 1664 ban and its repeal in 1668 relates to the politics of the Oboi regency. There is no evidence that the 1664 ban was ever implemented, let alone that it "failed" due to defiant opposition by footbinding women, or that it encouraged Han women to bind their feet to symbolize resistance to the Qing.[99]

Explanations for a continued spread of footbinding from the late Ming into the early and high Qing come not by looking to discontinuities caused by the dynastic transition but by attending to the continuities in commercialization and merchant and popular cultures that transcended the political rupture.[100] In the Qing, as in the Ming, definitions of beauty, desires for status and good marriages, and pressures to conform remained the motivating factors that led to binding.

CHAPTER 2

The Taiwan Census of 1905

OUR knowledge of the prevalence of the footbinding fashion in Ming-Qing China is almost wholly based on a very few comments made by Chinese literati and Western observers, as footbinding was ignored in the writings of a great majority of Chinese scholars, for whom the practice was both too undignified and too common to be worthy of notice. But in the eyes of Western traders, diplomats, and missionaries, footbinding was a curiosity (variously shocking or exotic) worthy of inquiry and comment. From the late nineteenth century on, the increasing numbers of Western sojourners in China produced the sizable body of anecdotal observations on the practice that have been mined by all modern students of footbinding to construct a picture of footbinding's distribution across the classes and regions of China. The censuses of Taiwan from the early Japanese colonial era are, however, the only systematic accounting of the practice of footbinding that was ever produced. The 1905 and 1915 censuses document the prevalence of footbinding across an entire population when the practice was still in its heyday.

The richly documented history of Taiwanese society, and Taiwan's rare census materials recording the custom, provides a unique opportunity to place footbinding in the full context of the local society that sustained its practice. The findings from a detailed local study can also inform analysis of various interpretations put forth by studies using other forms of documentation and focusing on other regional variants of China's complex society.

Major questions to be explored through the Taiwan data over the next several chapters are these: What are the main lines of ethnic difference with regard to footbinding in Taiwan? How do rates of binding vary by region and across generations? How did women and families react to the growing anti-binding sentiment and the prohibition of binding in 1915? Does binding advantage young women in the marriage market? What accounts for regional differences in the age at binding and the prevalence of binding? How did the presence of non-binding Hakka affect rates of binding among the Hoklo? Does wet versus dry agriculture or some other factor explain variations in binding prevalence? What is the relationship between binding and the handi-craft work women did?

HISTORICAL BACKGROUND

The origins of Taiwan's Chinese society date to the seventeenth century, when Chinese agriculturalists from the southeast coast of China (southern Fujian and northeastern Guangdong provinces) began to open up lands on the sparsely populated island only one hundred miles across the strait. Settlement began under the auspices of the Dutch East India Company (1624–61), was spurred on by the turbulence caused during the Manchu conquest of main-land China, and continued under the Ming loyalist regime of the Zhengs (1661–83). In 1683, the Zheng regime surrendered to the Manchu Qing dynasty, and Taiwan was incorporated into the Qing empire as a prefecture of Fujian Province.

Taiwan's Chinese population grew rapidly in the early 1700s, when the economy and population of the southeast coast recovered from losses suf-fered during the dynastic transition. Nearby Taiwan's open fields attracted increasing numbers of southeast coast immigrants seeking land to farm and to profit from the demand for rice and sugar across the strait. Over the next two centuries, the Chinese population and economy of Qing Taiwan contin-ued to grow. The majority of Taiwan's Chinese descended from settlers hailing from the Quanzhou and Zhangzhou Prefectures of southern Fujian. These settlers brought with them the footbinding culture of the Hoklos (the Hok-kien speakers of southeast Fujian and the Teochiu speakers on the northeast coast of Guangdong).[1] Smaller elements of Taiwan's population did not prac-tice footbinding; these were the Hakka, who immigrated from the interior of northeast Guangdong, and the plains aborigines, descendants of the original Austronesian population of Taiwan.

In 1887, the Qing government, concerned about foreign threats to southeast coast security, appointed a governor and raised Taiwan to provincial status. By 1895, when it became Japan's first colonial conquest, Taiwan was the site of a mature Chinese society in which female footbinding was widely practiced.[2]

The Meiji restoration in 1868 inaugurated an intensive effort by Japan to modernize its military, technology, and institutions to ward off the threat of Western encroachment. In only a few decades Japan became the leading industrial and military power in East Asia. By the early 1890s, the Japanese were seeking to assert equality with the Western powers, to curtail competing spheres of influence in Northeast Asia and the Pacific and to expand Japan's own spheres of influence. Nationalists perceived threats to Japanese security in Russian plans to build the trans-Siberian railroad to Vladivostok and Chinese opposition to Japanese influence in Korea.[3] To resolve the latter conflict, Japan declared war on Qing China in 1894. Japan's modernized navy and army won quick victories in China's northeast that brought the Sino-Japanese war to a swift conclusion in 1895.[4]

The Treaty of Shimonoseki, which ended the war, forced China to cede Taiwan to Japan. Japanese troops landed in northeast Taiwan in late May 1895 and proceeded to defeat a fragmented armed opposition as they swept down the western coastal plain, reaching the southern tip of the island by October.[5] A nascent colonial administration was installed and reconstruction along Japanese lines began.

The first military governors of the new colony were preoccupied with immediate challenges: suppressing guerrilla resistance, limiting the threat to their forces from the island's many diseases, creating an effective administration, and dealing with mounting expenses. They lacked a larger vision for the future administration and development of the colony. That changed in 1898 when Kodama Gentarō was appointed military governor and he selected Gotō Shimpei as his civilian chief. Kodama and Gotō seized the opportunity to develop Taiwan's agriculture and exploit the island's natural resources for Japan's benefit and, in the process, to remold Taiwan into a model colony. Their personal experience of rapid modernization in Japan gave them confidence in their ability to use the tools of government to reshape society, and they were intent on demonstrating their skill as colonialists to the Western powers.[6] Kodama and Gotō led an administration (1898–1906) committed to a "scientific colonialism" that based its development plans on detailed information gathered about the colony's society, population, and resources. As part of this effort they oversaw Taiwan's 1905 census, the first modern census in East Asia, which predated Japan's own first census by fifteen years.[7] In addition to designing the comprehensive census and household registration system (that produced the footbinding data analyzed herein), Kodama and

Gotō initiated an extensive land survey, reformed the system of taxation, and sponsored research on Taiwan's customary law.[8]

Japanese plans to develop Taiwan's economy and modernize its society required an orderly, disciplined, and productive colonial population. The Japanese viewed Taiwanese practices that reduced economic productivity, such as opium smoking, footbinding, and queue wearing, as both backward and degenerate.[9] Fukuzawa Yukichi, a leading Meiji intellectual, published editorials in 1895 in his influential newspaper *Jiji shinpō* expressing contempt for the Taiwanese in Japan's new colony. An August 14 editorial recommended radical corrective measures: "In order to pacify the island and develop the rich resources with the hands of our Japanese people, the goal of managing Taiwan should focus solely on the land while ignoring the natives. We should first issue orders to correct all the barbarous customs such as men's wearing pigtails and women's foot-binding. Opium smoking should be strictly prohibited."[10] Thus, from the beginning of their rule, the Japanese singled out "three degenerate practices," footbinding, queue wearing, and opium smoking, as obstacles to development.[11]

Footbinding and queue wearing clashed with Meiji-era Japanese (and Western) hair and dress standards. As part of the drive to modernize their own society, Japanese elites had adopted Western definitions of progress and backwardness, and these included notions about proper modern hair and dress styles. Western fashions in dress and hairstyles were seen as symbols of modernity, and the Meiji government encouraged their adoption and the abandonment of distinctive Japanese fashions. The samurai topknot was abolished, and both civil and military personnel were ordered to wear Western-style uniforms and suits in all professional settings. The empress set the example for Japanese women by abandoning shaved eyebrows and blackened teeth and making public appearances in Western dresses.[12] In East Asia, Western dress became a badge of Meiji Japan's progress and footbinding and queue wearing marks of China's backwardness. The new colonial elite brought these attitudes to Taiwan.

Taiwanese society proved less pliable than the colonialists at first imagined. Reforming the governmental administration, tax structure, and economy proved to be easier than changing deeply ingrained customs. Colonial policy makers soon abandoned ambitious plans to eradicate opium smoking in favor of controls over the opium supply. Because opium smoking depended on an import trade in opium that offered a means both to regulate the trade and to profit from it, the colonial government created an opium monopoly and instituted strict controls limiting sales to licensed smokers.[13] But foot-binding and queue wearing, as intimate aspects of female and male bodies and appearance closely linked to Hoklo Taiwanese notions of personhood, offered no easy or profitable means for government intervention.

Japanese colonial administrators believed that eradicating long-standing social customs such as footbinding and queue wearing could not be done by government fiat without raising serious grassroots opposition.[14] The Japanese were not able to eliminate the last pockets of guerrilla resistance to colonial rule until 1902 and were wary of needlessly stirring up renewed opposition. Thus the colonial authorities adopted a laissez-faire regulatory policy but a proactive educational approach to social reform. They gave support to indig-enous reform efforts led by Taiwanese elites and encouraged media criticisms of the practices as unnatural, backward, and unsanitary. They hoped that over time Taiwanese would be enlightened and "degenerate" customs would be abandoned.

Separation from China and incorporation into the Japanese empire caused prominent Taiwanese to rethink old customs. Taiwanese elites who made government-sponsored visits to Japan were impressed by the sight of natural-footed girls studying in schools and women taking active roles in society and industry. In preparation for trips abroad, some Taiwanese busi-nessmen and intellectuals cut their queues "to avoid being humiliated," a sign of increasing sensitivity in elite strata to negative foreign attitudes and notions of backwardness that stigmatized queue wearing and footbinding.[15]

Anti-footbinding attitudes were already making headway among Chinese elites in this era, and reform-minded Taiwanese adopted many of the arguments and strategies used by the anti-footbinding movement in Qing China. The first Taiwanese anti-footbinding association was launched in 1900 when Huang Yujie, an influential doctor of Chinese medicine in Taipei's mercantile center of Dadaocheng, organized the Taipei Natural Foot Society (Taibei Tianran Zu Hui). The society drew membership from progressive members of the Taipei elite (by 1903, membership had grown to 2,270) and received high-level official blessing. But the society's efforts were quickly frustrated by conservative atti-tudes in the broader society (where natural-footed women were ridiculed) as well as by opposition from women in the families of society members.

A delegation of influential gentry visiting the Fifth National Indus-trial Exhibition in Osaka, Japan, in 1903, was deeply impressed by Japan's economic and technical advances and its modernizing society. Delegates were also embarrassed when bound-footed women appeared in the Taiwan exhibition serving tea, and Chinese students in Japan complained about the shameful display of backwardness.[16] Convinced that broad societal reforms were needed, members of the delegation launched a second natural foot society in the southern center of Tainan on their return to Taiwan. As in mainland anti-footbinding societies, members of the anti-footbinding associations pledged not to bind daughters' feet and to arrange marriages for sons only to natural-footed women. The combined efforts of these societies, whose memberships reached at most a few thousand and which relied on families to voluntarily give up footbinding, had had very limited impact by the time of the 1905 census.[17]

Mothers, not fathers, oversaw the binding of daughters' feet. These women understood binding as part of a mother's duty to make daughters eligible for good marriages. Women, who were much less exposed to the information and pressures felt by their husbands, had yet to be convinced that natural-footed girls could find worthy husbands, would not be subjected to humiliating jibes when going out in public or in the families of their husbands, and would not be reduced to the status of servant girls and forced to perform outdoor labor reserved for the natural-footed. These strongly held beliefs would not be easily changed.

Confronting entrenched resistance, some local reformers decided that coercion (rather than gentlemen's agreements) was necessary to eliminate footbinding, but their efforts appear to have had little effect. In 1903, gentry councilors in Tainan Prefecture advocated using local mutual security organizations and agricultural associations to enforce an official prohibition.[18] In 1903, the Jiaobanian agricultural cooperative (located in present-day Yujing Township, Tainan), concerned that footbinding reduced agricultural productivity, reportedly forced all girls aged twelve years and under to release their bindings, and, after a few days of difficulty walking, it was claimed that their feet returned to their natural shape.[19] The results were not long lasting: the proportions of Fujian women ever-bound in this district in 1915 is the same as the all-Taiwan average and shows no effect of this attempt to eliminate binding.[20] The attempt nevertheless shows that the leaders of the agricultural association understood the costs of binding in lost labor to farm families. No prohibition of footbinding was forthcoming from the colonial government at this time; prohibition would have to wait until 1915.

In the first years of colonial rule, the Japanese battled armed resistance and, when that was suppressed, scattered outbreaks of banditry and rebellion. To minimize these threats, the security-conscious Japanese created a policing system that exercised close control over the subject Taiwanese population. They did this by creating a dense network of police stations and charging police with surveillance of households. In this task the police were aided by a neighborhood security system built on the Chinese system of self-policing (C: baojia, J: hokō) that held household heads mutually responsible for crimes committed in their locality. At the local police station, registers were maintained that recorded the names, birth dates, parentage, provenance, and other information of every member of each household in the district. Heads were required to report any changes in household membership, whether by birth, death, migration, adoption, or marriage. Movements of households and transfers of membership between households were carefully tracked in both sending and receiving registry offices. To ensure that the registers were kept up to date, the police regularly visited the households in their precincts to verify the information.[21]

In police hands, the household registers proved instrumental to guaranteeing local security, collecting taxes, and overseeing public works and sanitation. In addition, the registration system produced the demographic data required by economic development and administrative planning and in public health programming.

To better serve both development planning goals and the policing function, colonial administrators conducted a fully modern census of the population on October 1, 1905. In the preparations leading up to the census, the registry system was improved and new household registers were designed and adopted across the island.[22] A census bureaucracy trained census takers (many were police or schoolteachers) to verify the information in the police registers, enter it into census forms, and aggregate the data into census reports. Beginning in the final quarter of 1905, the changes in the population recorded through the household registration system were aggregated to produce annual vital statistics volumes and, at five- and ten-year intervals, detailed census reports on the status of the population. Census coverage was complete; the censuses registered and enumerated males and females of all ages and ethnicities, and no groups were overlooked.[23] Tests of consistency matching reports of births and deaths to successive census counts demonstrate the accuracy of the census's classification of the population by the key attributes of age and sex.[24] This system of continuously updated registration yielded the extremely high-quality demographic data available for Japanese-period Taiwan.[25] The Taiwan censuses are thus very different from (and superior in quality to) censuses conducted in parachute fashion once every ten years, such as the U.S. census.

The census schedule and the new household registers provided space to document two of the "three degenerate practices," opium smoking and footbinding, which were on the reform agenda of the colony. In the columns where each individual's name, birth date, parentage, and other details were to be recorded, blank spaces were provided to note whether the person was a licensed opium smoker and, in the case of females, whether the feet were currently or formerly bound (if the woman had never bound, no notation was made).[26] This collection of data made both practices a matter of police surveillance and record keeping, although in 1905 only opium licenses were actively regulated. When the prohibition of footbinding was decreed in 1915, the police would make use of the register information to enforce the ban. In both 1905 and 1915, the census schedules recorded the updated footbinding data collected in the household registers, thereby documenting both the dimensions of the social problem footbinding represented and the progress of anti-binding campaigns.[27] The registers also provided spaces to make note of other individual characteristics, including provenance (e.g., Fujian, Guangdong, plains aborigine), security ranking (determining the frequency of police inspection visits), smallpox vaccination, and disabilities (e.g., deaf, mute, blind, insane), all reflecting the interest of the police in monitoring the population.[28]

The 1905 and 1915 census reports presented the information gathered on footbinding in identically designed sets of tables. The most detailed footbinding data in the 1905 and 1915 censuses (from the *Detailed Tables* [Shūkei gempyō] census volumes) are included in two pairs of tables, reported for the island as a whole and then for each prefecture (twenty in 1905 and twelve in 1915). Two tables report information only for currently bound women (C: *chanzuzhe*, J: *tensokusha*), and two identically formatted tables report the same information for women who were once bound-footed but had since removed their bindings, who are labeled "released" (C: *jiechanzuzhe*, J: *kaitensokusha*). The use of the awkward "released" as a translation for this label is preferable to use of an ambiguous phrasing such as "unbound," which might be mistaken to include women whose feet had never been bound. The numbers of released women would only grow to significant size in 1915 as the campaign to abolish footbinding gained traction. Together, the currently bound and released Taiwanese women (numbering in 1905, 800,392 and 8,690, respectively) constitute the "ever-bound" portion of the female population. The footbinding tables do not report the number of women whose feet had never been bound at the time of the census; these natural-footed women will be referred to as the "never-bound." Comparing the footbinding tables to the corresponding tables for the female population as a whole reveals the numbers of females never-bound. The first pair of the footbinding tables reports the ages, marital status, and provenance of bound and released women. The second pair of tables reports the occupational categories of bound and released women.[29]

FOOTBINDING AND ETHNICITY

Any description of footbinding among the Taiwanese must begin by distinguishing the population subgroups that differed greatly in their reception of the practice. The colonial censuses distinguished the Han according to province of origin in China, Guangdong (*Yue ji*) and Fujian (*Min ji*), which for most individuals corresponded to speech group. This continued the Qing practice of differentiating the immigrant groups by provenance defined by administrative, not ethnic, criteria.[30] The census divided the non-Han populations of Austronesian descent between plains and mountain aborigines (labeled by the Japanese as civilized and non-civilized). Nineteenth-century Western sources (and Chinese sources concur) regularly report that footbinding in Taiwan was overwhelmingly practiced among the Hokkien-speaking majority (commonly called Hoklos), who traced their origins to southern Fujian Province, and almost never by the minority Hakka speakers from Guangdong Province and by the several groups of plains aborigines.[31] Table 2.1 shows a sharp contrast in footbinding between the populations hailing from Fujian and those of Guangdong and plains aborigine extraction.

As shown in the table, a sizable 68.7% of Fujian women were ever-bound, but only 1.6% of Guangdong and 0.6% of plains aborigine women. Overall, 99.6% of ever-bound Taiwanese women claimed provincial origin in Fujian, and only 0.4% claimed Guangdong. It comes as no surprise that Fujianese women in Taiwan bound their feet at high rates, for it is also known from late nineteenth-century accounts that footbinding in the Xiamen (Amoy) area, from which most Taiwan Hoklo hailed, was nearly universal, "with the exception of the slave girls."[32] But is it the case that all Fujian women are Hoklo and all Guangdong women Hakka? Does provincial origin always correspond to

	PROVENANCE			
	Taiwanese*	Fujian	Guangdong	Plains aborigine
Female population, all ages	1,405,732	1,172,818	190,496	23,724
% of Taiwanese female population	100.00	83.40	13.60	1.70
Bound, all ages	800,392	797,347	2,881	127
Released, all ages	8,690	8,429	250	10
Ever-bound, all ages	809,082	805,776	3,131	137
Never-bound, all ages	596,650	367,042	187,365	23,587
% ever-bound, by provenance	57.56	68.70	1.64	0.58
% of total ever bound	100.00	99.59	0.39	0.017

Sources: Census of 1905, Shūkei gempyō, zentō no bu 1907: tables 22, 24; Census of 1905, Kekka hyō 1908: tables 8, 9

* The "Taiwanese" census category ("islanders," C: bendaoren, J: hontōjin) includes all three provenance categories shown, plus two very small groups, Han from other provinces and mountain aborigines.

ethnolinguistic differences? The census data on footbinding classify the Taiwanese population by a combination of ethnic (e.g., Han, plains aborigine) and provenance categories (e.g., Fujian, Guangdong), not by speech group.

Fortunately, a second source of evidence bears on the correspondence between provenance and speech group. The 1905 census reported data on language in daily use (C: chang yong yu, J: jōyōgo), cross-classified by provenance.[33] This enables an assessment of the extent to which groups classified by provenance were also homogeneous speech groups. In Table 2.2, the data are given for women only, as only women had bound feet, and the purpose is to understand the cultural background of the female population that practiced footbinding. The census and household registers assigned provenance to a woman according to the provenance of her father (or, if the woman was illegitimate, her mother) and not her husband.

The data on language use confirm that very few Fujianese spoke a language other than Hokkien. Thus data referring to Fujianese identify a population culturally Hoklo. The data also show that a large preponderance of Guangdong settlers spoke Hakka (85%), although a minority spoke Hokkien (15%). The Guangdong category is thus overwhelmingly composed of Hakka

TABLE 2.2. Language in daily use among Taiwanese females, by provenance, 1905

Language in daily use	PROVENANCE					
	Fujian		Guangdong		Plains aborigine	
Hokkien	1,164,086	99.37%	29,012	15.25%	19,467	82.29%
Hakka	7,033	0.60%	161,100	84.67%	472	2.00%
Bango	294	0.03%	146	0.08%	3,719	15.72%

Source: Census of 1905, Shūkei gempyō, zentō no bu 1907: table 10, 1208–9

Note: A few speakers of Japanese and other Chinese languages are not shown in this table. The categories used in the language classification are clarified in SPCF 1905 (1909: 95); see also Hashimoto (1973: 24). Hokkien includes speakers of Teochiu (from Chaozhou Prefecture, Guangdong). Bango refers to several different Austronesian languages.

speakers, and, with a few precautions, data referring to Guangdongese can be used to characterize the Hakka ethnic group. The language data also show that the plains aborigine group had overwhelmingly adopted the majority Hokkien language and that only 18% spoke other languages. There is thus a strong correspondence between provenance and speech group in the Taiwan population that enables, in most instances, the interchangeable use of provenance and ethnic labels, Fujianese and Hoklo, on the one hand, and Guangdongese and Hakka, on the other.[34] The main exceptions were the culturally Hoklo peoples from the coastal areas of Guangdong's Chaozhou Prefecture, who were speakers of a variety of Hokkien known as Teochiu.

The 1905 census recorded only 8,429 Fujian women who had released their bindings, compared to 797,347 women whose feet remained bound. Of these 8,429, 4,842 were adult women (above age fifteen) who were widely scattered among the age-groups and prefectures. Although the census provides no hint as to why these few women released their bindings, they may have done so for any number of reasons: in response to anti-footbinding campaigns, because they needed to find outdoor work, or for health or other concerns. With respect to the 3,587 girls aged fifteen and younger who released their bindings, 86% of them were concentrated in only three prefectures: Zhanghua (55%) and Nantou (12%) in central Taiwan and Tainan (19%) in the south. It is possible that the campaign of the southern branch of the anti-footbinding movement may have influenced the families of the girls who had released their bindings. The Taipei branch of the anti-footbinding movement, which is discussed in great detail in the historical literature, appears to have had minimal impact by 1905. In the three prefectures with concentrations of young girls releasing, the proportions released of the total ever-bound at ages fifteen and younger were 20% in Zhanghua, 32% in Nantou, and only 7% in Tainan; thus large majorities of girls continued binding. Judging from the large increases in the proportion of girls binding between ages five and ten and ages eleven and fifteen reported in these three prefectures, there was little reduction in the numbers of young girls beginning to bind. In all three of these prefectures, more than 90% of adult women had bound feet, suggesting that the binding tradition was deeply rooted in social custom.

Footbinding among Guangdong Females

Although very few Guangdong women (3,131) were included among the eight hundred thousand ever-bound Taiwanese females, any footbinding among a population overwhelmingly Hakka appears anomalous. Reports of footbinding by prefecture show that over half (1,788) are located in only three prefectures (Zhanghua, Yanshuigang, and Penghu), having small populations of Guangdong females (2,712), 66% of whom were ever-bound.[35] Reports of language in daily use by provenance and prefecture show that over 99% of these women were Hokkien speakers.[36] Thus it is likely that these women either were speakers of Teochiu from the coastal areas of Chaozhou Prefecture or were from populations that, although Hakka in origin, have "Hoklorized."[37] In either case, it is not surprising that such culturally Hoklo Guangdong women would bind their feet; nineteenth-century sources confirm that footbinding was widespread among Hoklo around the port of Swatow (Shantou) and its hinterlands in Chaozhou Prefecture.[38] Five additional prefectures (Taibei, Jilong, Douliu, Tainan, and Fengshan) have small populations of Guangdongese (599 females in total), of whom an average of 68% are Hokkien speakers. These populations of Guangdongese average 28% ever-bound (168 women), and those who bound are also likely to be Chaozhou Hoklo or Hoklorized Hakka.

The remaining twelve prefectures contain the bulk of the Guangdongese population (187,185 females), of whom only 13.8% are Hokkien speakers and only 0.6% are ever-bound. Hakka predominate among the Guangdongese in these prefectures, as do natural feet, and it is likely that a goodly proportion of the remaining ever-bound women (1,175) come from the minority of Hokkien, not Hakka, speakers. A few very elite Hakka women are known to have bound their feet in the southern Hakka township of Meinong, apparently as a means of status display.[39] But, given that well over half of the ever-bound Guangdong women are Hokkien speakers, and the likelihood that Hokkien

FIGURE 2.1. Ethnicities in the population of Taiwan. Five groups are represented by figures proportional to their share of the population: Fujianese, Guangdongese, aborigines, Japanese, and foreigners. The Fujianese woman is represented as having bound feet and the Guangdong woman as having natural or bare feet. *Source: Taiwan tōkei zuhyō* 1912: 4.

speakers account for much of the rest, it is almost certain that only a handful at most of Hakka-speaking Guangdong women were ever-bound. Thus we can rely on the generalization that Taiwanese Hakka (almost) never bound. Figure 2.1 accordingly represents Fujianese women as bound-footed and Guangdongese women as natural-footed.

The Absence of Footbinding among Plains Aborigines

Why did Taiwan's plains aborigines, in many ways highly acculturated to Hoklo ways, never adopt footbinding, despite being surrounded by a dominant Hoklo footbinding culture? There are a number of possible explanations. First, as among the Hakka, the plains aborigine gender division of labor relied on significant female contributions to farming, which would be lost if footbinding were adopted.[40] Footbinding would also impede plains aborigine women's accustomed freedom of movement and, in contrast to family patriarchy among both Hakka and Hoklo, conflict with the authority plains aborigine women exercised in the household.[41] Second, despite their proficiency in Hokkien language and the adoption of many other Han practices, plains aborigines continued to be disparaged by their neighbors as "barbarians" (hoan-a) and poor farmers well into the late twentieth century.[42] The stigma of "barbarian" origins thwarted attempts to improve their status in Han eyes even after the abolition of footbinding in 1915. This suggests plains aborigines may well have judged that emulating Han footbinding (when it was fashionable) was unlikely to do much to improve their "barbarian" status. Third, plains aborigine numbers remained small in part due to an unfavorable marriage market for men and the loss of women through marriage to outsider Han. The high male sex ratios in the surrounding Chinese population, the result of a pattern of male immigrants coming without families and also of excess female mortality (due to female infanticide and daughter neglect) in the Han settler communities, created a high demand for brides, including aborigine brides.[43] In the competition for wives, better-off Chinese could offer incentives that plains aborigine men could not match. Plains aborigine populations thus experienced a slow drain of women into marriages to Han, which they only partly made up by importing wives from the mountain tribes and through the adoption of Hoklo girls unwanted by their families.[44] Given the drain of women to intermarriage, adopting footbinding would only have made plains aborigine women more acceptable to proud Hoklo families and further weakened aborigine communities demographically. In sum, both demographic and economic considerations reinforced the plains aborigine gender culture that empowered women and abhorred binding. Thus plains aborigines, despite the dominance of Hoklo binding culture in neighboring communities, never adopted footbinding.

FOOTBINDING AMONG FUJIANESE
BY AGE AND GENERATION

Sharp ethnic differences thus influenced the propensity to bind in Taiwan's population. Footbinding was a rarity among the Hakka and plains aborigines, but was extremely common among the Fujianese Hoklo, of whom 68.7% were ever-bound and who accounted for 99.6% of all ever-bound women in Taiwan.

Table 2.3 shows the numbers and proportions of Fujian women ever-bound in each age-group. The largest age-group, those between one and ten

TABLE 2.3. Proportions of Fujianese females with ever-bound feet, by age, 1905

Age and years of birth*	Number of Fujian females	Number of ever-bound	% ever-bound
1–10, 1896–1905	302,902	54,638	18.0
11–20, 1886–95	223,184	167,310	75.0
21–30, 1876–85	221,931	195,743	88.2
31–40, 1866–75	161,839	146,778	90.7
41–50, 1856–65	110,995	100,893	90.9
51–60, 1846–55	84,471	77,631	91.9
61–70, 1836–45	48,106	44,649	92.8
71+, before 1836	19,390	18,134	93.5
Total (all ages)	1,172,818	805,776	68.7
Total (5–10)	167,571	54,638	32.6
Total (>20)	646,732	583,828	90.3

Sources: Census of 1905, Shūkei gempyō, zentō no bu 1907: tables 22, 24; Census of 1905, Kekka hyō 1908: table 9

* The census reports "age" by year of birth, beginning with those born in the year of the census, 1905, who are listed as "sui age 1." There is no age "0" by this reckoning. Note that this measure of age by birth-year cohort does not correspond either to traditional Chinese sui or to Western measures of age at last birthday.

years old, is the youngest and has the smallest proportion ever-bound. This is because binding for girls begins at the earliest at age five, and there are large numbers of younger girls who have not yet begun binding. If the youngest girls are excluded from the calculation, the proportion bound at ages five through ten rises to 32.6%.

Measuring proportions bound by age corrects the mistaken impression conveyed by the crude measure of 68.7% ever-bound of all ages that seems to imply that over 30% of Fujianese women never bound. Families began to bind their daughters' feet at various ages, some as early as five, some just prior to marriage, and some natural-footed women bound their feet after marriage under pressure from their husbands' families. Thus the proportions ever-bound increase rapidly in the early age classes, most markedly in the eleven-to-twenty age-group (where 75% were bound, compared to 32.6% at ages five through ten), as women approached the age of marriage. Between ages twenty and thirty the proportions ever-bound reach a plateau and remain constant thereafter. The table shows that a strikingly high proportion of all Fujianese women (more than 90%) eventually bound their feet. Thus for Fujianese, footbinding was practiced by the overwhelming majority, and only a handful of women never bound. Clearly, footbinding was not a practice restricted to a privileged and aristocratic few. When 90% of women bound, the pressure to conform to the footbinding convention must have been enormous; not to bind under these conditions was unthinkable for respectable Fujianese.

The constant proportions ever-bound in the older age classes suggest that footbinding practices had not changed in the lifetimes of the women reported in the 1905 census. The proportions ever-bound in the older age classes reflect conditions prevailing when these women were young and their feet were bound. Once women entered middle and old age, they would rarely have acted to bind fully formed but never-bound feet; the few who loosened bindings are included in the ever-bound category.

The constant high proportions ever-bound in the older age classes controvert any claims that footbinding had only recently become the fashion among a frontier population of Taiwan Fujianese or that the proportions bound had changed in response to changing economic or political conditions in nineteenth-century Taiwan. That high proportions were bound in the earliest decades of the nineteenth century is corroborated by the eyewitness account of Captain Frank Denham, taken captive in Taiwan in 1842 after his ship wrecked on the north coast; Denham noted of the women he saw while he was marched south to Tainan: "They have almost all the small feet."[45] The high proportion ever-bound among adult Fujianese women is consistent with reports of high proportions bound in the native prefectures of Taiwan's Fujianese population in southeast coastal Fujian.[46] The proportion ever-bound among adult Fujianese women is also comparable to the 94% of adult women who bound in Ding County, Hebei, in North China.[47] Thus broad claims that proportions bound in South China were always much lower than in North China can be rejected.[48] The constant high proportions bound across the generations suggests that footbinding was a custom deeply entrenched in Hoklo culture, seemingly impervious to change, that each generation imposed on the next.

CONCLUSION

What accounts for the strong hold of the footbinding fashion among the Hoklo and its near absence among the Hakka? Can differences in gender hierarchies explain natural feet among Hakka and bound feet among Hoklo? Comparative studies of household registers from Hakka and Hoklo districts in Taiwan have repeatedly found overwhelming similarity in family structure, patterns of marriage and adoption, and rates of fertility and mortality.[49] Bound-footed Hoklo women and their natural-footed Hakka sisters lived out their lives in families of similar type. That Confucian patriarchy, gender hierarchy and work discipline, or mother-daughter bonding were only made possible by footbinding would have come as a surprise to natural-footed Hakka women. Ethnography affirms that although Hakka women engaged in tasks that natural feet made possible, this did little to change their position with respect to power in the family.[50] Patriarchy and the subordination of women thus fail to explain differences between Hoklo and Hakka.

The different foot cultures of the Hoklo and the Hakka must be traced to their different histories. A search for the origins of footbinding among Fujianese begins with the general notion that the fashion trickled down from the Song and successor courts, as status emulation by provincial elites gradually introduced the footbinding fashion into China's local societies.[51] Although observations about footbinding in Fujian in these early centuries have yet to be identified in the documentary record, it is known that Fujianese elites were closely attuned to court culture.[52] Fujian's remarkable success in producing holders of the highest degree (jinshi) in the civil service examinations in the Song, and the presence of large numbers of Song imperial clansmen, created a close connection between its provincial elite and the Song court in the period when the footbinding fashion was first taking hold.[53] The earliest evidence of footbinding in Fujian comes from the bowed shoes and bound feet preserved in the Song-period tomb of a woman (1227–1243) from a high-ranking official family, whose father had served as superintendent of maritime trade in Quanzhou and whose husband was a member of the imperial clan.[54] In southern Fujian, Quanzhou's prosperous seaborne trade generated much of the prosperity that funded investments in education and examination success in the province. Quanzhou's own elites invested in classical educations, won examination success, and adopted literati lifestyles that surely included footbinding for female family members.[55]

Building on academic traditions established in the Song, Ming-period Fujian repeated its success in winning the highest examination degree, ranking fourth among the provinces in numbers of jinshi (the Jiangnan provinces of Zhejiang and Jiangsu ranked first and second) and first when ranked by jinshi per million population.[56] Ming Fujian also ranked second highest among the provinces in mobility, measured by the proportion of jinshi whose families had failed to produce a holder of any official title in the previous three generations.[57] The high rates of upward mobility and the density of elite degree holders testify to the deep penetration of literati culture in the province.

During the sixteenth century, the revival of Fujian's overseas commerce and its coastal trade links to the wealthy Jiangnan region brought renewed prosperity to the province. This was a period of economic expansion, commercialization, growth of cities and craft industries, interregional trade, increased spatial and social mobility, growing literacy, and a popular culture celebrating elite fashions.[58]

Because no sumptuary laws forbade footbinding by commoners, and no legal barriers blocked their occupational mobility, status competition was given free rein, enabling binding to spread throughout society.[59] Upwardly mobile merchant families often went to extremes in their striving for status, whether through success in the examination system, by material display and consumption, or by demonstrations of conspicuous morality, especially by female kin (e.g., widow suicide, the cult of widow chastity).[60] Wealthy families seeking to enhance their status invested in sons' educations so they could succeed in the civil service examinations and expected daughters to acquire the attributes of beauty and refinement, which included bound feet.

As new wealth replaced old, and prosperity put luxuries within reach, competition for status led to conspicuous consumption.[61] This process accelerated in the sixteenth and seventeenth centuries, especially in areas where the growth of an urban, commercialized society increased opportunities for social mobility. The scholars Hu Yinglin (1551–1602) and Ye Mengzhu (1623–1693) linked the downward spread of footbinding in the prosperous Jiangnan region to the emergence of a fashion-conscious society in this era.[62]

The coastal prefectures of southeast Fujian from which Taiwan's Hoklo settlers emigrated, Zhangzhou and Quanzhou, were among the centers of this urban mercantile culture. Their international trade prospered in Ming times, generating wealth and social mobility. As a result, these south Fujian prefectures again achieved exceptional success in the civil service examinations.[63] At the same time, they also ranked high in the number of widow suicides in elite families.[64] Both are indicative of an intense competition for status among literati and merchant families, in which footbinding became deeply rooted in Hoklo culture. The revival of southeast coast economies after the Qing dynastic transition reinforced these cultural patterns.[65] This historical background likely explains the hegemonic status and the deep penetration of the footbinding custom in the Hoklo culture Fujianese immigrants reproduced in Taiwan.

Why did Hakka reject binding for natural feet? The Hakka homeland was in northeast Guangdong's hill country, a region of relatively poor farms and undeveloped commerce. The factors most frequently invoked to explain non-binding among the Hakka include male sojourning that left women in charge of home farms and their own defense, women taking over fieldwork to free men to study for the civil service examinations, intermarriage with non-Han hill peoples (She), and ethnic pride and boundary marking.[66] In his 1815 work "Miscellaneous Notes from Fenghu" (Fenghu zaji), the Hakka scholar Xu Xuzeng (1751–1819) suggests that the hardships Hakka suffered during the dynastic transition convinced them of the harms of footbinding (*zi jing guobian jianku beichang shi zhi chanzu zhi hai*). From then on, Hakka women, rich and poor, abstained from footbinding. Xu lists the many farming and domestic tasks performed by Hakka women and praises their skills at household management.[67] All those who have studied the Hakka stress the incompatibility of footbinding with the active roles Hakka expected women to assume in farmwork. Although male sojourners were able to find work as laborers and peddlers in the more vibrant coastal economies, relative poverty and life in the landlocked hill country insulated Hakka women from the footbinding fashions popular in the status-striving merchant culture of the coast. Natural feet were as much a social convention among Hakka women as bound feet were among the Hoklo. This appears to have been true from the earliest days of Hakka settlement in Taiwan and was as much a source of pride as embarrassment.

CHAPTER 3

The 1915 Prohibition

THE Japanese colonial government considered footbinding to be culturally backward (along with men's queues) and an impediment to the full mobilization of female labor and Taiwan's economic development. But it prudently hesitated to risk intervening in so intimate a practice until it was sure that a ban would not be opposed by influential Taiwanese. Only in 1915, after twenty years of rule, and years of support for the efforts of Taiwanese opposed to footbinding, did the colonial government take the step of forbidding the binding of young girls' feet and ordering adult women to loosen their bindings.

In the years following 1905, attitudes toward footbinding and wearing the queue changed slowly, but then accelerated in 1911. Major events outside Taiwan played important roles in destabilizing old social values. Japan's defeat of a European power in the 1905 Russo-Japanese war solidified the status of Japan as a rising power and a beacon of Asia's future. In mainland China, growing dissatisfaction with Qing rule spurred numerous small uprisings in the years leading up to 1911. Holding the queue to be a symbol of subservience to the Manchu dynasty, Chinese revolutionaries signaled their defiance by cutting their queues. The October 1911 revolution and the collapse of Qing rule in China led to a wave of queue cutting in the Chinese population at large.[1] To Taiwanese, these events highlighted the backwardness of the old society and further undermined conservative resistance to change in outdated customs such as queue wearing and footbinding.

In early 1911, the leader of the Taipei anti-footbinding movement, Huang Yujie, organized a queue-cutting society, with high-level official blessing, and the society held a collective queue-cutting ceremony in Taipei's commercial center, Dadaocheng. Cutting queues became fashionable among students in Taipei, and the practice spread gradually among the upper levels of society. In November, over ninety-eight hundred students in Taichung cut their queues. Reformers hoped the enthusiasm for queue cutting would spread to the anti-footbinding cause. With encouragement, wives from prominent families in Taipei's Mengjia District organized the Society for Releasing Bindings (Jiechan Hui) in 1911, the first time Taiwanese women took a lead role in reform. Schoolgirls (still a small population, but overwhelmingly the daughters of better-off progressives) abandoned binding in rapidly increasing numbers over the next few years. Textbooks for male and female students taught the evils of both footbinding and queues, which were characterized as backward and unsanitary practices. Taiwan's newspapers also carried reports of the anti-footbinding movement in mainland China.[2] Student support for reform ideas reflected the rise of a younger generation raised under Japanese rule, educated in a modern curriculum, and ready to take on roles in a modern society freed of the legacy of old customs.[3]

In some locales, the push for reform moved beyond voluntary and educational approaches to obtain compliance. Coercive measures were contemplated when Tainan Prefecture promulgated *baojia* regulations in 1911 mandating the release of bindings for all women under twenty years of age and imposing fines on those who failed to comply. Beginning in 1912, Yilan Prefecture directed the use of *baojia* security groups to pressure women to unbind. These more aggressive uses of government power reflect a growing self-confidence on the part of colonial officials and reform leaders, impatience with purely voluntary methods, and the weakening of entrenched resistance to change.[4]

The reform movement gained momentum in 1914, when efforts encouraging queue cutting and unbinding intensified with the formation of new customs reform societies (*fengsu gailiang hui*) by members of the social elite. A large-scale meeting to release bound feet (*jie chanzu hui*) was held in 1914 at Wufeng, Taizhong, the seat of the wealthy and socially prominent reform leader Lin Xiantang. The meeting celebrated the release of bindings by Lin family women in a large ceremony attended by many Japanese officials, their wives, and reform leaders. Lin's activism coincided with his leading role in the short-lived Taiwan Assimilation Society (J: Taiwan Dōkakai, C: Taiwan Tonghua Hui), which advocated cultural reform as a path to Taiwanese equality with Japanese (and thereby fell afoul of Japanese interests anxious to preserve their privileged position in the colony). The Assimilation Society, founded with the participation of Itagaki Taisuke, a prominent elder statesman and founder of Japan's Liberal Party, attracted many leading Taiwanese and created an upsurge of enthusiasm for cultural reforms.[5]

In late 1914, the *Taiwan Daily News* (Taiwan Nichinichi shinpō) announced an essay contest on the topic of "footbinding, its harms and how to relieve them." The response was overwhelming, and the newspaper published forty-four of the best essays from January 1 to April 16, 1915. The essays demonstrated near unanimity among the Taiwanese male intellectual elite, whether educated under the new or old regime, that footbinding was a corrupt practice in need of elimination. The essays criticized footbinding as an unsanitary practice that damaged women's health, endangered them in emergencies, weakened their offspring, and limited their contribution to family budgets. To achieve reform, the essay writers supported educational efforts to overcome social attitudes that ridiculed natural feet and considered bound feet a prerequisite for a good marriage. The writers stressed the responsibility of the elite to lead the way by making an example of their own families, and not a few advocated official action to prohibit binding and reward unbinding.[6] The same publisher sought to reach a female audience by publishing the essays in the Chinese-language issues of the journal *Patriotic Women of Taiwan*. Although the readership of such a journal must have reached at most a literate elite stratum, publishing the essays for female readers represented an intensified effort to persuade key opinion makers of the need for reform. The journal also published full-page photographs of selected township meetings celebrating the release of bindings.[7]

In early 1915, officials and reform society leaders organized ceremonies to celebrate the release of bindings in numerous localities; photographs and newspaper articles ensured broad media coverage of these events. Given the positive reception to these well-orchestrated efforts, and intellectuals' support for an active government role in reform, the Government-General of Taiwan adopted a regulation effective April 15, 1915, prohibiting the binding of feet (and the queue). This made it the responsibility of local *baojia* leaders and the police to enforce the prohibition and levy fines on violators. The work of enforcement was to be completed by June 17, 1915, the twentieth anniversary of Japanese rule in the island.[8] The regulations allowed older women whose feet were too misshapen and who would find it difficult to walk without bindings to remain bound (men over age sixty were also allowed to keep their queues).[9]

Several elderly Taiwanese women were interviewed in 1960 and 1961 about their experiences unbinding their feet in response to the 1915 prohibition.

Some of the women reported that as wives of local officials and employees of Japanese firms they felt pressured to unbind, as they were expected to serve as models for others. One reported that if the Japanese police discovered a woman continuing to bind her feet, they would humiliate her by forcing her to unbind her feet in public. One of the women who resisted the order to unbind reported having been beaten by the Japanese police. Several of the women reported having unbound to satisfy the police, but later rebinding because they found walking on unbound feet too painful. Some of the rebinding was done with police permission and some, done surreptitiously, was not. The women recounted a variety of methods by which released feet could be coaxed to return to more natural shapes, but disagreed on whether these could be successful. All the women expressed regret that, having bound their feet and achieved a pleasing shape, they were forced to unbind.[10]

The long educational campaign against footbinding, and the activities of reform groups organized with elite male participation and government support, prepared the way for the final coercive push to prohibit binding. Much of the reformers' effort directed at male opinion makers served to preempt the possibility of organized opposition, and none arose to oppose the ban. The only resistance to the prohibition was by older women acting alone. The vast majority of women lived in rural areas, and the chances of changing the opinions of nonliterate older Hoklo women were slight. Their strongly held beliefs in the importance of binding for their own and their daughters' status could not be easily changed, although some at least may have been relieved to be freed of the burden of binding young daughters' feet. More easily enlisted in the reform cause were literate family members and village leaders, as well as younger women who welcomed the prohibition. Undoubtedly a few men lamented the end of footbinding, but none appear to have raised their voices in public opposition. A rare example is a conservative male whose complaints were more about queue cutting than the ban on footbinding.[11] With no hope of any outside support, the great majority of women accepted the inevitable and acquiesced. Many must have welcomed the assurance that all other women were being forced to unbind as well.

BINDING AND UNBINDING IN THE CENSUS OF 1915

The 1915 census was taken on October 1, several months after the June 17 deadline for completing enforcement of the footbinding ban. The census thus provides a record by which the success of the anti-footbinding campaign and the

TABLE 3.1. Proportions of Fujianese females with ever-bound feet, by age, 1905 and 1915

Age	Number of Fujianese females, 1915	% ever-bound, 1905	% ever-bound, 1915	% released of ever-bound, 1915
1–10	380,172	18.0	3.4	89.4
11–20	265,905	75.0	50.1	83.1
21–30	199,292	88.2	84.2	74.8
31–40	187,477	90.7	89.6	68.4
41–50	130,569	90.9	92.2	56.3
51–60	83,012	91.9	93.2	35.8
61–70	52,913	92.8	93.6	25.5
71+	23,676	93.5	94.2	14.1
Total (all ages)	1,323,016	68.7	56.8	63.0
Total (>10)	942,844	86.3	78.3	62.6
Total (>20)	676,939	90.3	89.4	58.1

Sources: Census of 1905, Shūkei gempyō, zentō no bu 1907: tables 2, 22, 24; Census of 1905, Kekka hyō 1908: table 8; Census of 1915, Shūkei gempyō, zentō no bu 1917: tables 2, 23, 25

ban can be measured. The ban had two elements, a prospective prohibition on binding, which most affected young girls, and a mandate that women already bound release their bindings (with allowance for women too old or severely bound who could not adjust if the bindings were released). The 1915 census reveals that although binding continued in the ten years from 1905 to 1915, the proportion who had begun binding their feet in the youngest (and largest) cohorts had significantly declined in the years leading up to the census (Table 3.1). As a result, the proportion of Fujian women (all ages) ever-bound declined from 68.7% in 1905 to 56.8% in 1915. The census also shows that a very large number of women had released their bindings in compliance with police orders; these women remain in the measure of the ever-bound. Thus the proportions ever-bound in the older age ranges remain in excess of 90%. The distribution of the ever-bound population among the provenance groups remains unchanged, with Fujianese accounting for 99.7% of ever-bound women in 1915.

The significant decline in the proportions of Fujianese females with ever-bound feet in the youngest age-groups between 1905 and 1915 suggests that the anti-footbinding campaigns had succeeded in convincing families to abandon the binding of daughters' feet. Only 3.4% of Fujianese girls aged one to ten years had initiated binding in 1915, compared to 18% of girls at the same age in 1905. Since binding begins at the earliest at age five, these are girls who would have started binding after 1910, when the anti-footbinding campaigns intensified. A very high proportion of the few girls who had started binding (89.4%) released their bindings in response to the 1915 prohibition, and returning to a more natural shape must have been relatively easy for feet that had only begun the process and were still growing. The dramatic decline in binding in this age-group is evidence of families' voluntary response to the anti-footbinding campaign leading up to the 1915 ban.

In the next older age-group, eleven to twenty years, the proportion ever-bound in 1915 of 50.1% is also considerably lower than the 75% of girls eleven to twenty in 1905. But when these girls are traced back to 1905, it can be seen that over the ten years from 1905 to 1915, the proportion ever-bound has increased from 18% to 50.1%. Thus for a significant number of the girls aged eleven to twenty in 1915, binding had been initiated in the prior decade despite the anti-footbinding campaigns. Because the censuses report binding by five-year age-groups above age ten, changes in proportions bound from 1905 to 1915 in this age-group can be observed in greater detail (Table 3.2). The proportion ever-bound of girls aged eleven to fifteen in 1915 has risen to only 35%, compared to the 67% of girls eleven to fifteen in 1905. The proportion ever-bound of girls aged sixteen to twenty in 1915 has risen to only 67.5%, compared to 81.6% of girls sixteen to twenty in 1905. Thus both groups show significant declines in the rate of new binding by 1915, especially the younger eleven-to-fifteen group. But in both groups, many have also started to bind. Girls aged eleven to twenty, who likely were themselves (and not their mothers) binding their feet, were approaching marriageable ages and averse to taking chances on finding a mother-in-law who would accept a daughter-in-law without bound feet. These older girls may also have felt both peer pressure and some competitiveness with other girls their age that pushed them to bind, despite exposure to anti-footbinding propaganda. Nevertheless, the significant decline in the rate of new binding is strong evidence that the anti-footbinding campaign was having an effect before the 1915 prohibition was imposed. Very high proportions of these girls (87.9% of those eleven to fifteen and 80.3% of those sixteen to twenty) released their bindings in response to the 1915 prohibition, and their youth must have made returning to a more natural shape relatively easy, except for those with the most severe binding.

Concerns about marriageability and peer pressure also likely explain why the proportion ever-bound of those aged twenty-one to thirty in 1915 increased

TABLE 3.2. Proportions of Fujianese females with ever-bound feet, by birth cohorts, 1905 and 1915

	1905 CENSUS		1915 CENSUS		
Years cohort born	Age, 1905	% Fujianese ever-bound	Age, 1915	% Fujianese ever-bound	% released of Fujianese ever-bound
1906–15	—	—	≤10	3.4	89.4
1901–5	≤10	18	11–15	35.0	87.9
1896–1900			16–20	67.5	80.3
1891–95	11–15	67.0	21–25	82.1	75.4
1886–90	16–20	81.6	26–30	86.4	74.2
1881–85	21–25	87.4	31–35	88.6	70.2
1876–80	26–30	90.5	36–40	90.8	66.2

Sources: Census of 1905, Shūkei gempyō, zentō no bu 1907: tables 2, 22, 24; Census of 1905, Kekka hyō 1908: table 8; Census of 1915, Shūkei gempyō, zentō no bu 1917: tables 2, 23, 25; Census of 1915, Kijutsu hōbun 1918: table 31

from an already high 75% in 1905 (when they were eleven to twenty) to 84.2% in 1915, only 4% lower than women twenty-one to thirty in 1905. In 1915, the proportions ever-bound at ages above thirty remain comparable to those in 1905, when the rates of binding in those birth cohorts had already reached the range of 90%. But these older women would feel the impact of the 1915 prohibition when forced to unbind. Allowances for the difficulty of adjusting to an unbound state meant that the proportions of Fujian women released decreased as age and the difficulty of unbinding increase (see Table 3.1).

The 1905 census report provides an insightful discussion of the effect of age on the willingness of parents, girls, and young women to release bindings:

> The reason why this difference is produced by age is probably as follows: The children being in the first stage of compression, and not yet used to it, feel the greatest pain, so that their parents who are awakened to the sense of its evil do not hesitate to unbind their feet. Furthermore, children being far from a marriageable age do not attract much public notice and are consequently less liable to be ridiculed as rustic and unrefined, whereas in adolescence women are vain and sensitive and matrimony comes in to deter them from loosening their feet, the unmarried, through fear of making a favorable marriage more difficult, and the married, through the desire to keep a coquettish appearance and to gratify their parents-in-law.[12]

In the dramatically reduced proportions ever-bound and in the high proportions released, at ages one to ten and eleven to fifteen, there is broad uniformity among the twelve 1915 prefectures, although Taibei and Yilan are partial exceptions. The proportions ever-bound at ages one to ten and eleven to fifteen are much higher in Taibei (11.2% and 75.2%) and Yilan (20.7% and 92.3%) than the all-Taiwan averages of 3.4% and 35%. Compared to the other prefectures, Taibei and Yilan were both slow to reduce the proportions initiating binding at these ages. Yilan corrected that by doing better than average at unbinding the feet of young girls, but Taibei only managed to release below-average proportions (83.2% released at ages one to ten, compared to the all-Taiwan average of 89.4%, and 78.7% released at ages eleven to fifteen, compared to the all-Taiwan average of 87.9%). In the proportion of released women (all ages), both Taibei (46.1%) and Yilan (55.9%) fell below the all-Taiwan average of 63%. Taibei and Yilan were among the prefectures having younger average ages at binding and more severe binding (as shown in chapter 5), and this may have contributed to the higher proportion bound in the youngest ages, one to ten, and a lower release rate at all ages for severely bound feet. Nevertheless, Taibei, as the metropolitan prefecture of the Japanese colony, and site of the oldest natural foot society, was surprisingly slow in moving toward natural feet. Although both Taibei and Yilan have been mentioned as sites of elite anti-footbinding activism, the census data reveal that conservative attitudes were able to retard the progress of the anti-footbinding prohibition in those prefectures. A very different outcome for anti-footbinding activism is seen in the very high rates of release across all the age-groups in Taizhong (84.7% compared to the all-Taiwan average of 63%), which likely reflects the impact of native son Lin Xiantang's reform efforts.

CONCLUSION

In sum, many families continued to prepare their daughters for marriage and adult life by binding their feet between 1905 and 1915. But the data from the youngest cohorts also show that many families who would have begun binding the feet of girls under conditions prevailing in 1905 had stopped binding them in the years leading up to 1915. Perhaps awareness that others were abandoning the custom, along with their daughters' tears, made parents receptive to anti-footbinding propaganda in the case of their youngest daughters. In any case, the 1915 prohibition stopped families binding the feet of young daughters and, in addition, forced the majority (63%, all ages) of those who had bound to unbind.

The combined effect of reduced binding and high rates of forced release meant that only a very small number of girls aged fifteen and younger remained bound in any of the prefectures. High rates of release (80.3%) also greatly reduced the numbers left bound in the ages between sixteen and twenty. By the time of the 1915 census, 473,874 Fujianese women had released their bindings. As a result of the anti-footbinding policies, the total number of Fujianese women remaining bound-footed fell to 277,780 (from the 1915 total ever-bound of 751,654), representing only 21% of the 1,323,016 Fujianese women of all ages. From the point of view of the colonial state, this must be considered a tremendous success.

CHAPTER 4

Footbinding for Marriage

NEARLY every account of footbinding mentions that parents justified the suffering of young girls undergoing footbinding by telling them (and themselves) that binding was necessary to improve a girl's marriage prospects. From the parents' point of view, binding was a service they provided daughters to ensure marriage into a family of equal, if not higher, standing. Because binding was a mark of a girl's respectability, if not gentility, a bound-footed woman would be more attractive to families seeking brides and would attract interest from better-quality families. And proud status-conscious families expected daughters-in-law to have bound feet. According to the 1905 census report: "The idea, pernicious as it is, is deeply rooted in the mind of the people that the smaller a girl's feet are, the easier it will be for her to find a suitor in marriage. The larger footed, and especially those whose feet have never been bound, are ridiculed as 'rustic and unrefined' and consequently find it difficult to get married. For this reason, all parents make it a point of honor to have their daughters' feet compressed at the proper age, whether they are good-looking or not."[1]

The quality of a prospective bride's binding and the fineness of her embroidered shoes might also be indicators of the girl's own character, her ability to endure pain, her diligence, and her craftsmanship.[2] In areas where the cultural hegemony of the custom was secure, conformity to the footbinding fashion overrode almost all gradations of status and conditions of life except for the excluded lowest class of servants. Where footbinding was nearly universal, natural feet marked a girl from an otherwise respectable family as an incorrigible or as a weak-willed female incapable of self-discipline and unable to endure hardship. At the other extreme, the smallest foot in a prospective bride, while a source of bragging rights, may also indicate an excessive vanity and self-indulgence that would interfere with the hard work expected of married women. Discerning parents needed to beware of both possibilities when selecting brides for their sons. While bound feet were also reputed to be sexually attractive, such considerations did not play a role in parents' selection of a daughter-in-law for a son (but they might in an adult male's selection of a concubine for himself).[3]

The anti-footbinding societies understood very well the close connection between marriageability and footbinding in the minds of parents. Families could not be convinced to stop binding unless they could be ensured of the marriageability of natural-footed daughters. Society members were therefore required to match pledges not to bind daughters' feet with pledges not to marry sons to bound-footed women.[4] Only when families could be confident that others would stand by their pledges would footbinding be abandoned. Until that trust could be established, parents could not risk not binding daughters' feet.

Arranging a marriage depends on many variables, for example, the current state of the family's economy and its reputation, the negotiated amounts of bride-price and dowry and their net affordability, the number of siblings nearing marriage age and competing for family resources, and the assessment of both the economic and the noneconomic qualities of the prospective in-laws. One way of interpreting the claim that footbinding improved a girl's marriage prospects is to look for better economic conditions in a woman's marital family compared to her natal family at the time of the marriage. How often did families manage to marry their daughters into better-off households?[5]

Retrospective interviews of elderly bound-footed women in several provinces of mainland China have been used to assess the relative economic status of natal and marital families at the time of marriage. One study, using informants' reports of landownership (acreage was not reported), tenancy, and labor from a large Sichuan sample, found that ever-bound girls in Sichuan were slightly more likely to marry into economically better-off (23%) than into economically worse-off (17%) families; the great majority (60%) married into families of similar economic standing.[6] Another study, using informants' recollections of ownership of house, land (double weighted), and draft animals as indicators of wealth, found a statistically significant pattern of marriage into better-off households for women bound at marriage in the Sichuan sample, but reported no such pattern in the much smaller samples of later-born cohorts (married after 1924) from sites in northern, central, and southwestern China.[7] Women, regardless of binding status, were most likely to marry into families whose economic standing was similar to that of their natal households in all the regions. There could be no guarantee that women whose feet were bound would see an improvement in their economic circumstances following marriage.

AGE AT MARRIAGE

In the traditional cultural environment, parents rarely considered delaying a nubile daughter's marriage to allow her to continue her education or to work for her own account. Unless a daughter was needed to help out at home, the sooner after menarche a marriage could be arranged the better. Any delay would increase the risk of an affair outside of marriage and the damage to reputation caused by rumors or an illegitimate pregnancy. Grooms' families, especially mothers-in-law-to-be, desired younger daughters-in-law, who would be more compliant and tractable than older, more mature, and self-confident women, yet not so young as to be incapable of childbearing. Thus competition for fecund brides in the marriage market was greatest for the prospects of prime age, and it was for them that inquiries from matchmakers were most frequent and bride-prices highest. Because grooms' families preferred younger girls, those past the prime age of marriage began to lose value and often had to settle for less desirable matches (even large dowries might not be able to overcome the disadvantages of older age).[8]

On both sides of the marriage negotiations, family priorities took precedence over the desires and wishes of grooms and brides. Weddings involved considerable expense for both families, and financial distress on one side might impair that family's ability to conclude a desirable match. From the bride's family's point of view, issues important to the future life of their daughter, such as the reputation and prosperity of the groom's family and the personality of the prospective mother-in-law, might be overridden by pressing economic or other concerns (including worries that advancing age and the rarity of offers would leave the daughter a spinster) that counseled accepting a less desirable match.[9] The Taiwan census data do not provide indicators of wealth, but they do enable one to show that ever-bound women enjoyed an important advantage: they were able to marry earlier than the never-bound.

Table 4.1 compares the proportions ever-married (currently married, widowed, and divorced) by age and the mean ages at first marriage, for

TABLE 4.1. Proportions of Fujianese females ever-married by age, mean age at marriage, and footbinding status, 1915

	FUJIANESE FEMALES, 1915			% EVER-MARRIED, FUJIANESE FEMALES, 1915		
Age	Total	Ever-bound	Never-bound	Total	Ever-bound	Never-bound
≤10	380,172	12,972	367,200	0.0	0.0	0.0
11–15	141,991	49,650	92,341	0.7	1.4	0.3
16–20	123,914	83,627	40,287	35.0	40.0	24.7
21–25	102,469	84,128	18,341	88.2	90.1	79.4
26–30	96,823	83,613	13,210	97.0	97.7	92.8
31–35	100,612	89,127	11,485	98.7	99.0	96.6
36–40	86,865	78,857	8,008	99.2	99.4	97.4
41+	290,170	269,680	20,490	99.7	99.8	98.5
Total	1,323,016	751,654	571,362			
Mean age at first marriage, Fujianese, 1915				19.05	18.61	20.41
Mean age at first marriage, Guangdongese, 1915				19.55	19.45	19.55
Mean age at first marriage, Taiwanese, 1915				19.14	18.62	20.00
Mean age at first marriage, Taiwanese, 1905				18.02	17.02	18.72

Sources: Census of 1915, Shūkei gempyō, zentō no bu 1917: tables 2, 23, 25; Census of 1905, Shūkei gempyō, zentō no bu 1907: tables 22, 24; Census of 1915, Kijutsu hōbun 1918: table 31

ever-bound and natural-footed females in 1915 and 1905. As the proportions of ever-married Fujianese women above age thirty make clear, both the ever-bound and the natural-footed ultimately married in extraordinarily high proportions (99%). For Fujianese (and all Taiwanese) women in 1915, marriage was an inescapable event, regardless of footbinding status. Nevertheless, although marriage was as certain for natural-footed women as for bound-footed women, it is also clear that from age sixteen to age thirty, a higher proportion of the bound-footed were married than the natural-footed were. As a result, the mean age at marriage of the ever-bound Fujianese in 1915 is estimated at 18.61, younger than that of 20.41 for the natural-footed by a significant margin of 1.8 years. A similar advantage of at least 1.7 years was enjoyed by ever-bound Taiwanese in 1905.[10] This confirms that bound-footed Fujianese girls enjoyed an advantage in the marriage market that led to the earlier conclusion of their marriages. Thus many young women approaching marriage age and anxious about their prospects continued to bind despite increased anti-footbinding pressures in the years leading up to 1915, as shown in Table 3.2. In a market where girls lose competitive advantage as they age, the earlier timing of bound-footed girls' marriages reflects their families' greater bargaining power, greater choice, and the higher likelihood of a quality match. The higher bride-price that natal families obtained for daughters with well-bound feet was an additional incentive to conclude early marriages for their daughters.[11]

Between 1905 and 1915, the average marriage age has risen for all Taiwanese females, from 18.0 to 19.1. This reflects a decline in the sex ratios (males per one hundred females) of marriage-age Taiwanese of all ethnicities due to declining mortality rates for young girls. High sex ratios sharpen competition for scarce brides and that drives down their age at marriage. The declining sex ratio increased the supply of brides, eased competition in the marriage market, and reduced the ability of families to marry off daughters as early as possible. This effect led to a gradual rise in the age at marriage for females throughout the Japanese period.[12]

Of course, there may well be factors other than binding alone that favor bound-footed girls and that contribute to the pattern of earlier marriage. For example, the parents of bound-footed girls may be more prosperous and thus better able to offer business connections and attractive dowries to possible suitors. Daughters of better-off parents may also enjoy better health and nutrition that make them more attractive candidates than the weak and sickly. But when over 90% of Fujianese women above age thirty have bound feet, the bound-footed cannot come from an exclusive economic elite. Even if those binding are the better-off 90%, there will still be many very poor families among those who have chosen to bind their daughters' feet. Late marriages to men who had failed to win a bound-footed woman for a bride were likely not the only disadvantage faced by Hoklo girls whose feet were never bound. Their families likely had them doing heavier, outdoor labor from an early age and, if their earnings were important to the family budget, perhaps kept them unmarried for some years. Families who married their daughters at a higher age may also have had to settle for sons-in-law who not only had few resources but were much older or had been divorced or widowed.[13]

The data on age at marriage offer testimony to the power of self-fulfilling prophecies, of cultural presuppositions to create the facts that then confirm their truth. When a majority of parents tell daughters that not binding will reduce their marriage options, and favor the bound-footed as brides for their sons, then girls who do not bind will indeed suffer delay and disadvantage in the marriage market.[14]

FORMS OF MARRIAGE

It is the prospects of life in a husband's family (major marriage) that parents cite when they admonish their daughters to endure the pain of footbinding. But families also bound the feet of girls they were raising as little daughters-in-law (*sim-pua*) to marry their sons (minor marriage) and daughters kept for uxorilocal marriages to an in-marrying son-in-law. Minor and uxorilocal marriages often constituted a significant percentage of all marriages in Taiwanese localities.[15] In the case of the little daughter-in-law being fostered in her future husband's family, footbinding could not enhance the possibility or improve the quality of a marriage that had been arranged since early childhood. Thus binding the feet of a little daughter-in-law could not have been motivated by her foster mother's desire to enhance the girl's chances of marrying. Indeed, binding, by making her more attractive on the wider marriage market, may have increased the risk that the little daughter-in-law would refuse to marry her foster brother.[16] But the desire to enhance marriage prospects could explain binding the feet of girls marrying uxorilocally, for they are raised with the expectation of marrying out. The circumstances that resulted in uxorilocal marriage (e.g., loss of a brother) often arose after the girl was past the age of binding, and bound feet might still be useful in attracting an in-marrying son-in-law. Accordingly, one might expect lower proportions ever-bound among little daughters-in-law and the same higher proportions among girls marrying in the major fashion and uxorilocally. The census data do not report footbinding by marriage form, but such data have been compiled from the household registers of selected communities. The proportions bound among Hoklo by form of marriage in Haishan (Taibei basin) and Xinzhu show women in minor marriages bound at the same rate as women in major and uxorilocal marriages.[17] Analysis of ten additional Hoklo majority sites from the Taiwan Household Register Database confirms that women married for the first time in the major, minor, and uxorilocal modes during the period 1906–16 were bound in similar proportions in each of the sites.[18]

What explains binding the feet of little daughters-in-law when a desire to enhance their marriage prospects cannot be the answer? Taiwan anthropologists Arthur P. Wolf and Huang Chieh-shan conclude that "most people who raised wives for their sons were wealthy enough to be concerned about appearances and bound the feet of their *sim-pua* because small feet were fashionable."[19] Where footbinding as a fashion predominated, bound feet were a prerequisite to respectability for all women. Thus one woman who was betrothed at age nine reported: "I went to their house to serve as a daughter-in-law in the home of my future husband. My mother-in-law bound my feet much more tightly than mother ever had, saying that I still hadn't achieved the standard."[20] For women raised with the expectation of marrying out, bound feet, by making them respectable, enhanced their marriage prospects compared to the never-bound; for little daughters-in-law, marriage prospects were beside the point, but respectability was not. At stake here was pride (or at least the avoidance of ridicule), not a concern for beauty per se.

APPEARANCES MATTERED

Women were particularly sensitive about the appearance of their feet on their wedding day, when their feet would be subjected to public viewing and comment. Brides feared being shamed on account of large or poorly bound feet in the wedding day rituals. Women interviewed in 1960 and 1961 in Taiwan reported that other women examining the bride's trousseau of bowed shoes openly commented on their size and the bride's shoe-making skills.[21] Friends and neighbors inspected the bride's foot size on her arrival at her groom's home and offered either praise or scorn, delighting or mortifying the groom and his father.[22] One of the North Chinese women interviewed in the 1980s in the documentary *Small Happiness* described such a scene: "After a wedding they'd show the bride off around the village. She'd sit in a cart with her legs crossed, everyone gathered around. Some would shout: 'New bride, new bride. . . . Hey, let's see the feet.' If the feet were big, they'd say, 'The face isn't half bad, but get a load of those feet.' And they'd walk off."[23]

Women who had lightly bound "cucumber" feet or who had let out their bindings before marriage often took pains to squeeze their feet into the smallest shoes possible for their wedding day.[24] Natural-footed Chaozhou women are reported to have bound their feet just before their marriage and undone them after the wedding.[25] Another of the *Small Happiness* women regretted not doing this: "My red wedding shoes, they were this long. I was so ashamed. One day my in-laws were sitting in the doorway. As I walked toward them I overheard them saying, 'Just look at this, the person hasn't shown up yet and her two feet have already arrived.' Those awful big feet. So I took a year and bound them up again."[26]

When they passed judgment on a new bride's feet in the wedding rituals, men revealed their active role in enforcing conformity to the footbinding fashion. These public rituals exposed not just the bride but the men of the groom's family to the threat of ridicule and humiliation. Because providing sons with bound-footed brides was important to their own status, fathers were intent that their sons "have a wife as modish as the next."[27] Men, too, were affected by the face, won or lost, through the footbinding of the family's female members.

MARITAL STATUS AND BINDING

Would women, after they had been married for many years or had left a marriage either as widows or in divorce, unbind their feet? Surely, the force of arguments that tie binding to marriage prospects would carry little weight for such women. Younger widows and divorcées might retain their bindings, if they felt binding were important to enhance their chances of remarrying. But one might expect older women of any marital status to want to free themselves of crippled feet and to feel less constrained by social norms that would keep them bound. And if husbands were a force keeping wives' feet bound, then at least widows and divorcées could make an independent decision free of spousal pressure. These speculations need not presume that unbinding feet would be painless and would allow feet to return to their natural shape, assumptions that would be false, especially for the severely bound. Any decision to remove bindings must have factored in the pain and continued crippling involved and would not have been taken lightly.

Did such women who had loosened their bindings and let their feet return to more natural states exist? The footbinding status of these women might be reported as "released" (only 8,690 women in 1905, likely if the bindings were recently loosened) or as "never-bound," if they had unbound many years before and appeared natural-footed at the time of the census. In either case, if they were numerous, they would reduce the numbers reported as currently bound. The proportions currently bound among those aged twenty-one to seventy for Taiwanese women of all ethnicities in 1905 (data by age and marital status restricted to Fujian women are not available for 1905) was 75.2%

for the married, 79.3% for the widowed, and only 55.1% for the divorced.[28] The data show no consistent trend for proportions currently bound to decline with age in any of the marital statuses, as the chances of remarriage decline. Widows even have higher proportions bound than still-married women of comparable age. Thus it appears that the sign of respectability that came with bound feet was as important to older women as it was to the young.

Why do divorced women, who until recently were married, have rates of binding so much lower than the married? The data do not reveal whether the divorced women not currently bound were natural-footed when they divorced or had been bound-footed during marriage and only removed their bindings following divorce. This uncertainty and the very small numbers of divorced women (5,416, ages twenty-one to seventy) caution against drawing many conclusions from these data. Nevertheless, it is conceivable that some divorcées, already deprived of their respectability by divorce and forced to earn an independent living, found advantage in removing their bindings following divorce or, if natural-footed, no advantage in adopting binding. One learns from the biography of one working-class woman that women forced to fend for themselves might abandon bindings and see their feet spread.[29]

Overall, it appears that Taiwanese Hoklo women maintained their bindings no matter how their circumstances might have changed after marriage. They appear to have met economic hardships with a determination to maintain the respectability that binding conferred. In the previously mentioned Sichuan sample, many women undid their bindings in order to do heavier, outdoor labor for their natal or their marital families.[30] Such a pattern has not been reported in Taiwan, nor is it seen in the census data. Whatever work Taiwanese Hoklo women were expected to do, they seem to have managed it with bound feet.

CONCLUSION

Maintaining respectability in a society that valued small bound feet, fear of ridicule if feet were ill-bound or never bound, and a concern for marriage prospects motivated parents to bind their daughters' feet for however short a time they could manage. When family pride favored bound-footed brides for sons, mothers were not wrong to tell daughters that binding would improve their chances of a good marriage. As the Taiwan census data establish, in a competitive marriage market, families succeeded in concluding earlier and more desirable marriages when they had bound their daughters' feet.

The finding that mothers-in-law also bound the feet of girls (little daughters-in-law) they adopted to marry their sons suggests that concerns for the groom's family's face dictated binding even when improving the marriage chances of the girl was beside the point. Weddings, when the bride's feet were subject to public scrutiny and judgments, were very sensitive occasions for the face not only of the bride, but of both families. The ethnographic accounts document not just a concern for status but a fear of ridicule should the feet not measure up. Where the practice was near universal, as it was among Taiwan's Hoklo, binding served more to prevent humiliation and loss of respectability, than to elevate a woman's status above her peers.

CHAPTER 5

Regional Variations among the Hoklo Fujianese

I N 1905, the Fujianese majority accounted for 99.6% of ever-bound Taiwanese women, and an average of 68.7% of Fujianese women of all ages were ever-bound. But the proportions ever-bound of Fujianese were not uniform across the island. In some prefectures the proportions of Fujianese females with ever-bound feet were substantially below average and in others substantially above. What accounts for the differences among localities in the proportions bound?

Table 5.1 presents several indicators describing aspects of the Fujianese female population for each of the twenty prefectures and for Taiwan as a whole in 1905. Prefectures are listed in a generally north-to-south order, starting with Taibei (also the seat of the colonial capital) and Jilong in the north, followed by Yilan in the northeast corner of the island, then proceeding south along the west coast, veering east in the cases of Nantou, Fanshuliao, and Taidong, and at the end, including the island prefecture of Penghu (Map 5.1).

The female populations of the twenty prefectures in 1905 varied greatly in size and ethnic makeup. Eight prefectures had total populations of Fujianese females numbering less than 30,000 (the populations of Fujianese women in Hengchun and Taidong are especially small), and three have populations four times as large (Taibei, Zhanghua, and Yanshuigang). Guangdongese (13.6% of the total female population) were a majority in Xinzhu and Miaoli and made up significant proportions of the populations of five other prefectures, Taoyuan and Taizhong in the northwest and center and Fanshuliao, Ahou, and Hengchun in the southern hills. Plains aborigines (only 1.7% of the total female population) were a small but significant presence in Fanshuliao,

TABLE 5.1. Footbinding among Fujianese females, by prefecture, 1905

Prefecture	Number of Fujian females*	% of Taiwanese females Fujianese*	Number of Fujian females ever-bound†	% Fujian females all ages ever-bound†	% crop area devoted to dry field crops‡	% of Fujianese listed as Zhang-zhou, 1926§	Ratio, all bilinguals per 100 Fujian females#
Taibei	125,987	99.6	97,307	77.2	20.8	18.8	1.3
Jilong	47,665	99.5	37,161	78.0	39.4	54.9	0.1
Yilan	50,991	97.2	42,641	83.6	9.1	92.9	0.6
Shenkeng	20,626	99.8	15,025	72.8	46.4	9.5	0.3
Taoyuan	53,757	**55.0**	21,899	**40.7**	34.3	68.2	**36.7**
Xinzhu	29,614	**36.5**	6,604	**22.3**	22.2	8.4	**49.7**
Miaoli	28,017	**40.2**	10,472	**37.4**	19.4	14.0	**63.3**
Taizhong	76,700	**80.9**	43,559	**56.8**	13.7	53.0	**15.4**
Zhanghua	126,657	98.1	89,512	70.7	24.1	36.0	0.1
Nantou	28,436	86.9	18,121	63.7	33.4	92.9	6.3
Douliu	99,292	99.8	74,052	74.6	71.8	53.1	6.1
Jiayi	92,094	99.9	73,351	79.6	62.4	57.8	0.7
Yanshuigang	124,753	98.6	100,856	80.8	72.5	33.8	0.0
Tainan	84,938	97.7	62,753	73.9	72.6	34.8	0.2
Fanshuliao	10,745	**45.6**	5,541	**51.6**	36.1	30.9	**16.1**
Fengshan	83,298	99.7	61,956	74.4	56.3	34.8	0.2
Ahou	53,146	**66.6**	20,823	**39.2**	40.7	32.0	**16.9**
Hengchun	6,150	**66.6**	193	**3.1**	43.0	32.0	**22.2**
Taidong	1,852	**7.8**	690	**37.3**	72.0	41.2	**49.7**
Penghu	28,100	100.0	23,260	82.8	100.0	12.8	0.1
All-Taiwan	1,172,818	83.4	805,776	68.7	39.3	42.3	7.5

Note: Boldfaced numbers identify prefectures having low proportions Fujianese, low proportions Fujianese ever-bound, and high ratios of bilinguals.

* *Census of 1905, Kekka hyō 1908: table 8, females only*

† *Census of 1905, Shūkei gempyō, zentō no bu 1907: tables 22, 24; Census of 1905, Shūkei gempyō, chihō no bu 1907: tables 34, 36; Census of 1905, Kekka hyō 1908: table 8*

‡ *Taiwan Sōtokufu tōkeisho 1905: 518–31, 532–48, 569–80, 705–10*

§ *Taiwan zaiseki kan'minzoku kyōkanbetsu chōsa 1928*

Census of 1905, Shūkei gempyō, zentō no bu 1907: table 10; Census of 1905, Shūkei gempyō, chihō no bu 1907: table 18; Census of 1905, Kekka hyō 1908: table 8

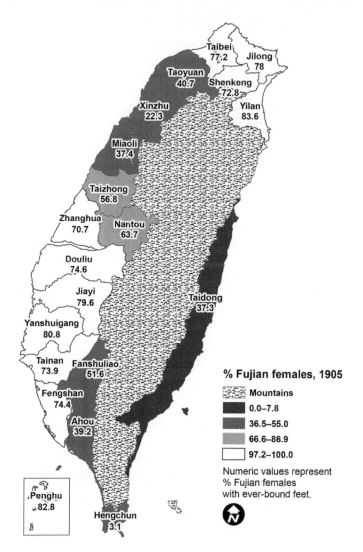

MAP 5.1. Proportions of Fujianese females with ever-bound feet and proportions of females Fujianese, 1905 (20 prefectures). Lighter shading indicates higher proportions Fujianese; numbers indicate the proportion ever-bound. (Penghu shown in inset.)

Hengchun, and the east coast prefecture of Taidong. Fujianese were a majority in all but four prefectures and constituted greater than 97% of the population in eleven prefectures, which accounted for 884,401 women and 75% of the total Fujian female population.

The prefectural data in Table 5.1 reveal some intriguing regional variations in the proportions ever-bound among Fujianese. Eleven of the twenty prefectures, ranging from Taibei in the north to Fengshan in the south, and including the Penghu Islands, report above-average proportions ever-bound. Nine prefectures report below-average proportions, three in the northwest (Taoyuan, Xinzhu, and Miaoli), two in the north-central area (Taizhong and Nantou), and four more (Fanshuliao, Ahou, Hengchun, and Taidong) in the southern hills and along the east coast. The highest proportion of Fujianese ever-bound is found in Yilan, at 83.6%, and the lowest in Hengchun, at 3.1%. So there is considerable variation in the extent of footbinding within the Fujianese population of Taiwan. What accounts for this variation?

Explanations for the variation in footbinding rates among Fujianese potentially include differences in class structure, female labor requirements, and urban-rural divisions (to be discussed in chapter 6), but here the focus is on the effects of provenance and ethnicity. More than 99% of Fujianese were Hokkien speakers, so language differences cannot explain this variation. Taiwan's Fujianese population is divided between two large groups that trace their origin to the two coastal prefectures of southern Fujian, Quanzhou and Zhangzhou. According to the 1926 survey of Han provenance, the Quanzhou settlers accounted for 54.0% of the Fujianese total, and the Zhangzhou settlers 42.3%.[1] Could cultural differences regarding footbinding between the populations hailing from these two regions account for any of the prefectural variation within Taiwan? Yilan reports the highest proportion ever-bound (83.6%) and is also one of the most solidly Zhangzhou prefectures (92.9%). Yet Yanshuigang and Penghu report nearly as high proportions ever-bound (80.8% and 82.8%, respectively) but have much lower proportions Zhangzhou (33.8% and 12.8%). And Nantou, with as high a proportion Zhangzhou as Yilan, reports a below-average 63.7% ever-bound. Thus differences between those of Quanzhou and Zhangzhou origins do not explain the substantial variation among the Fujianese.

The proportion of Fujianese in each prefecture better accounts for proportions of ever-bound Fujianese. The eleven prefectures with above-average proportions ever-bound among Fujianese have greater than 97% Fujianese populations, account for 75% of all Fujian females and 84% of all Fujianese ever-bound, and report an average 77% ever-bound. These prefectures are clustered in the upper right of the scatter diagram, or scattergram, in Figure 5.1.[2] All nine of the prefectures with below-average proportions ever-bound among Fujianese are also below average in the proportions Fujianese. And the effect appears to be somewhat proportional at this low end. Middling proportions Fujianese (81%–87%) correspond to middling proportions ever-bound

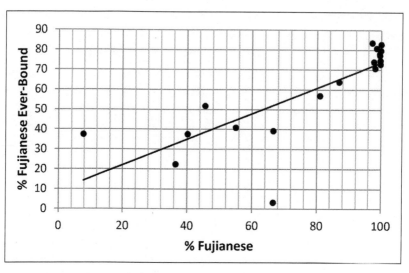

FIGURE 5.1. Proportions of Fujianese females with ever-bound feet by proportion of Fujianese females, 1905 (20 prefectures; r = 0.79). *Source*: Table 5.1.

(57%–64%) in the cases of Taizhong and Nantou. Low proportions Fujianese (37%–67%) correspond to low proportions of Fujianese ever-bound (22%–52%) in the cases of Taoyuan, Xinzhu, and Miaoli in the north and Fanshuliao and Ahou in the south. One stark exception to this pattern is the curious case of Hengchun, which, with a proportion Fujianese (66.6%) comparable to that of its neighbor Ahou, reports only 3.1% of its women ever-bound. Taidong is also somewhat anomalous; its Fujianese population reports an ever-bound proportion in the low range (37.3%), which is proportional to its Fujianese proportion of Han at 62%, but not to the Fujianese proportion of its total Taiwanese population (8%). Because Taidong has a large aboriginal population, it reports a much lower proportion when Fujianese are measured as a proportion of all Taiwanese in 1905. The nine prefectures with below-average proportions ever-bound account for 25% of the Fujian female population but only 16% of the Fujianese ever-bound and have an average 44% ever-bound.

CROSS-CULTURAL INFLUENCES

Where proportions of Fujianese are low, proportions of Guangdongese (85% of whom are Hakka speakers [see Table 2.2]), and aborigines, especially on the east coast, are high. The lower rates of binding in prefectures with lower proportions Fujianese suggest that cultural influence coming from non-footbinding Hakka in the north and center, and both Hakka and non-footbinding aborigines in the southern hills and east coast, may contribute to a lower rate of binding among neighboring Fujianese. The usual assumption is that rival ethnic groups seek to accentuate and take pride in their differences, not borrow the despised habits of the opposing group. This perspective emphasizes the rivalry and hostility between neighboring ethnic groups, and Hakka-Hoklo communal strife was certainly a well-known feature of the history of these areas.[3] According to the ethnic marker hypothesis, ethnic hostility would lead opposing groups to create homogeneous solidary units and clear ethnic boundaries. This hypothesis predicts that footbinding should serve as a distinctive ethnic marker and that Fujianese, facing non-binding Hakka rivals, would preserve, if not accentuate, their customary practice of binding and Hakka would even more assiduously avoid binding. But this is the opposite of what the rates suggest, at least in the case of the Fujianese, whose rates of binding are lower where they share territory with Hakka neighbors and highest in prefectures where Fujianese are most concentrated.

Communal strife also suggests an opposite prediction more in line with the data: that the dangers of raids and dislocation should put a premium on mobility. Women should avoid binding in order to be able to escape on foot from emergencies and the dangers of civil conflict.[4] This suggests that the Fujianese may have been forced to abandon footbinding if they were not to see their women kidnapped, or worse, by Hakka braves in times of strife. This theory explains low rates of Fujianese binding as a consciously adopted strategy rather than as the result of Hakka cultural influence. However, it would be mistaken to assume that Fujianese were under constant siege in the north Taiwan Hakka areas: communal strife involving communities in the Xinzhu area in the nineteenth century was rarely internal. Rather, ethnically based militia were mobilized to suppress conflicts occurring outside the Xinzhu area, and ethnic strife within Xinzhu was avoided.[5] Local magistrates took steps to ensure cross-ethnic cooperation in the building of the Xinzhu city wall and in frontier reclamation enterprises such as Jin-Guang-Fu.[6] And why, if civil strife leads to reduced rates of binding, did rates of binding remain high in wholly Fujianese areas, which continued to suffer from disorder caused by intra-Hoklo Zhang-Quan and surname group strife?[7] Hypotheses depending on communal strife, whether leading to the ethnic marker or the mobility adaptation theory, offer contradictory predictions, none of which match all the facts.

Instead, as Figure 5.1 demonstrates, the greater the proportion of Fujianese in a prefecture, the more likely are Fujian women to bind their feet. Rates of binding are highest where Fujianese most dominate the population and the pressure to conform to the footbinding fashion is most intense. It is Hoklo against Hoklo status competition that drives up the rate of binding, not interethnic strife. The lower the proportion of Fujianese in a prefecture, the fewer Fujianese who bind. Sharing a locality with a non-binding population undermines Hoklo cultural hegemony and makes conformity to the footbinding fashion no longer compulsory.

If Hakka cultural influence is to be considered a plausible cause of low rates of Fujianese binding in prefectures of mixed ethnicity, how such cross-cultural influence operated needs to be explained. If the Hakka and Hoklo lived in isolated enclaves with little contact across the ethnic boundary, their incorporation into the same districts, and statistics that show low proportions of Fujianese, could be no more than accidents of administrative geography, not indicators of proximity that led to mutual influence. Is it correct to assume there was only minimal contact between these intermittently hostile communal groups?

Another possibility is that despite occasional violence, the members of the two groups in fact interacted frequently and were well acquainted with the cultural similarities and differences between them. In this way, Fujianese could learn not just that Hakka did not bind (part of the Hakka stereotype known to most Chinese) but that despite their women's natural feet, Hakka families could maintain patriarchal order, husbands could be found for Hakka girls, and natural-footed women could be economic assets. The presence of a non-binding population nearby surely made it somewhat more difficult for parents to convince their daughters and themselves that the excruciating pain of footbinding had to be endured for the sake of prestige and bright marriage prospects. It also made obvious the economic sacrifice imposed by footbinding when labor shortages in the busy season could not be filled by family women. In these circumstances binding could no longer be an act of unthinking conformity, but required a conscious choice. The presence of the Hakka made it impossible for Fujianese to assume that there was no alternative to binding.

If cross-ethnic group interaction was substantial, it would have been facilitated by use of a common language. The Fujianese and plains aborigines were both predominantly Hokkien speakers; thus language was no impediment to their interaction. The Hakka and Hoklo, however, spoke different and mutually unintelligible languages, which impeded cross-ethnic communication. Fortunately, the 1905 census provides evidence in its language-use tables on how the gap was bridged. In addition to the data on language in daily use, the census reports the use of secondary or supplemental languages. This makes it possible to identify Hakka-Hokkien bilinguals in the Fujianese and Guangdongese communities. Any of these bilinguals, of either sex, would have had considerable knowledge of and contact with both cultural groups and thus might have shared accounts of Hakka lifeways with footbinding Hoklo.

In both provenance groups, males were about one and a half times more likely than females to have acquired a second language, which is not surprising given the more prominent role of men in trade and all activities outside the domestic sphere. The largest numbers of bilinguals in both groups were in the prefectures where there were substantial proportions of Guangdong-ese Fujianese dominated commerce and the markets in all the prefectures (as shopkeepers, peddlers, buyers, and wholesalers), so in prefectures with substantial Guangdong populations, both provenance groups, but especially the Guangdongese, could benefit by learning the other's language. In all Taiwan, there were more than three times as many Guangdongese bilinguals as Fujianese bilinguals. In the eleven prefectures where they constituted at least 97% of the population, Fujianese had little reason to learn a second language.[8]

While data on bilinguals alone cannot establish that bilinguals were a means by which Hakka values influenced Hoklo footbinding, the data can serve as a valuable indicator of the degree of interaction and communication between the two groups. The right-most column of Table 5.1 presents the ratio of all bilinguals (both male and female, Fujianese and Guangdongese) to the population of Fujianese females in each prefecture. This is an indicator of the maximum possible exposure of Fujianese females to persons who would have personal knowledge of Hakka lifeways and who were capable of communicating that knowledge to Hokkien-speaking Fujianese females (and their families), whether directly or indirectly. The substantial ratios in the prefectures having sizable proportions Guangdongese suggest that the two speech communities were by no means isolated from each other and were in frequent contact. Not surprisingly, the table shows that the eight prefectures with the highest ratio of bilinguals are the prefectures with the lowest proportions of Fujianese ever-bound.

Although Hakka were much more likely to learn the Hokkien language than Hoklo were to learn Hakka, the cultural influence hypothesis requires the influence concerning footbinding to move in the opposite direction. Hakka bilinguals were undoubtedly exposed to Hoklo values and were perhaps made desirous of emulating the economically superior Hoklo. However, despite the high proportions of Hakka speakers who learned Hokkien, the data show this interaction only rarely led to Hakka footbinding (see chapter 2). Paradoxically, although it was the Hakka who learned the Hokkien language, it appears that it was the Hoklo who were influenced by Hakka attitudes toward binding. At the very least, these data show that cross-cultural communication was substantial in areas of mixed ethnicity and that the image of isolated ethnic enclaves is an erroneous one.

VARIATIONS IN AGE AT BINDING
AND SEVERITY OF BINDING

Although only 32.6% of Taiwan Fujianese girls aged five to ten in 1905 were ever-bound, 90.3% of Fujianese women older than twenty were ever-bound (see Table 2.3). Table 5.2 presents the proportions ever-bound of Fujianese by age and by prefecture, revealing that prefectures vary not just in the eventual proportions ever-bound but in the ages at which binding begins and the rates at which it is adopted as girls mature.[9]

This variation can be seen in Table 5.2 by comparing the proportions bound of girls aged five to ten among prefectures having similar proportions ultimately bound. Twelve prefectures report 94% or more of women bound in ages twenty-six to thirty; six of these (Shenkeng, Zhanghua, Nantou, Douliu, Tainan, and Fengshan) show less than 35% bound in ages five to ten. The remaining six prefectures report much higher proportions bound in ages five to ten; four report more than 55% (Taibei, Yilan, Yanshuigang, and Penghu), and two report 46%–49% bound of girls ages five to ten (Jilong and Jiayi). The prefectures where binding starts early also approach their peak levels at a faster rate: the six prefectures with higher proportions bound in ages five to ten (plus Shenkeng) all have at least 84% bound in ages eleven to fifteen. Table 5.2 and Figure 5.2 show important variations in the speed at which different Fujianese populations achieved high proportions ever-bound.

What about the ages at binding in the remaining prefectures with lower proportions ultimately bound? Although the proportions ultimately bound vary widely among the prefectures, this variation can be controlled by calculating a mean age at footbinding from the proportions ever-bound by age in each prefecture.[10] The right-most column of Table 5.2 and Figure 5.3 present the mean ages at binding for the prefectures.

Prefecture	% EVER-BOUND BY AGE, FUJIANESE FEMALES					SMAB
	5–10	11–15	16–20	21–25	26–30	
Taibei	56.9	85.9	91.8	95.3	95.6	7.4
Jilong	45.9	92.5	98.1	98.7	98.8	7.9
Yilan	83.5	97.7	99.1	98.6	99.0	6.0
Shenkeng	34.8	84.3	93.8	95.1	96.7	9.0
Taoyuan	13.2	30.0	40.3	51.1	56.1	12.9
Xinzhu	4.4	6.8	13.2	22.4	37.5	18.7
Miaoli	6.0	21.9	36.1	48.6	56.6	15.0
Taizhong	18.4	46.5	61.3	72.5	79.7	12.4
Zhanghua	13.3	66.8	91.0	96.5	98.1	11.3
Nantou	4.6	45.0	85.1	93.0	94.4	12.9
Douliu	21.7	69.4	94.6	98.4	99.0	10.6
Jiayi	49.2	89.7	96.4	98.1	98.2	7.8
Yanshuigang	55.7	89.2	96.3	97.9	98.6	7.3
Tainan	27.7	71.8	90.9	95.5	97.0	10.0
Fanshuliao	2.3	20.2	53.6	69.7	73.3	15.0
Fengshan	30.8	68.2	89.9	96.6	98.1	10.2
Ahou	3.3	21.7	43.1	46.6	56.6	14.8
Hengchun	0.0	0.7	1.1	1.2	2.5	18.7
Taidong	3.8	13.3	46.7	59.2	61.2	14.9
Penghu	56.1	95.2	99.1	99.2	99.5	7.2
All-Taiwan	32.6	67.0	81.6	87.4	90.5	10.0

Sources: Census of 1905, Shūkei gempyō, zentō no bu 1907: tables 2, 22, 24; Census of 1905, Shūkei gempyō, chihō no bu 1907: tables 2, 34, 36; Census of 1905, Kekka hyō 1908: table 8.

Note: The proportion bound at ages five to ten is calculated assuming no binding takes place before five years of age. SMAB = singulate mean age at binding.

Mean age at binding adds a significant dimension to the picture of foot-binding so far constructed only from proportions ever-bound. To appreciate this significance requires explaining in greater detail the process by which girls' feet were bound. Binding was achieved in two distinct and painful stages. The first stage involved wrapping the binding cloth over the four small toes to bend them under the sole of the foot, leaving the big toe straight (Figure 5.4 [*left*]). Flattening the toes under the sole of the foot was accomplished

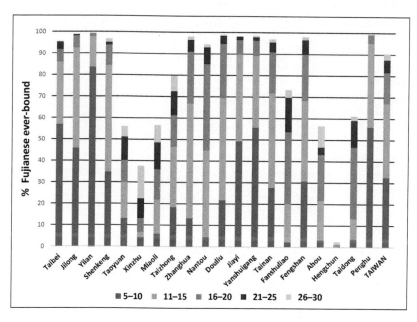

FIGURE 5.2. Proportions of Fujianese females with ever-bound feet, by age-group, 1905 (20 prefectures). *Source:* Table 5.2.

gradually by repeatedly rewrapping and tightening the binding cloth. A small pointed shoe was worn over the bound foot. For some girls, this stage might begin as early as five years of age. The second, more painful stage would begin two or more years later (at ages seven to eight). It involved using the binding cloth to compress the foot by drawing the heel and forefoot forcefully together. This causes the instep to bulge out in front of the ankle bone and raises the arch. Taiwanese women interviewed in the 1960s reported that binding usually started around age six, although some began as young as three or as old as twelve, and that the two stages of binding could take five to six years to complete.[11]

To achieve the smallest foot, the classic "three-inch lotus," it was necessary to begin binding at the earliest possible age and to continue the binding process unforgivingly. If the foot was allowed to grow naturally and binding postponed to higher ages, a larger "cucumber" foot was likely the best that could be achieved. If circumstances warranted, both binding stages could be postponed and only loose bindings used to approximate the second, more severe stage. Certain shoe styles could improve the appearance and mask the size of the cucumber foot. A bound-foot shoe popular in Taiwan that incorporated

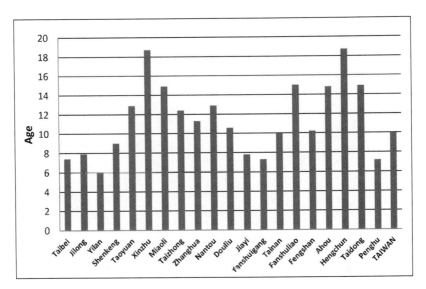

FIGURE 5.3. Mean age at binding of Fujianese females, by prefecture, 1905. *Source*:
Table 5.2.

a high heel is an example (Figure 5.4 [*right*]). The large toe was inserted into
the pointed tip of the shoe, and the heel rested on a platform that extended
beyond the raised heel of the shoe; leggings were used to hide both heel and
bowed arch from view. Such a shoe could accommodate a foot of five to six
inches and make it look smaller.[12]

Accounts of footbinding among the Hoklo in the Swatow area of Chaozhou
frequently noted variation in the age and severity of binding according to circumstances. The anti-footbinding crusader Mrs. Archibald Little reported in
1908: "At Swatow . . . people do not shorten the child's feet, always the most
painful part of the process. In order to get some field work out of the children
they do not bind their feet till twelve, often not till thirteen, when the foot is
already too much formed for it to be possible to do more than narrow it by
binding all the toes but the big one underneath the foot. An abnormally high
heel is however worn, and this gives to the foot, placed slanting upon it, the
appearance of being short."[13]

The missionary Adele Fielde, writing in the 1880s, also noted that in Swatow "the rich bind the feet of their daughters at six or eight years; the poor, at
thirteen or fourteen."[14] Taiwanese women in the 1960s recalled differences in
binding between the leisured and the working classes: "Women with three-
inch feet could not walk long distances. When they left their homes, most of

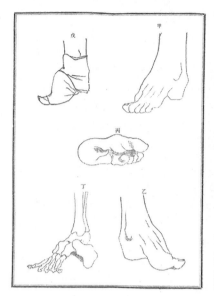

FIGURE 5.4. Bound feet (*left*) and shoes (*right*). A shoe resembling the one pictured has a sole measuring 11.1 centimeters (4.375 inches) in length and a raised heel measuring 4.4 centimeters (1.75 inches) in height. *Source*: Ino 1905: 309–10.

them rode in sedan chairs. But poor women had to go out to the streets to work. Their feet were often five to six inches long, the so-called semi-large tiny foot." [15]

Although over 90% of Fujianese adult women had bound feet (the census reports only whether feet were bound or not, not the size of feet or degree of binding), there was considerable variation in the age at binding and the degree of binding among them. Early binding led to more severe binding and smaller feet, and later binding meant less severe binding and larger feet. The mean ages at binding are thus a valuable indicator of the severity of binding in the various prefectures.

Six prefectures report mean ages at binding of less than eight years (6.0–7.9): Taibei, Jilong, Yilan, Jiayi, Yanshuigang, and Penghu. In these prefectures, a majority of girls who bound started at quite young ages, and if an early age at footbinding corresponds to tighter binding, then their bindings were also the most severe. Five more prefectures report mean ages at binding at slightly later ages (9.0–11.3): these are Shenkeng, Zhanghua, Douliu, Tainan, and Fengshan. In these prefectures, some girls began binding relatively late, and a smaller proportion must have had the more severe form of binding.

The prefectures with average ages at binding below 11.3 are the eleven heavily Fujianese prefectures reporting 95% or more of women ages twenty-six to thirty ever-bound. These prefectures all attain the same high proportion of women ultimately bound, but do so at different rates of binding through the young ages.

Of the remaining nine prefectures, seven (Taoyuan, Miaoli, Taizhong, Nantou, Fanshuliao, Ahou, and Taidong) report mean ages at binding at much higher ages (12.4–15.0), and two prefectures, Xinzhu and Hengchun, report very high means of 18.7. In these prefectures, a much larger proportion of girls who ultimately bound began to bind only at a relatively late age, and they probably bound in a much less severe fashion (toes bent under but the arch not broken, with the heel supported by a "false" shoe). Some may have started to bind just prior to marrying. These are the prefectures with lower proportions of Hoklo ever bound, and with lower proportions of Fujianese, and apparently a weakened Hoklo cultural hegemony. This set of prefectures also includes the prefectures where a Hakka cultural influence reduced binding. Here, although binding was still practiced overwhelmingly by Fujianese, the binding started later, was less severe, and occurred in lower proportions, than in the prefectures heavily dominated by the Fujianese.

Figure 5.5 shows a strong correlation in Taiwan between the proportion of Fujianese who ultimately bind (those over age thirty) and the mean age at binding.[16] Where the proportion of Fujianese ultimately binding is high, there is considerable social pressure to begin binding early and strong competition to achieve the smaller, more "beautiful" foot. But as the proportion of Fujianese ultimately binding declines, and social pressure and the intensity of status competition ease, the mean age at binding rises, and the severity of binding declines.

VARIATIONS IN FOOTBINDING BY TOWNSHIP, 1915

The 1905 census only allowed comparisons of the twenty prefectures, which obscures variation among smaller areas, especially in the largest prefectures. Because the 1915 census enables the proportions Fujianese and Fujianese ever-bound to be calculated for each of 284 townships, a finer-grained picture of regional differentials in the prevalence of footbinding among Fujianese can be produced.[17]

Map 5.2 shows the proportions of Fujianese ever-bound by township. Large areas of white, indicating above-average proportions bound, are found

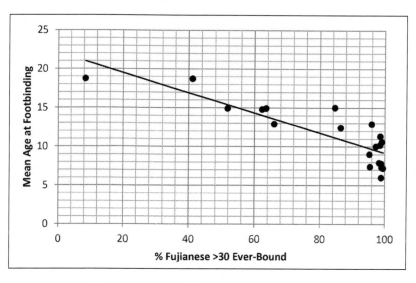

FIGURE 5.5. Mean age at binding by proportion of Fujianese females older than 30 with ever-bound feet, 1905 (20 prefectures; $r = -0.87$). *Source*: Table 5.2.

in the north in Taibei and Yilan, on the west coast in Zhanghua, and on the southwest coast from Jiayi to Tainan. The darker shades indicating low proportions of Fujianese ever-bound are concentrated in three main regions: the northwest Hakka area in Taoyuan, Xinzhu, and Miaoli; the southern Hakka area in Ahou; and the sparsely populated and ethnically mixed areas of Hengchun and the east coast.

The scattergram in Figure 5.6 of the 284 township data shows the same positive relationship between proportion of Fujianese and proportion Fujianese ever-bound, as found in the 1905 twenty prefecture data (see Figure 5.1), reinforcing the conclusion that the pressures of conformity and intra-Hoklo status competition were key mechanisms enforcing the footbinding fashion. But the 284 township data gives a much more detailed picture of local variation than the large prefectural averages could reveal. The distribution of townships by proportion Fujianese is strongly bipolar. Two clusters of townships, one solidly Fujianese and the other of townships having very few Fujianese, reflect the ethnic segregation that is a product of Taiwan's history of settlement and communal strife. The cluster in the upper right of the scattergram, where the women are greater than 80% Fujianese and greater than 40% ever-bound, contains 179 townships that account for 85% of the total Fujianese female population and 93% of the Fujianese ever-bound. An average of 62.5% of Fujianese women in

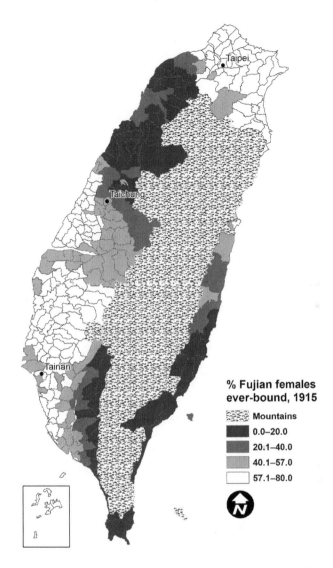

**% Fujian females
ever-bound, 1915**

Mountains
0.0–20.0
20.1–40.0
40.1–57.0
57.1–80.0

MAP 5.2. Proportions of Fujianese females with ever-bound feet, by township, 1915.
(Penghu shown in inset.)

these 179 townships are ever-bound (higher than the all-Taiwan average for
Fujianese ever-bound of 56.8% in 1915). The remaining 105 townships account
for 15% of the Fujianese females and only 7% of the Fujianese ever-bound; an
average of only 26.4% of Fujianese women in these townships are ever-bound.
The townships whose populations are less than 50% Fujianese have large numbers of Guangdongese and, especially on the east coast, Austronesians. The

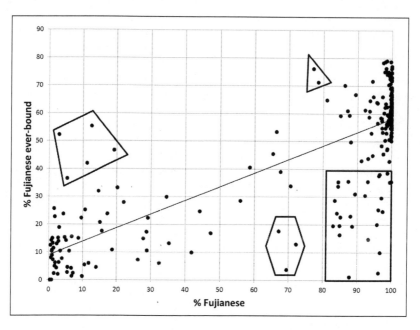

FIGURE 5.6. Proportions of Fujianese females with ever-bound feet by proportion of Fujianese females, 1915 (284 townships; r = 0.80). *Source: Census of 1915, Gairan hyō 1917:* tables I.3, III.3.

Guangdongese in these townships are overwhelmingly Hakka and at least 85% Hakka speaking (see Table 2.2).[18]

Township-level data afford the opportunity to examine the circumstances of specific localities and identify the factors affecting the proportions ever-bound. The most interesting exercise in this regard is to determine what factors are causing a number of townships to diverge from the general pattern that correlates proportion Fujianese to proportion ever-bound. Four areas of the scattergram in Figure 5.6 show clusters of outlier townships at some distance from the trend line.

What causes these townships to diverge from the strong overall positive correlation of proportions Fujianese and proportions Fujianese ever-bound? In the triangle in the upper right are two townships whose proportions Fujianese are only 77%–78%, yet the proportions ever-bound (76% and 71%) are as high as townships having 99% Fujianese. These are two Zhanghua townships (Zhutang and Tianwei) containing Hoklorized Guangdongese who bound; the proportions are artificially high because only Fujianese women are included in the denominator. As 99.7% of all Taiwanese women binding in 1915 are Fujianese, the calculation assumes that only Fujianese are binding. That assumption is contradicted in the few cases where there are concentrations of Guangdongese who bind, as in these two townships. If both Fujianese and Guangdongese are included in the denominator, the proportions ever-bound in these townships become 56% and 59%, still above but much closer to the trend line.[19]

In the trapezoid in the upper left of the scattergram are five townships with unexpectedly high proportions bound given their low proportions Fujianese. Four of these townships are in Hualian, on the east coast, where migrants from Taiwan's west coast have only recently arrived.[20] The fifth is a west coast frontier township (Shigang, in the hills east of Fengyuan, in modern Taizhong). It appears the already bound Fujianese women who moved into these townships have not yet been influenced by their minority status in new environments.

In the rectangle in the lower right, below the trend line, are twenty-seven townships having greater than 83% Fujianese but lower than expected proportions (less than 40%) Fujianese ever-bound (these twenty-seven townships account for 10% of the total Fujianese female population). Locating these townships on the map (Map 5.3) shows they are far from randomly distributed. Twenty-three of twenty-seven are adjacent to Fujian minority townships (all less than 30% Fujianese, except for one case of 47%) having Guangdong majorities (in one case, 47% Guangdong and 37% plains aborigine).[21] That the Guangdongese in these townships are Hakka (and not Chaozhou Hoklo) is confirmed by recent surveys.[22] Three more townships having middling proportions Fujianese (67%–72%) and lower than expected proportions of Fujianese ever-bound (less than 18%) are designated by the hexagon in Figure 5.6. All three of these townships are also adjacent to Hakka-dominant townships.

If bordering a Hakka-dominant and Fujian-minority township helps explain why twenty-six of these thirty Fujian-majority townships have lower than expected proportions ever-bound, what is the effect of adjacency in the sample as a whole? There are eight more (for a total of thirty-four) Fujian-majority townships that are "Hakka adjacent"; thirty-two of the thirty-four have proportions ever-bound that are below the trend line, and twenty-seven are less than 40% ever-bound. Sharing a border with a Hakka-dominant township appears to have an effect on Fujianese similar to co-residing with Hakka in the same township: the example of non-binding Hakka nearby reduces the proportion binding among Fujianese, despite being surrounded by a solid majority of Hoklo families in their own township.

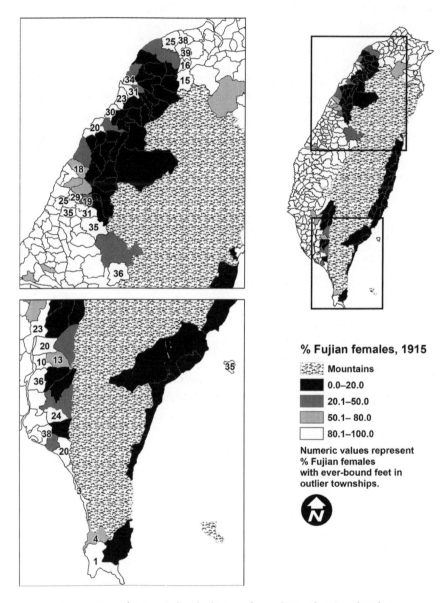

% Fujian females, 1915

Mountains
0.0–20.0
20.1–50.0
50.1– 80.0
80.1–100.0

Numeric values represent
% Fujian females
with ever-bound feet in
outlier townships.

MAP 5.3. Proportions of Fujianese females by township and 30 outlier townships having low proportions of Fujianese females with ever-bound feet, 1915

The definition of "Hakka adjacent" is simple and crude: when a Fujian-majority township shares a border with a Hakka-dominant township having a Fujian minority, the Fujian-majority township is considered Hakka adjacent. No attempt has been made to judge the quality or intensity of the interaction between adjacent townships, a very complicated issue beyond the scope of this exercise (and for which 1915 data are likely unavailable).[23]

HAKKAIZED HOKLO AND THE DEMONSTRATION EFFECT

In an environment dominated by fellow footbinding Fujianese, two factors, fear of ridicule and competition for status, intensified the pressure to conform to the footbinding fashion. Elite adherence to the footbinding fashion was essential to maintaining the hegemonic identification of elite status with notions of beauty that included bound feet. A vicious circle then reinforced the custom: as more people competed for status by binding, the threat of ridicule for not binding grew greater. In these circumstances, natural feet were not a neutral option, but a stigma to be avoided. The role of Hakka adjacency brings out another dimension important to maintaining that conformity: the absence in areas dominated by Fujianese of any model offering a respectable alternative to footbinding. Where Fujianese lived in localities with significant numbers of Hakka, not only were fear of ridicule and status competition less intense, but the cultural hegemony of the footbinding fashion was undermined by a competing model, the example of peers who had natural feet. Where Fujianese co-resided with Hakka, binding was less prevalent (see Figures 5.1 and 5.6), began later, and was less severe (see Figure 5.5). The Fujianese-majority townships having lower than expected proportions ever-bound reveal that proximity without co-residence was sufficient for the Hakka example to weaken the cultural hegemony of the footbinding fashion (see Map 5.3).

How did the example of Hakka natural feet have its "demonstration effect"? In prefectures where Hakka were a significant presence, there were sizable numbers of bilinguals facilitating communication between the speech groups and increasing awareness of differences with respect to female labor and footbinding. Through what mechanisms did this mutual awareness operate to reduce footbinding?

Did cross-ethnic marriage and adoption play a role in lowering proportions ever-bound? It seems likely that Hakka women who married into Hoklo families would resist pressures to bind their Hoklo daughters' feet and that

Hakka women adopting Hoklo girls would be unlikely to bind their feet. The Taiwan Household Register Database contains one site, Zhubei, in Xinzhu, that, with a mixed population of Hoklo and Hakka, can be used to assess whether such a pattern can account for lower rates of binding.[24] The Zhubei site contains villages from two 1915 townships, the Hoklo-dominant but Hakka-adjacent Jiugang (84.5% Fujianese and 33.8% Fujianese ever-bound, one of the outliers) and the Hakka-dominated Liujia (29.2% Fujianese and 22.3% Fujianese ever-bound).[25] The proportions ever-bound among Fujianese in both townships are significantly below the 1915 all-Taiwan average of 56.8%.[26] The high average age at binding in Xinzhu in 1905 also suggests that severe forms of binding were uncommon in these districts. The low rate of binding among Hoklo was not due to the presence of women whose fathers were Hoklo (conferring Hoklo provenance on their daughters) but whose mothers were Hakka and averse to binding their daughters' feet. Of 252 never-bound Fujianese women born before 1906 for whom mother's provenance is known, 242 had Fujianese mothers and only ten had Guangdong mothers. Nor was adoption by Hakka a reason for failure to bind. Of 220 never-bound Fujianese women born before 1906 for whom adoptive parents' provenance is known, 211 were adopted by Fujianese and only nine were adopted by Guangdongese. Thus failure to bind among Fujianese cannot be attributed to Hakka mothers of Hoklo daughters, whether natural or adopted.

A stronger hypothesis is that Hoklo families came to perceive the advantages of not binding through observing the benefits Hakka families enjoyed from female labor. Several Western observers in Taiwan claimed that the ability of the Hakka to make fuller use of female labor gave them an edge in competing with the Hoklo. According to one missionary: "The women do not bind their feet, and as a result are stronger and more robust than their Hok-lo sisters. They help their husbands on the farm and in all outside work, and are remarkably industrious. In consequence of this the Hak-kas will thrive and become wealthy where the Hoklos would fail."[27] Chinese sources also praise the health and industriousness of Hakka women compared to their crippled and vain Hoklo sisters. A selection from the *Classified Anthology of Qing Anecdotes* (Qingbai leichao) singles out for praise the Hakka women of Dapu County in Chaozhou, Guangdong, "who because they do not bind their feet, their bodies are strong and robust, their movement free, and they have no use for cosmetics or flowers in their hair; they begin work at sunrise and do not rest until sunset, they are modest and frugal, never idle or wasteful, and proud to be known as diligent and thrifty." After listing the numerous jobs Hakka women perform barefooted (weeding, fertilizing, portering, gardening, pottery manufacture, peddling, collecting brush from hillsides, weaving their own clothes), the author observes that "the women's ability to do every kind of work lightens the burden of the men."[28] Hoklo are said to have claimed about the Hakka: "Hakka women are more capable than their husbands. They can do everything. They don't care whether they have a husband or not."[29] This backhanded compliment (satirizing Hakka men) testifies to Hoklo awareness of the advantages their gender division of labor conferred on the Hakka.

Hoklo respect for the farming skills of non-binding Hakka did not extend to the non-binding plains aborigines, whose women also farmed. Plains aborigines had a reputation as indifferent farmers, and Hoklo disparaged them more than they did Hakka. Thus, while the presence of plains aborigines may have helped undermine the hegemony of the footbinding fashion, they were unlikely to be seen by Hoklo as worthy competitors, and their low status limited any cultural influence they might have had on neighboring Hoklo. There is no evidence in these data to support the suggestion (reflecting the ethnic marker, boundary maintenance theory) that footbinding in Taiwan was a way to "reinforce a claim to Han identity" somehow brought into question by nearby aborigine populations.[30] The township data show the highest rates of binding were in areas of Hoklo supermajorities, not where Hoklo dominance was weak due to the presence of aboriginal populations.

If indeed Hoklo who neighbored Hakka came to feel they were losing out, they might well have determined to level the playing field by abandoning footbinding (some by binding later and looser, others by not binding at all). Many situations might drive home the disadvantages of footbinding. If during the busy season a Hakka family is able to harvest and replant its rice fields in a shorter time, and with less expense from the hiring of laborers, it may enjoy a significant advantage. Hiring Hakka female field labor was common in some areas, and for hard-pressed farmers it may have come to be perceived as an unnecessary and unaffordable expense, when female family members (if no longer bound-footed) could do those jobs. If a Hoklo farmer fell ill, his fields and crops might suffer damage and neglect, while a Hakka farmer in the same situation could rely on the womenfolk in his family to complete the necessary work.[31] All these situations would impress on Hoklo families how unnecessary the costs imposed by footbinding were. Men and perhaps some senior women may well have seen the advantage never-bound wives, daughters, and daughters-in-law might bring to the family farm.

There is no need to assume that all family members so readily endorsed not binding. It is doubtful that Hoklo women saw not binding so favorably: this meant giving up the dream that their daughters, if their feet were tightly bound, might marry up the status ladder. Not binding might spare their daughters the pain of the binding process, but it might also condemn their daughters to lives of misery. Natural feet would make them eligible for drudgery, doing jobs only Hakka women did, such as labor in wet paddy fields (transplanting or weeding) and carrying heavy loads as porters. Nor should it be assumed that Hakka women rejoiced in their unbound freedom: Hakka women were well aware that they were expected to do many onerous tasks that Hoklo women were not.[32] Proud Hoklo families cited the workload of Hakka wives as reasons for refusing to marry their daughters to Hakka men.[33] To overcome these objections, the argument for economic advantage would have to be strong and the pressure to conform to the footbinding culture weak, conditions likely met when whole neighborhoods were both aware of the Hakka example and motivated to reduce the costs of binding. In such localities, if Hoklo families daring to break ranks by loosening bindings were seen to clearly benefit, then instead of being ridiculed they might be followed by others; if sufficient numbers joined the new trend, then a tipping point could be reached in which conformist pressure, instead of favoring binding, worked against it.[34]

That binding's importance to women's sense of pride might conflict with men's desire to increase family income is illustrated by a lawsuit in which a husband faced accusations when his wife drowned herself after they fought. The husband successfully defended himself by bringing "into court a very small woman's shoe, explaining that he had scolded his wife for wearing so small a one, which unfitted her for work. He alleged she then reviled him, for which he struck her."[35] The husband valued more the labor lost due to his wife's binding than binding's importance to his wife's social standing.

The 1905 census correctly observed of the few who had recently loosened their bindings: "In localities where the majority are natural footed, the influence of custom being little felt and the daily intercourse with the natural footed making the people sensible of the disadvantages of the bound feet, they little hesitate to loosen their feet; whereas in places where the foot-bound are in a majority, many who may have been convinced of the advantages of having natural feet would not be able, under the powerful influence of the old custom, to loosen their feet at once."[36]

High proportions of Hoklo subscribing to the footbinding fashion intensified conformist pressure and status competition and led to higher proportions binding, earlier ages at binding, and more severe binding. These circumstances solidified the hegemony of the footbinding fashion. But when Hoklo did not dominate the population in the locality, and when they lived mixed with or adjacent to non-binding Hakka, they were less likely to bind, postponed binding to higher ages, and bound less severely. The presence of Hakka highlighted the high costs and low benefits of binding and undermined the mechanisms of conformity.

Adele Fielde documents the impact the Hakka example had on footbinding neighbors in her 1887 book *Pagoda Shadows*. Fielde was an acute observer of the Chinese women she came to know as a missionary while based in Swatow, a treaty port on the coast of Chaozhou Prefecture. Fielde had worked more than five years among Teochiu (Chaozhou) emigrants in Thailand (1866–72) and acquired fluency in Teochiu before postings in Swatow, in 1873–83 and 1885–89.[37] Fielde's many years of missionary work took her to rural mission stations spread across the countryside outside Swatow. The lowland and coastal hinterland of Chaozhou consisted of an area occupied by a Teochiu-speaking and footbinding population, but inland, toward the border with the Hakka-dominated Jiayingzhou Prefecture, lay a band of mixed Teochiu and Hakka settlement.[38] Many of the Hakka residing in this border area were bilingual, which made it easy for Teochiu-speaking missionaries to begin work among them.[39] Map 5.4 shows the boundary between areas of Hakka (to the north and west) and Teochiu (to the south and east) settlement in Chaozhou Prefecture. Having worked in the cultural borderland between Teochiu and Hakka, Fielde had observed the influence of the Hakka on footbinding among their Teochiu neighbors:

> The Hakka women do not bind their feet; they lead a vigorous physical life, working chiefly in the open air. The better custom of these people influences those living on their borders, and the country women in their vicinity do not bind their feet. On their side of Tie Chiu [Chaozhou], among those who live in hamlets and small villages, the custom is slowly dying out. In one cluster of hamlets where twenty years ago every girl's feet were bound, no one now binds a daughter's feet. This laxity is unfortunately confined to the country villages in the neighbourhood of the Hakkas. In the cities and large towns, all women, except slaves and bond-servants, have deformed feet.[40]

Fielde's observation describes a situation that matches the one found in Taiwan. In Fielde's view, the presence of non-binding neighbors (even those

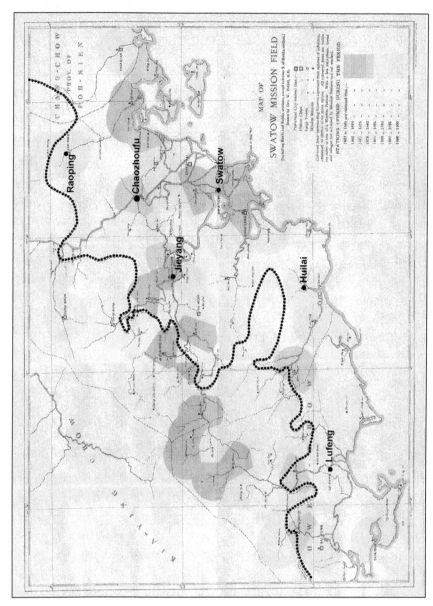

MAP 5.4.
Borderland between
Hakka and Teochiu,
circa 1901. The dotted
line marks the bound-
ary between Hakka
(to the north and
west) and Teochiu on
the coastal plain. Note
how the area of Hakka
settlement advances
on high ground
between valleys and
recedes along valley
floors. *Source:* Riddell
1901 (boundary line
and place-names
enhanced by author).

who speak another language) provided an example that undermined families' rationale for binding. But in places where there was no troubling Hakka presence, the cultural hegemony of the binding fashion went unchallenged.

The Hakka adjacency hypothesis does not claim that Hakka were seen as culturally superior in the Hoklo-majority townships where binding was attenuated. Hoklo culture remained dominant, and it was not the case that Hoklo were emulating Hakka as status superiors or even equals or with respect to features other than natural feet. Many more Hakka learned to speak the Hoklo language, than vice versa, and Hoklo were dominant in commerce. Hoklo considered themselves superior to the Hakka and, in the right company, laughed at big-footed Hakka women and ridiculed lazy Hakka husbands.[41] The effect of Hakka presence was restricted to undermining the footbinding fashion. That only footbinding was undermined points to factors specific to footbinding: the weakening of conformist pressures that maintained the fashion and economic motivations encouraging its rejection.

CONCLUSION

Thus far it has been shown that the greater the proportion of Fujianese in a locality, the higher the proportion of Fujianese ever-bound (see Figures 5.1 and 5.6), and the higher the proportion of Fujianese ever-bound, the younger the age at which binding began and the more severe the binding (see Figure 5.5). The pressure to conform to the footbinding fashion was greatest where Hoklo dominated, Hoklo cultural hegemony was unchallenged, and Hoklo competed for status against fellow Hoklo. When over 90% of adult Hoklo women bound their feet, binding, while no guarantee of respectability, was nevertheless a requisite of those who would aspire to respectability. To be one of the non-binding 10% put one in the ranks of the lowest and most despised classes.[42] Where Fujianese domination of the local population was weaker, and Fujianese shared a locality with non-binding populations of Hakka, the pressure to conform to the footbinding fashion eased, lower proportions of Fujianese bound, and those who did bind began binding at later ages and bound less severely.

Two social mechanisms enforced conformity to the footbinding fashion: fear of ridicule and competition for "face." Many reports of women who sought to unbind their feet in the early stages of the anti-binding movement tell of the harsh treatment they received in public places, where their natural feet were mocked and passersby freely insulted them. There were many degrading terms for women whose feet were unbound or poorly bound, for example, "slave girl," "flat-footed laboring woman," "bigfoot barbarian," "half Guanyin" (H: *ca-bo-kan-a, pingjiao sao, dajiao manpo, ban Guanyin*).[43] John Macgowan, the missionary who founded China's first anti-binding society in Amoy (Xiamen) in 1874, reports what women told him if they should stop binding a daughter's feet:

> What would happen to her then? Her life would become intolerable to her, and she would be laughed at and despised and treated as a slave-girl. When she appeared on the street she would not be allowed to do up her hair in the beautiful artistic fashion that is permitted to the women with bound feet. Neither would she be allowed to wear the embroidered skirts nor the beautiful dresses that the women love in China. She would have to submit to the rules laid down by society for the conduct of slave-women. Any attempt to evade these would arouse the anger of the people on the street, who would certainly mob her and tear her finery from her back.[44]

Women who did not bind were shamed and stigmatized. To counter the fear of ridicule in Taiwan, anti-binding groups proposed the government issue "badges of honor" to reward those who released their bindings or never bound.[45]

In the 1960s, Howard Levy interviewed several elderly Taiwanese women who had bound their feet as children and who believed that "everyone would laugh at the girl who had natural, unbound feet." These women reported binding their feet "to show others that they were neither the daughters of poor families nor maid servants."[46] Fielde describes several stratagems large-footed Swatow (Chaozhou) women undertook to escape ridicule: "Many whose feet are apparently bound have natural shaped feet, merely dressed in the style of the bound-footed. In some villages, the girls have their feet slightly bound just before marriage, and unbind them soon after the wedding festivities are past. In some hamlets the women are all large-footed, and wade streams and walk long distances bare-footed; but on approaching a town and on gala days, they do up their feet, more or less successfully, in the aristocratic style."[47] Fielde notes that "women would be laughed at and despised if their feet were like men's."[48]

Competition for status drew on the desires of women to be attractive (and more beautiful than others), as defined by the dictates of the footbinding fashion. Fielde took note of the fashion victims: "For a Chinese woman the greatest of sorrows is that of having no sons; the next to the greatest is that of being unlike her neighbours. The smallest feet are made by those who determine to be elegant at any cost, and these draw their own foot-ligatures tighter than anyone else would draw them. Religion is not the only sentiment which has its martyrs."[49] Macgowan reports from Amoy what a daughter bent on distinction would say to her mother: "I shall try and hold back my screams, but still keep on until my feet shall be compressed into so small a compass that no girl in all the street shall have any to be compared with mine."[50]

Mothers determined to bind their daughters' feet often had to use force in the initial stages, but gradually a girl's own desire to have beautiful feet made coercion unnecessary.[51] Mrs. Chen of Longjing, Taiwan, told Levy: "At first I suffered very much, and often spent sleepless nights because of the pain. But I did it to be beautiful. [Did you ever stealthily loosen the bandages?] The women of my family all bound their feet. I, in the hope of being beautiful, never loosened the bandage because of the pain and gradually got used to it. Other girls loosened the bindings, but if caught they were beaten and forced to bind them tightly again. I didn't dare do this, and suffered from beginning to end."[52]

Mrs. Chen of Taichung, another of Levy's Taiwanese informants, reported: "I never stealthily removed the bandages, as I wanted to be beautiful. I liked making the shoes very much. Because my family was relatively well-off, I often competed with my sisters to see whose foot was the prettiest and who made the most elegantly embroidered shoes."[53] Mrs. Yang of Qingshui, Taiwan, recalled: "When I saw how pretty the tiny feet of others were, I liked that very much. My cousin told me that no one wanted to marry a woman with big feet, while a woman with tiny feet was considered most beautiful."[54] The concern for beauty expressed in these interviews refers not to pursuit of an abstract aesthetic, but is always accompanied by a concern for status and the regard of others.

John Ross observed of footbinding: "For after all it is a fashion. The men everywhere declare they do not want it. The women everywhere declare they must have it; for they cannot have their daughters different from the daughters of other respectable people. The girls themselves at a certain age demand it, so that they may be equally fashionable with their neighbours."[55] There is no need to follow Ross in absolving men of responsibility for the maintenance of the custom, for they were not slow to look down on or ridicule women with unbound feet or to reject them as potential brides for their sons (or concubines for themselves). Fathers' pride could be stung by criticism of a bride's feet, and they were also well aware that a higher bride-price could be obtained for a daughter with well-bound feet.[56] But there seems to be little evidence that the patriarchal or erotic urges of men (rather than their status anxieties) were directly responsible for the maintenance of a custom often costly to family budgets.[57]

Girls who believed, as they were told, that only the smallest footed would be thought beautiful and marry the best husbands resolved to endure the years of pain required to achieve the smallest, most elegant feet. As adults they took pride in the beauty of their small feet. Fear of ridicule and desire for distinction enforced the footbinding fashion, not commitment to ideals of modesty and morality or sentiment engendered in mother-daughter relationships.[58] In Taiwan, the strength of these conformist pressures among the Hoklo is revealed by the close correlation of the proportions Fujianese to the proportions ever-bound and of the proportions ever-bound to early age at binding and severe binding. Where the cultural dominance of the Hoklo and the hegemony of the footbinding fashion went unchallenged, the practice achieved its greatest hold on the population.

CHAPTER 6

Women's Labor in Agriculture

S EVERAL hypotheses have been proposed that link the proportions of bound-footed women to aspects of their economic role or status. The upper classes are held to have bound earliest and in highest proportions to signal their wealth and refinement. For the elite, footbinding was an act of conspicuous consumption, even connoisseurship; the smallest bound feet stood as proof of cultural superiority and the ability to support a life of leisure for the family's women.[1] Families with more modest resources desired the respectability that the bound feet of daughters and daughters-in-law conferred, but were constrained by the need to gainfully employ their female members. If daughters could contribute income by performing labor that did not require mobility or lifting, such as spinning and weaving, then their feet could be bound with little economic loss.[2] If daughters were needed for field labor, binding need not be abandoned; it could be postponed, and a less severe form of binding adopted.[3] And farm families that needed female labor in the fields would be better able to maintain binding if they practiced dry and not wet field agriculture (where bound feet would sink into the mud).[4]

Sociologist Edward Alsworth Ross was one of many who observed a general contrast between near-universal and tight binding in the north of China and lower frequencies and looser binding in the south.[5] But severe binding did not exempt northern women from fieldwork. When traveling in China in 1910, Ross was struck by the awkwardness and pain North Chinese women with tightly bound feet endured when working in the fields: "On the Mongolian frontier the field women work kneeling, with great pads over the knees to protect them from the damp soil. . . . In Shansi and Shensi, I saw the women wielding the sickle, not stooping—that would hurt their poor feet too much—but sitting, and hitching themselves along as they reaped. The women had to be carried to the wheat field on wheelbarrow or cart." In some southerly areas of China, by contrast, Ross saw loosely bound girls taking an active part in threshing, and in Guangdong he found only daughters of the well-to-do had bound feet.[6] Ross, although aware of differences in the agricultural economies of North and South China, saw the regional contrasts in footbinding as the result of cultural, not economic, differences. A similar conclusion follows from the observations of travelers who, leaving the Guangzhou (Canton) region, where farm women did much outdoor work and rarely bound, report being struck by the sudden change to footbinding and indoor work when entering Hunan and Chaozhou.[7] This suggests that cultural divides, rather than economic gradients, determined the prevalence of footbinding.

More recent scholars, exploiting agricultural surveys from the 1930s, have stressed a more direct connection between the prevalence of footbinding and women's employment in different agricultural regimes. In the north, a shorter growing season left long winters for sedentary handicraft work compatible with binding, although even bound-footed women were called out to the fields in the busy periods of planting and harvesting. In the south, longer growing seasons and multiple cropping meant greater and more continuous demand for female field labor and, as a consequence, lower rates of binding and looser binding.[8] Also affecting binding rates was the great difficulty of working "in wet rice fields with bound feet," whereas "women could work in dry wheat fields even if on their knees."[9] These insights point to a connection between the dry field agriculture and widespread binding characterizing the north and the wet fields and limited binding characterizing the south.

In some instances, the contrast between dry and wet field regimes does not align with north-south climatic differences in length of growing season, but occurs within a single region. In Jiangbei (the area of Jiangsu north of the Yangzi), for example, footbinding was common in the upland, well-drained, dry farming areas east of the Fangong dike, but rare in the soggy, low-lying Xiahe area to the west, where natural-footed women worked in paddy fields.[10] In Jiangnan (the area south of the Yangzi), footbinding kept women out of flooded paddies but not dry cotton fields.[11] These examples support the presumption that binding is compatible with female labor in dry fields but not in wet fields and flooded rice paddies. Ding Xian, a North China area of dry cropping and high proportions bound, fits the north-south pattern, but the high rates of binding among Taiwan's Fujianese contradict the pattern of low binding predicted for a southern region.[12] Do Taiwan's high proportions bound result from a pattern of dry agriculture, despite its southern location?

Data from ethnography and agricultural surveys enable a comparison of binding practices in wet and dry farming areas within Taiwan. A common conceit among Hoklo claims that, unlike Hakka, bound-footed Hoklo women did not labor in the fields.[13] But numerous sources confirm that bound-footed Hoklo women in dry field areas of southern Taiwan worked at a wide variety of field tasks. Women from the Hoklo village of Kongliao in Yanshui Township (a dry field area) told anthropologist Ruth Ann Sando in the late 1970s: "Most of the women in K'ung-liao worked in the fields. If they were born into a rich family and brought a maid with them when they married, they did not work outside in the fields. Those who did work wore bamboo shoes to prevent the wrappings on their bound feet from getting wet. Thus when it rained they were not able to work."[14]

In Kongliao, bound-footed women performed only certain jobs, as one of Sando's informants explained: "When I was young even women with bound feet worked, but women did only simple tasks like weeding, not harvesting or transplanting."[15] The naturalist Joseph Steere traveled in the same general area, between Tainan and Jiayi, in October 1873, and observed "men, women and children . . . busy with the rice harvest." "The women generally were of the small footed variety, and wore broad triangular slippers of palm leaves to keep their feet from sinking into the soft ground of rice fields."[16] These sources thus confirm that in dry field areas, although it was difficult, bound-footed women could find ways to work even in damp fields. Steere found bound-footed Hoklo women doing some of the heaviest agricultural labor in the Penghu Islands (also a dry field area), where men were occupied full-time in fishing: "The feet of all the women are small, though their hard and laborious life must make this custom troublesome enough. I saw one small-footed woman ploughing and driving the buffalo."[17] It is likely that the Penghu case was exceptional and that women, whether Hoklo or Hakka, rarely plowed fields. In the Hoklo sugar town of Kio-a-thau, lying between Tainan and Gaoxiong, anthropologist Cheng-yuan Liu's informants recalled that their bound-footed grandmothers "could do most of the field chores except some laborious tasks such as ploughing fields and driving ox-carts."[18] Even natural-footed Hakka women were not reported plowing; according to

FIGURE 6.1. Hakka women weeding a flooded field. Image courtesy of Special Collections and College Archives, Skillman Library, Lafayette College, and the East Asia Image Collection (http://digital.lafayette.edu/collections/eastasia).

anthropologist Myron Cohen's study of Hakka in south Taiwan's Meinong Township: "During rice cultivation initial weeding is usually restricted to women and plowing to men, but both sexes transplant and harvest the crop."[19] Natural-footed Hakka women regularly transplanted rice in rain-soaked and flooded fields (Figure 6.1). But no report says bound-footed Hoklo women could do so.

So it seems that Hoklo women in dry field areas could bind feet and still contribute to farm field labor, so long as the fields were not flooded. Were Hoklo women in wet field areas unable to make similar labor contributions and therefore inhibited from binding their feet or forced to delay binding and bind less severely? Or were families forced to adjust the gender division of labor to accommodate the footbinding custom? The ethnography from northern wet rice areas of Taiwan suggests that Hoklo women customarily did not work in the fields as in the south, and the observations just reviewed suggest that weeding flooded paddies and harvesting in still-wet paddies would have been difficult for bound-footed women.[20] Even bound-footed women, however, worked in flooded paddy fields in parts of Yunnan.[21] In wet field areas in Taiwan, the general norm exempted bound-footed women from most field labor, making it possible (though costly to family budgets) to maintain binding. But not all northern Taiwan fields were wet or wet all the time, and ethnographic reports document northern Hoklo women working in the fields in more recent times.[22] Although the field labor of bound-footed northern Hoklo women may have been more intermittent and less conspicuous than that of their southern counterparts, it likely was not absent.

Tea growing was a form of dry field agriculture common in the wetter north of Taiwan and provided employment for many bound-footed Hoklo women in what were otherwise wet field areas. Picking tea was a female task, and despite tea being grown on hillsides, bound-footed women climbed to the fields to pick tea. In 1915, when bound-footed women were ordered to release their bindings, local leaders in tea areas in Taibei Prefecture debated whether to ask for postponement of the ban until after tea-picking season to avoid discomforting the tea pickers.[23] Families in wet field areas apparently found that tea picking and other side employments made sufficient use of female labor to allow footbinding to continue, despite women's diminished ability to contribute to wet rice cultivation.

Although data from 1905 that directly measure female participation in the agricultural process, the hours worked, or the financial contribution of women to the household are not available, reports of crop areas for dry crops and wet rice provide a measure that corresponds to labor requirements in different types of agriculture. Table 5.1 presents data on the proportion of the total cropping area devoted to dry field crops and the proportions of Fujianese females with ever-bound feet in each prefecture in 1905.

Dry field crops include dry rice, tea, sugarcane, sweet potatoes, peanuts, sesame, beans, barley, wheat, and millets. Sweet potatoes, an important staple, were everywhere a significant proportion of the total dry crop area. In general, the higher proportions of dry crop areas are found in the less well watered southwestern prefectures, from Douliu south to Ahou, along with the Penghu Islands. Dry field rice was particularly significant in Jiayi (where dry rice occupied 41% of the dry crop area), Yanshuigang (36%), Fengshan (35%), Ahou (27%), and Tainan (23%); peanuts and sugarcane were also important in these prefectures. The main dry field crop in the better-watered north of Taiwan, besides sweet potatoes, was tea. The largest tea-producing areas were in Taoyuan (where tea occupied 60% of the dry crop area), Taibei (44%), Jilong (52%), and Shenkeng (70%). Dry field crops appear least significant in Yilan and in central Taiwan, from Xinzhu south to Nantou.[24]

Is there evidence in Table 5.1 for a positive relationship between footbinding and dry cropping and a negative relationship with wet cropping? Did the drier south have higher proportions bound and the wetter north, where footbinding might interfere with female field labor, lower proportions? To answer these questions, it is useful to focus on the tension between footbinding and the female field labor contribution in the prefectures overwhelmingly Fujianese (greater than 97%); this puts aside the issue of Hakka influence. High proportions ever-bound (73.9%–82.8%) go together with high rates of dry cropping (56.3%–100%) in the southern prefectures of Douliu, Jiayi, Yanshuigang, Tainan, and Fengshan and in Penghu. But equally high proportions ever-bound can be found in the northern prefectures of Taibei, Jilong, Shenkeng, and Yilan and in centrally located Zhanghua (70.7%–83.6%), all prefectures where the dry cropping area is much smaller (9.1%–46.4%) and wet cropping predominates. In sum, *all* the prefectures with Fujianese supermajorities, whether they have high rates of dry or wet cropping, have high rates of footbinding. The Pearson's correlation coefficient of proportions Fujianese ever-bound and proportions dry crop area is for all twenty prefectures 0.27 and for the eleven prefectures more than 97% Fujianese 0.14, both weak.

What about differences in the mean age of footbinding (see Table 5.2) and the severity of binding? Is there a correlation between high mean ages at binding, less severe binding, and wet fields and crops? The lowest mean ages at binding are found in both the north and south: Jiayi, Yanshuigang, and Penghu in the south have high rates of dry cropping (62.4%–100%), and Taibei, Jilong, and Yilan in the north have low rates of dry cropping (9.1%–39.4%), but all six prefectures have mean ages at binding of less than eight years old. Middling ages at binding can also be found in both north and south: Douliu, Tainan, and Fengshan in the south have high rates of dry cropping (56.3%–72.6%), and Shenkeng and Zhanghua in the north have low rates of dry cropping (24.1%–46.4%), but all have ages at binding between 9.0 and 11.3. The Pearson's correlation coefficient of proportions dry crop area and average age at binding is for all twenty prefectures −0.26 and for the eleven prefectures more than 97% Fujianese 0.03, both weak.

The prefectures having high proportions Hakka—Taoyuan, Xinzhu, Miaoli, and Ahou—have low rates of dry cropping (19.4%–40.7%), low proportions ever-bound (22.3%–40.7%), and high average ages at binding (12.9–18.7) among the Fujianese living there. But the rates of dry cropping are as low in Taibei, Yilan, and Zhanghua (9.1%–24.1%), which have high proportions bound (70.7%–83.6%) and lower ages at binding (6.0–11.3). Hakka influences, not wet crops, account for low rates of binding among Hoklo in these Hakka-dominant prefectures.

In Hoklo-dominated areas of Taiwan, dry cropping does not raise rates of binding, nor does wet cropping depress rates of binding. Nor does wet cropping raise the age at binding and lower the severity of binding. If the "dry crop—more binding, wet crop—less binding" hypothesis fails, the connection needs rethinking. Where irrigated paddy fields produce the highest yields of the most valuable crop, prosperous wet rice farmers may be able to forgo a female field labor contribution. Side-employments suitable for sedentary bound-footed females may have been more common in the wet crop area. Females in dry crop areas do field labor *despite* their bound feet, and females in wet rice areas avoid field labor *because* of their bound feet, but their families employ them in other tasks and can afford to do without their field labor contribution. This could explain why the same high rates of footbinding are found in both the drier southern prefectures and the wetter northern ones. What varies across the agricultural regions of Taiwan is not the rate of binding or the strength of the footbinding fashion, but the tasks bound-footed women were required to do. The economy adapted to the culture of footbinding, not vice versa.

VARIATIONS AMONG TOWNSHIPS

A finer-grained view of regional variations in both footbinding and local economies is achieved by combining the 1915 footbinding data with agricultural statistics for the 284 townships. For each township, cropping areas (wet versus dry), proportions of owner-farmed land, and comparisons of urban versus rural townships provide good indicators of differences in modes of economic production.

The scattergrams in Figures 6.2 and 6.3 display the distribution of townships according to proportion Fujianese ever-bound, and one of the economic variables, and compute a simple correlation between the two measures. In the scattergrams, the townships falling below the 40% Fujianese ever-bound line fall into two categories. One category is the set of townships with substantial Hakka populations where Hakka influence *within* the township reduces the proportions of Fujianese ever-bound. In the townships where Fujianese live among a Hakka majority, use of township-level indicators assumes that there are no systematic differences between the Fujianese farms and the Hakka farms within a township. The other category is the set of thirty outlier townships having majority Hoklo populations where Hakka influence coming from *without* the township (Hakka adjacency) is the major factor reducing the proportion Fujianese ever-bound (see Figure 5.6). Showing the outlier townships having high proportions Fujianese as squares (rather than circles) in Figures 6.2 and 6.3 facilitates checking whether variables other than Hakka adjacency might account for their surprisingly low proportions ever-bound. The thirty outlier townships occupy a wide variety of ecologies (see Map 5.3); the Taoyuan plain (5 townships); the Xinzhu-Miaoli coast (6); foothills in Taizhong (6) and Nantou (1); the Pingdong plain (7); the Pingdong coast (4); and an island off Taidong (1). Given the wide variety of locations, it would be surprising to find that the outlier Hoklo-majority townships with markedly lower proportions ever-bound are all affected by some distinctive economic characteristics. It is reasonable, nevertheless, to ask whether any of the economic variables might explain, better than the Hakka adjacency hypothesis, the outliers' divergence from the high-binding Hoklo-majority townships.

Dry Cropping

The discussion of prefectural variation in 1905 tested the hypothesis that dry farming, because it made it easier to take advantage of the field labor of bound-footed women, lowered the cost of binding and resulted in higher rates of women ever-bound in dry farming areas and that wet farming raised the cost of binding and lowered binding rates in wet farming areas. Township-level data on proportions of dry versus wet crop area from an agricultural survey conducted in 1921 can be used to test the same hypothesis.[25] The 1921 data provide useful measures of conditions circa 1915 because major irrigation construction in Taiwan did not come on line until the 1930s and changes in proportions irrigated up to 1921 had yet to change earlier farming patterns.[26] The scattergram in Figure 6.2 (no cropping-area data were reported for 3 of the 284 townships) reveals no significant relationship between the proportions of Fujianese women ever-bound and the proportion of dry cropping area, confirming the earlier conclusion that dry farming, despite any advantage it may provide by facilitating greater female participation in agriculture, does not increase the proportions ever-bound, nor does wet farming depress rates of footbinding. The scattergram also confirms that the outlier townships

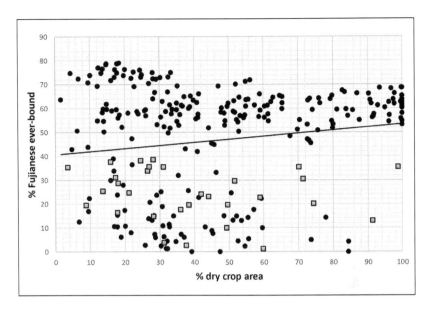

FIGURE 6.2. Proportions of Fujianese females with ever-bound feet, 1915; by % dry crop area, 1921 (281 townships; r = 0.15). Squares represent the outlier townships having high proportions Fujianese and low proportions bound. *Sources: Census of 1915, Gairan hyō* 1917: tables I.3, III.3; *Nōgyō kihon chōsasho* 1923b.

are widely distributed with respect to dry crop area and are not characterized by a distinctive agricultural regime. The correlation for all 281 townships of percent dry crop area to percent ever-bound is a weak 0.15.[27]

Owners versus Tenants

Many observers found that footbinding was less severe among the working poor than among the wealthy and the higher classes, and it is often assumed that binding of any kind was less common among the poor.[28] In an agrarian economy like Taiwan's in 1915, an important indicator of wealth was land-ownership. Wealthy Taiwanese with large holdings rented land to tenants and collected rents. If landlordism and tenancy were common in a township, more poor tenants (along with a few rich landlords) should be expected to reside there than in a township where owner-farmers predominated. The 1921 agricultural survey reports whether fields were rented to tenants or farmed by owners.[29] The proportion of owner-operated field area can be used as a proxy

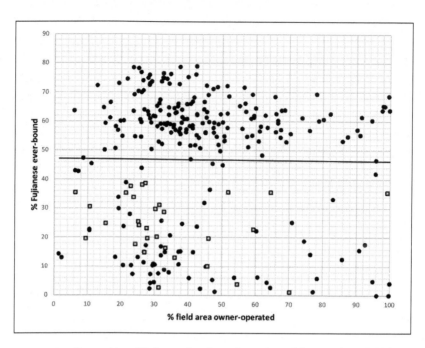

FIGURE 6.3. Proportions of Fujianese females with ever-bound feet, 1915; by % field area owner-operated, 1921 (280 townships; $r = -0.008$). Squares represent the outlier townships having high proportions Fujianese and low proportions bound. *Sources: Census of 1915, Gairan hyō 1917:* tables I.3, III.3; *Nōgyō kihon chōsasho* 1923a.

for the proportion of owner-farmers in a township. Do areas dominated by prosperous owner-farmers have higher proportions bound than areas dominated by poor tenants, who needed unencumbered female labor to make ends meet? Care must be taken not to assume owner-farmer-dominated populations are better-off in every case: owner-operated farms may be substituting poor farm laborers for tenants, and owner-operated farms may be more common on poor-quality land (and tenancy more common on high-quality land that attracted landlord investment). But whether owner-farmers or tenants beholden to a landlord are more common in a township is a reasonable indicator of its degree of stratification and division into classes.

Figure 6.3 shows there is no relationship between the proportion of owner-operated fields (or its inverse, tenanted fields) and the proportion of Fujianese females ever-bound (no data were reported for four of the townships). The scattergram also confirms that the outlier townships are widely distributed with respect to proportion owner-operated, with a concentration in the range

20%–50% similar to the distribution of the non-outliers. The correlation for all 280 townships of percent owner-operated to percent ever-bound is an extremely weak −0.008.

Urban versus Rural Differences

Did cities in Taiwan, with their concentrations of commercial and political elites, and despite what must have been large populations of urban laborers, have higher rates of binding? Many observers of footbinding in China noted that urban populations bound at higher rates than the surrounding farming populations. For instance, the missionary Justus Doolittle, who lived in and around Fuzhou, Fujian's provincial capital, from 1850 to 1864, before writing *Social Life of the Chinese*, observed:

> In some parts of China all the females have bandaged feet, but it is not thus here. There is a large proportion of the inhabitants of the country, and also about six or seven tenths of the population of the suburbs of this city, according to the estimate of some, whose females have feet of natural size. It is said that probably more than nine tenths of the females who are brought up in the city have bandaged feet. Necessity lays an interdict on many families, obliging them to rear their daughters with feet of the size and shape which Nature gave them, so that they can labor in the fields and carry heavy burdens, thus earning a living, or, at least contributing largely toward the maintenance of their families.[30]

Doolittle thus posits a sharp contrast between near-universal binding in the city and much lower rates in the Fuzhou countryside, a contrast he attributes to the economic necessities of female employment in rural areas. Adele Fielde, working in the vicinity of Swatow, also contrasted lower rates in the countryside to high rates of binding in the cities: "In the cities and large towns, all women, except slaves and bond-servants, have deformed feet."[31] A similar urban-rural gap in footbinding was noted for major Qing cities, such as Suzhou and Yangzhou, and some provincial capitals in the late eighteenth century.[32]

The report of the 1905 Taiwan census also endorsed an urban-rural contrast (uncontrolled for age and provenance): "In towns where the inhabitants are mostly in trade and technical industry there is much ostentation and foot-binding is fashionable, where the contrary is the case in villages where most of the inhabitants are farmers."[33] Thus a combination of the lighter labor requirements of urban occupations and the intensity of status competition in the cities is thought to have led to higher rates and more severe forms of binding.[34] None of Taiwan's cities reached the size of major centers such as Fuzhou, Suzhou, and Yangzhou. Taiwan's major cities were all quite small in 1915; the largest were Taipei (100,000 Taiwanese, 38,000 Japanese) and Tainan (56,000 Taiwanese, 10,000 Japanese). Taiwan's low rate of urbanization meant the transition from country to town was a gradual one that allowed few sharp contrasts between rural and urban life.[35]

The 1915 township-level data make it possible to test the hypothesis that urban populations bound at higher rates. The administrative label assigned to each basic-level unit can be used to identify cities, towns, and rural districts.[36] To control for the effect that living intermixed with Hakka reduces the propensity of Fujianese to bind, the sample is restricted to the 206 townships having female populations that are a minimum of 80% Fujianese, a subset that still includes the townships (all rural) affected by Hakka adjacency. Because commerce and urban occupations in Taiwan were dominated by the Fujianese majority, and few non-Fujianese lived in towns of any size, the full force of the mechanisms of conformity can be expected to enforce the footbinding custom in the cities. Comparison 1 in Table 6.1 shows the results of a comparison of an urban set of townships (composed of Taipei, Tainan, and nine other prefectural capitals and three port towns, Jilong, Lugang, and Gaoxiong) to the remaining 192 more rural districts. The results show that Fujianese females in the urban districts were bound at rates only 1.4% higher than those residing in the remaining rural districts, a negligible differential. The urban districts were also slightly (0.7%) more Fujianese than the rural ones. Thus in Taiwan, urban residence alone accounted for little difference in the strength of the footbinding fashion among Fujianese. This is confirmed by comparing key local cities to their hinterlands in regions dominated by Fujianese. Prefectures including Hakka—Taoyuan, Xinzhu, Nantou, and Ahou—have been excluded. Six areas have been isolated, all with greater than 96.8% Fujianese populations, and the results presented in comparisons 2–7 in Table 6.1. In three regions, the urban rate of ever-bound Fujianese exceeds the rural, and in three the opposite is the case; in all cases, the differences are quite small, less than 3.6%, as are the differences in proportions Fujianese. Urban Yilan accounts for both the largest difference in proportions ever-bound (3.6%) and the largest difference in proportions Fujianese (2.5%).

Table 6.1 reveals that in 1915 the major differences in proportions ever-bound are not urban versus rural within regions, but across the regions; the percentages range from the 70s (Yilan and Taibei) to the mid-50s, close to

TABLE 6.1. Proportions of Fujianese with ever-bound feet and proportions Fujianese in urban and rural districts, 1915 (206 townships)

Number of Cities, towns, and rural districts	% Taiwanese female population in 206 districts	% Fujianese females	% Fujianese females ever-bound
COMPARISON 1			
11 prefectural capitals and 3 port towns	15.2	98.7	59.8
192 rural districts	84.8	98.0	58.4
COMPARISON 2			
Taipei, Jilong	5.0	99.5	71.1
Taipei hinterland	13.5	99.7	70.5
COMPARISON 3			
Yilan, Luodong	1.1	99.3	78.8
Yilan hinterland	3.7	96.8	75.2
COMPARISON 4			
Taichung, Lugang	1.7	99.2	56.1
Taichung hinterland	16.7	97.5	54.2
COMPARISON 5			
Jiayi	1.1	99.8	58.1
Jiayi hinterland	16.6	99.6	60.6
COMPARISON 6			
Tainan, Gaoxiong	3.1	99.8	58.1
Tainan hinterland	20.4	98.7	61.0
COMPARISON 7			
Magong (Penghu)	0.7	100.0	63.8
Magong hinterland	1.7	100.0	65.6

Sources: *Census of 1915, Gairan hyō* 1917: tables I.3, III.3; *Census of 1920, Yōran hyō* 1922: table I.3

the all-Taiwan average of 56.8% ever-bound. As discussed in chapter 3, the above-average proportions ever-bound in Yilan and Taibei result from their continuing to bind the feet of young girls in the years leading up to 1915.

There remains the possibility that the measure, the proportions ever-bound, misses important differences in age and severity of binding. Could urban populations be binding at the same rates as rural areas, but more severely, as Fielde,

Doolittle, and others have implied?[37] Unfortunately, the 1915 township-level data do not report binding by age. But note that the 1905 prefectures having the youngest mean ages at binding, and likely the most severe binding—Yilan (6.0), Penghu (7.2), Yanshuigang (7.3), and Taibei (7.4)—are not, with the exception of Taibei, areas that included major urban centers. In sum, among Taiwan's Hoklo population, rural folk were as likely to bind as the urban dwellers in the nearest city. Overall, the footbinding fashion appears as deeply entrenched in rural areas as in the cities of Taiwan.

CONCLUSION

Hypotheses tying footbinding to the availability of female fieldwork compatible with bound feet fail to account for Taiwan. High proportions ever-bound make Taiwan an important exception to the broad regional generalization that binding was more prevalent in North China's dry fields than South China's wet ones. And within Taiwan, there is no significant correlation between spatial variations in proportions bound among Fujianese and cropping pattern, farm tenancy, and urban-rural residence. The constant proportions bound in the older age cohorts, some born as early as the 1830s (see Table 2.3), also suggest that the many changes in Taiwan's economy over the second half of the nineteenth century (e.g., the tea and camphor booms and the expansion of sugar production) had little impact on proportions bound.[38] Thus factors related to the agricultural economy have failed to explain both spatial and temporal patterns of footbinding within Taiwan. What did not change in Hoklo-dominated areas, over time or space, was the importance of binding to women's social status.

Hoklo families accommodated female labor requirements and footbinding in a wide variety of agricultural regimes. Footbinding interfered with field labor less than is usually assumed, and bound-footed women worked in the fields as their families needed, despite awkwardness and discomfort. Whatever the costs in lost labor contribution binding may have imposed, families deemed those costs bearable. Giving up binding was simply not an option where Hoklo cultural hegemony reigned unchallenged and the pressure to conform was intense. Only where the pressures of conformity and the tyranny of fashion were weakened by the presence of Hakka could Hoklo families make other choices.

CHAPTER 7

Women's Labor in Handicrafts

B ECAUSE of the importance of women's labor to family budgets, economic theories propose that where women's work is compatible with footbinding, the practice will be widespread, but where women's work and footbinding are incompatible, fewer women will be bound. The failure to find higher rates of binding in the dry farming areas of Taiwan casts doubt on the economic approach. Recent scholarship, however, has emphasized the significant economic contributions made by women's labor in handicrafts rather than agriculture. To evaluate the connection between footbinding and women's handicraft work, data on handicraft production and footbinding surveys for Liaoning and Hebei Provinces in North China, as well as Taiwan, are analyzed here.

SOURCES OF QUANTITATIVE DATA
ON FOOTBINDING IN CHINA

China's first twentieth-century census, undertaken in 1908–11, produced counts of county populations by sex and by ethnicity, but no counts of bound-footed women.[1] The collapse of the Qing dynasty and the rise of the warlord era meant that the 1908–11 census was the last national census until 1928, although individual provinces and cities continued in some instances to update census counts.

After the Northern Expedition weakened warlord power and reunified China in 1928, the Republican government instructed local governments to compile counts of the population as part of its planning for national reconstruction.[2] Sixteen provinces and six cities submitted reports over the next year.[3] County-level census reports made by a group of northern jurisdictions have been preserved in issues of the *Bulletin of the Ministry of the Interior* (Neizheng gongbao) for 1929 and 1930.[4] To aid in monitoring the progress of Republican policies banning footbinding, several of these jurisdictions used a census reporting form that called for enumeration of the numbers of women still binding their feet.[5] These reports provide one of the few sources of quantitative data on footbinding in Republican China.

The 1928 census data must be used with care. Historian Ping-ti Ho, in his assessment of Republican-period population figures, judged that due to the inadequacies of subcounty administration (insufficient local police, weak self-governing bodies) and the paltry resources devoted to surveying the population, the administrative machinery producing the census statistics in most jurisdictions in the years 1927–34 was incapable of producing accurate population figures.[6] Thus, before using any province's census report, it is important to establish the competence of its police bureaus and census-taking machinery.

The history of the police systems in Hebei (Zhili) and Liaoning (Fengtian), whose footbinding data are relevant here, indicates that they were capable of conducting reliable counts of their populations.[7] Following the Boxer catastrophe, the return of Beijing to Chinese control required assuring the foreign powers that local security could be maintained.[8] To accomplish this, Prince Qing arranged for the training of a Beijing police force by a group of Japanese instructors, beginning in 1901.[9] Zhili governor-general Yuan Shikai followed this up in 1902 when he initiated a vigorous effort to create modern police forces throughout Zhili Province. Yuan first implemented police reforms and training under Japanese instructors in Baoding, then shifted his operations to Tianjin, where he established the Zhili Police Academy. Chinese students were sent to Japan for police training, and Japanese-style police regulations were adopted.[10] Historian Stephen MacKinnon reports that based on success in Baoding and Tianjin, Yuan took steps to "extend police reform to the province at large. Indeed, during the late Qing, there was no other province where police reform penetrated the countryside as it did in Zhili. Crucial to this success . . . was the vigor with which local magistrates pursued police reform and the willingness of local gentry to support financially and to take part in the administration of police forces in their home *xian* [county]."[11] Counties were ordered to send representatives to the provincial police academy for training, and local-level police training institutes were also established. Maintaining population registers was made a police responsibility.[12]

The quality of the 1928 census surveys for Beijing, Tianjin, and Hebei and Chahar Provinces benefited from the foundation laid in the late Qing years

TABLE 7.1. Proportions of females (all ages) with bound feet, northern provinces and cities of Republican China, 1928

Jurisdiction and vol. of *Neizheng gongbao*	Total districts	Reporting districts	% of districts reporting	Female population of reporting districts	Bound-footed population of reporting districts	% bound-footed, reporting districts
PROVINCES						
Hebei, 2.7	129	127	98.0	12,636,525	6,396,704	50.6
Chahar, 2.3	17	17	100.0	827,010	429,609	52.0
Liaoning, 3.1	61	54	89.0	6,048,071	491,375	8.1
Municipalities						
Beijing, 2.1	15	15	100.0	525,369	61,149	11.6
Tianjin, 3.3	16	16	100.0	536,281	121,313	22.6

Sources: *Neizheng gongbao* 1929–30.

Note: "Reporting districts" includes districts that report both the number bound-footed and the female population. Districts correspond to counties in provinces and police precincts in cities.

that institutionalized modern policing along Japanese lines.[13] Hebei Province invested in police administration through the 1920s, and as a result Hebei had more ward-level police offices and more police and spent a higher proportion of county expenditures on policing than twenty-three other provinces.[14] Police regulations providing for fines and detention of those who failed to report births, deaths, and other population movements to the local police office helped ensure the accuracy of the registers.[15] Hebei's success in extracting revenues from localities owed much to its use of police-maintained population registers to allocate tax burdens to villages.[16]

The police forces of Hebei's two large cities, Beijing and Tianjin, also earned reputations for effective policing through the years of Republican governments following 1911. Tianjin was the early center of Yuan Shikai's efforts to institutionalize modern policing, including police-administered population surveys.[17] Its population reporting was regularized when Tianjin was made a special municipality with a separate police force by the Republican government in 1928.[18] The high quality of the police census machinery in Beijing and Liaoning is discussed in chapter 8.

Table 7.1 displays the percentages of the female population currently bound as reported in 1928 for Hebei, Chahar, Liaoning, Beijing, and Tianjin.[19] As females of all ages, including large numbers of girls too young to have started binding, are included in the denominators, the percentages reported underestimate the proportions of adult women bound. Note also that only females currently bound are reported and that this does not include those who have released their bindings (who are included in the proportions ever-bound that have been used in discussing Taiwan). By 1928, after decades of anti-footbinding campaigns and Republican efforts to eliminate the custom, the proportions currently bound should have declined in most jurisdictions from what they were at their high point in the Qing period, especially among younger women most affected by the changing attitudes toward binding and the primary target of government attempts to end the practice.[20]

In addition to the 1928 surveys, two other sources provide valuable quantitative information on footbinding in North China in the Republican period, the Ding County studies and the retrospective surveys conducted by Hill Gates, Laurel Bossen, and Melissa Brown.

Ding County

Sidney D. Gamble's study of footbinding in Ding County, Hebei, is one contemporary study of footbinding that produced numerical data of a highly reliable quality. Gamble drew data from the research area that was the focus of an intensive sociological study by the Chinese Mass Education movement.[21] Collected in 1929, the Ding County sample reported the numbers of females having bound feet in five-year age-groups up to age forty and in a final age-group of those forty and older. Of the 1,736 females of all ages included in the sample, 52.4% had bound feet. But the average proportion bound disguises tremendous differences among the age-groups. Among those thirty and older (40.5% of the female population), born before 1900, greater than 94% had bound feet in 1929. For those women under thirty, the proportions bound drop precipitately in each younger five-year age-group, to 81.5% among those twenty-five to twenty-nine, to 59.7% among those twenty to twenty-four, to 19.5% among those fifteen to nineteen, to only 5.6% in those ten to fourteen, and zero among those younger than ten. The hold of the custom over the population gradually and then rapidly weakened in the tumultuous years from 1900 to 1920, when binding young girls ceased. The proportion bound of 52.4% in the Ding County sample suggests that the similar average levels reported bound in Hebei and Chahar in 1928 (see Table 7.1) indicate a comparable pattern of very high rates of binding among adult women in those populations, combined with accelerating trends away from binding among younger women. Assuming equally high proportions bound among the oldest cohorts, counties experiencing more gradual declines begun only recently would have higher than average rates. Counties that began to abandon footbinding earlier, or did so more precipitately, would have below-average rates.

Recent Survey Data

An important contribution repairing the dearth of demographic data on footbinding in mainland China comes from the retrospective surveys of elderly women conducted by Gates, Bossen, and Brown in villages scattered across several provinces of mainland China. These surveys make an important contribution to studies of footbinding and represent the last chance to learn directly from women whose feet were bound in the early decades of the twentieth century. The investigators have cast a wide net by seeking information on all aspects of these women's lives both as children and as married women. Particularly important is the documentation of the economic contributions young girls made to their natal families through their labor in handicraft and other industries, contributions that have rarely been adequately recognized in the economic literature.

Anthropologist Hill Gates's survey in Sichuan was conducted in the early 1990s and included five thousand women born in the earliest decades of the twentieth century.[22] The smaller surveys conducted by Gates, and anthropologists Laurel Bossen and Melissa Brown in the 2000s, were lucky to include women born as early as 1915–20.[23] Their samples represent the experiences of the last cohorts of women subjected to binding, few of whom bound their own daughters' feet. Gates extended the time depth of her survey by asking about the binding status of her informants' close senior-generation kin.[24] But the perspective is primarily one of women whose feet were bound (and occasionally what they understood of their mothers' motivations in binding their feet), not the perspective of those deciding whether to bind their daughters' feet.

An advantage of these data is that they report the proportions bound by birth cohorts, as in the Ding County and Taiwan data. Bossen and Gates's interview samples from localities in Hebei and other North China plain provinces confirm the impression given by anecdotal literature and by Gamble's Ding County study: that in excess of 90% of adult women born at the beginning of the twentieth century had had their feet bound at some point in their lives.[25]

THE HANDICRAFT HYPOTHESES:
LIGHT LABOR AND LABOR DISCIPLINE

Several analysts have posited a connection between the spread of cotton culti-vation and cotton textile handicrafts and the spread of footbinding.[26] Because home spinning and weaving as sedentary occupations were compatible with footbinding (even if many other chores were not), little productivity might be lost when daughters' feet were bound. This, coupled with a high economic value of women's handicrafts, made binding less costly for families desiring the prestige and respectability that the footbinding fashion conferred. Bind-ing thus became feasible for increasing numbers of families at the lower ends of the social hierarchy.

Binding has been assumed to be incompatible with heavy labor, such as carrying loads, and work in wet paddies, but compatible with light labor tasks such as home handicrafts and lighter forms of fieldwork that did not put pain-ful load-bearing pressure on bound feet. Shifting focus away from agricultural tasks to the nature and value of women's handicraft production, a "light labor hypothesis" is used to explain regional variations in the prevalence of bind-ing: "Where women produced more value in light than in heavy labor, the status-emulation pressures of footbinding were hard to resist and the custom spread through the class ranks."[27] But in areas where girls were needed to help out by carrying loads and working in fields, tasks that required nimble and not crippled feet, footbinding would be costly to family budgets; in such cases, binding would be more frequently avoided or a less severe form of binding adopted.

Although these approaches envision families deciding to bind daughters' feet after assessing the trade-off between the economic costs of binding and its status benefits, the adoption of binding was not necessarily voluntary. The approach stressing the compatibility of footbinding and handicrafts fails to take into account the coercive nature of conformist pressure that demeaned those who failed to bind. It was not only families well positioned to keep daughters and wives occupied in light labor tasks who bound. Families who needed their womenfolk to work at heavy tasks, in the fields or elsewhere, also felt the pressure to bind. Women with tightly bound feet are reported working in soggy fields and scavenging firewood on hillsides, even though binding made such work awkward and painful. Thus there is reason to doubt that binding was restricted only to those families and regions where binding was compatible with the economic advantages of handicrafts. Where the binding fashion became the local convention, families, regardless of their circumstances, were forced to bind if they were to maintain respectability.

Recent arguments for what will be called the "labor discipline hypothesis" propose that where budgets depended on income from the sale of handicraft commodities, families used footbinding to maximize the productivity of young girls.[28] Although the domestic practice of spinning, weaving, and sewing to clothe family members was nearly universal, production for the market intensified the need for discipline. Hobbling a daughter engaged in the sedentary tasks of spinning, weaving, and raw materials processing ensured long hours of steady work at a cost of only a minor inconvenience (to parents).[29] According to the light labor hypothesis, when binding was compatible with handicraft labor, it could be adopted to enhance status. According to the labor discipline hypothesis, binding was *necessary* to maximize the productivity of girls' handicraft labor.

Female child labor is a common feature of historical as well as contemporary societies, and such societies range across a wide variety of cultures.[30] Families in many of these societies share an interest in maximizing the labor contributions of daughters, often in the kinds of spinning and weaving tasks common to female labor in imperial and Republican China. These societies use many methods to discipline and intimidate girls and keep them hard at work (methods also used in China), but only Chinese families resorted to binding feet. Footbinding is a culturally arbitrary practice, specific to historic periods of Chinese society. The decision to bind a girl's feet reflects cultural pressures and not a simple economic calculus. If binding is an economic choice, why should society have punished not binding with ridicule and shaming? The labor discipline hypothesis fails to account for this important attribute of the footbinding fashion wherever it is found.

Contrary to the assumption that binding increases the labor that can be extracted from a daughter, it more likely had the opposite effect. Many of the chores girls can perform to help their mothers, such as carrying loads, running errands, chasing down little brothers, picking cotton, gathering fuel, fetching water, weeding gardens, tending to chickens and pigs, are non-sedentary and made more arduous by the binding of feet. Focusing only on the work of girls in tedious sedentary jobs such as spinning yarn adopts too narrow a view of girls' labor contributions. From the economic point of view, hobbling a daughter is shortsighted and foolish: it prevents her helping out in tasks where carrying loads is important and thus impedes flexible use of her labor power. Conditions that once made binding economically feasible may change. Textile prices may plummet and other tasks that require full use of feet and legs prove more lucrative; members of the family who have in the past performed tasks requiring mobility and load bearing may fall ill and need to be replaced by daughters. Binding leaves daughters crippled for life and makes it difficult to adjust to new circumstances. Because of its long-lasting effects, binding for economic reasons is a poor choice. Promise of status and fear of ridicule, on the other hand, make a costly and economically inefficient practice such as binding tolerable, if not desirable.

Hakka parents saw no need to use footbinding when other means of discipline could achieve the same degree of concentration, hard work, and submissiveness without the crippling that limited the number of tasks a daughter could perform. What proponents of the labor discipline hypothesis portray as economically efficient, Hakka parents saw as highly inefficient. Parents who bound the feet of their daughters did so because they were captive to a cultural hegemony that valued binding as a status symbol; from this point of view, crippling in the artful form of footbinding added value to daughters despite the economic loss.

Chinese families recognized the inefficiency of binding by postponing binding, and letting out bindings already in place, when girls and women were needed in tasks requiring them to move about and carry heavy loads.[31] At other times, women were sent to work in the fields despite being bound and were expected to endure the pain. Mothers bound daughters' feet *despite* the loss in labor hobbling caused, because families lived within a culturally determined status order that demeaned those who failed to conform to the footbinding fashion. To see binding as something done to maximize handicraft labor confuses cause and effect: once a girl was hobbled, the work she was best able to do was limited to sedentary tasks, whether valuable or not.[32] Without question, the contributions made by female handicraft and other labor to household incomes were economically important, but it does not follow that sedentary labor required footbinding.

The hypothesis also fails to account for the widespread binding of women's feet in areas where cloth was imported and yarn and cloth production, and other forms of handicraft production of commodities, were unimportant. This issue is addressed in the analysis of regional variations in footbinding and handicraft production below. Because both the labor discipline and the light labor hypotheses predict footbinding will be most prevalent where handicraft production is most intense, they will be referred to collectively as the "handicraft hypothesis" when considering spatial and temporal variations in footbinding.

HANDICRAFTS IN LIAONING AND TAIWAN

What relevance can the handicraft hypothesis have for places such as Taiwan and Liaoning that imported cloth rather than produced it? Since its resettlement in the eighteenth century, Liaoning was a cloth-importing rather than a cotton-growing and cloth-producing region. Only a few of Liaoning's coastal counties had growing seasons long enough to cultivate cotton, and the cotton they produced was insufficient to support a market-oriented cotton textile handicraft industry.[33] Instead of producing cloth locally, "Manchuria imported woven cotton cloth and exported coarse grains such as millet and sorghum as well as raw soybeans and some soybean beancake."[34] Favorable terms of trade for its large grain surpluses enabled Liaoning's farmers to purchase factory yarn and handwoven cloth imported from cloth-producing districts in Hebei, Shandong, and Jiangnan.[35] What little weaving was done was for domestic use; the *Customs Trade Reports* note that farm families in the northeast bought raw cotton for wadding and factory yarn for weaving to produce the clothes needed by family members.[36]

The low rates of binding in Liaoning (8.1% currently bound), however, could be taken as support for the handicraft hypothesis—no handicrafts, no footbinding. Conceivably, the bound-footed women from the cloth-producing provinces of Hebei and Shandong who immigrated to Liaoning found that under the new economic conditions in the northeast, their work in handicraft cloth production was no longer needed, enabling them to abandon footbinding. At least two objections to this possibility present themselves. As will be shown in the analysis of footbinding and handicrafts in Hebei below, the connection between spinning and footbinding is extremely weak; if footbinding is done for reasons unconnected to spinning, then it cannot be the absence of spinning work that removes the motivation to bind. A second objection relates to the case of Chahar, in 1928 the province directly north of Hebei, where rates of footbinding (52% currently bound) were nearly the same as those in Hebei (51%) (see Table 7.1). In 1910, Edward Alsworth Ross observed women with bound feet in Chahar and reported that "at Kalgan on the Mongolian frontier the field women work kneeling with great pads over the knees to protect them from the damp soil."[37]

Chahar, like Liaoning, was a target of considerable immigration of farm families from Hebei in the early decades of the twentieth century.[38] Both Chahar and Liaoning lie to the north of Hebei and beyond the climatic zone where cotton can be easily grown.[39] In 1936, it was estimated that only 0.1% of rural households in Chahar engaged in spinning and/or weaving of cotton (compared to 30.1% in Hebei and 36.7% in Shandong).[40] Chahar, like Liaoning, made up for the absence of local production by importing cloth. Chahar was the most important market for the cloth produced in Hebei's Ding County and a significant consumer of cloth from Hebei's Gaoyang weaving district.[41] If the absence of spinning predicts an abandonment of footbinding, then why did footbinding rates among the immigrants to Chahar remain at the same level as those in Hebei, when those in Liaoning fell to very low levels? The difference that accounts for continued binding in Chahar and the abandonment of binding in Liaoning lies in the differences in local status hierarchies. Han immigrants in Liaoning confronted non-binding Manchu elites, whose superior social status they recognized and emulated.[42] Han immigrants in Chahar confronted non-binding Mongol banner populations, who they looked down on, and maintained binding "in order to set themselves apart from the Mongols."[43] The result was that Chinese immigrants continued binding in Chahar and abandoned binding in Liaoning.

How did Fujian and Taiwan come to be cloth-importing regions and fail to develop the local cotton textile handicraft production for the market that is a prerequisite of the handicraft hypothesis? The southeast coast climate was certainly warm enough to make cotton cultivation possible. In the sixteenth and early seventeenth centuries, Fujian's coastal prefecture of Zhangzhou grew cotton (of inferior quality) and produced cotton textiles for the market. However, the southeast coast, blessed by a long growing season, was able to raise sugarcane, tea, and two crops of rice, crops that brought profitable returns in interregional trade. As the coastal trade flourished in the late Ming and early Qing, families preferred to devote their land and labor to these more valuable crops, leading to a decline in cotton cultivation and cloth production for market. To satisfy their needs for cloth, some families grew small amounts of cotton for use in home weaving, while others purchased cloth in the market. The local demand for cotton and cloth was supplied by Fujianese traders who purchased supplies from cotton-producing districts in Jiangnan in exchange for refined sugar.[44] Cloth woven in the late nineteenth century in Fujian localities, such as Tong'an, incorporated good amounts of machine-spun yarn, reducing the reliance on home spinning. Consumers in the warmer climates of Fujian and Taiwan were less concerned with the issues of warmth that required that cloth for export to northern localities such as Manchuria be made of the heavier homespun.[45] In 1936, it was estimated that only 5.1% of rural households in Fujian engaged in spinning and/or weaving of cotton.[46]

The southeast coast immigrants to Taiwan in the eighteenth century recreated the pattern of commercialized agriculture they had known in their home counties. Taiwan's comparative advantage was to export rice and sugar in exchange for imports of cloth and a large variety of handicraft goods supplied by a coastal shipping network stretching all the way to Tianjin.[47] In the late nineteenth century, Taiwan's booming exports of tea and camphor reinforced these patterns of trade. From 1868 to 1896, imports of cottons and woolens accounted for a substantial 12%–16% by value of total imports to Taiwan.[48] The *Customs Trade Reports* confirm that little to no cotton cloth was produced in Taiwan, that imports of handwoven cloth (nankeens incorporating machine yarn warps) supplied the needs of the "labouring classes," and that only a very coarse cloth of palm fibers was produced locally.[49]

The absence of market-oriented textile handicrafts in Taiwan, coupled with high rates of footbinding, appears to controvert the handicraft hypothesis. Perhaps other lines of home handicraft production resembled spinning and required long hours of sedentary work by young girls?

Given Taiwan's dependence on imported textiles, it is not surprising that the missionary George Leslie Mackay found "no hemp, flax or cotton" cultivated in north Taiwan.[50] But there were a large number of small-scale handicraft industries processing the fibers that grew in a variety of localities. The chapter on economical plants contained in Consul James Davidson's 1903 treatise on Taiwan gives a very extensive account of the processing of such fibers in Taiwan, work that often employed women. One of the most important fibers cultivated was China grass, from whose stalks Taiwanese women extracted ribbons for export to China. The ribbons were not retained to produce grass cloth (comfortable in warm climates), for the "considerable" local demand was instead met through imports.[51] Davidson gives accounts of several other fibers (jute, pineapple fiber, and the pith-paper plant), the bulk of which were locally processed and exported rather than retained for finishing.[52] Handicraft labor also produced coarse wrapping paper from bamboo, umbrellas and lanterns from the paper mulberry, and raincoats and sun hats from the fan palm.[53] There were thus a large number of handicrafts enlisting the labor of women and men, but they appear to have been by-employments, and there are no data quantifying the hours of labor they required or their economic importance to family incomes. None appear to have required the intense, sedentary spinning, weaving, and plaiting contemplated by the handicraft hypotheses.

One large and economically important handicraft industry was an exception: the weaving of rush sleeping mats from the fine-quality rushes growing in the Yuanli area of north-central Taiwan.[54] When in the early nineteenth century local Chinese recognized the value of what was originally a plains aborigine specialty, the mat-weaving industry grew to commercial proportions. The industry spread to nearby Dajia, and because of that town's marketing and transport advantages, the mats came to be called Dajia mats.[55] The reputation of these bed mats for softness and pliability created a demand large enough to support a sizable industry. Davidson reports that in the Dajia District, "there are some 165 houses and over a thousand females steadily employed in the manufacture. Yenri [Yuanli], Taika [Dajia] and Taiankang [Da'an gang] are the villages chiefly engaged in the industry. In addition there are many farm girls who give their spare time to the work. It is estimated that there are some 1,300 houses and 3,000 females engaged thus in irregular manufacture."[56] Davidson reports that "at 8 or 9 years of age the children receive their first lessons in weaving, and as a rule are fairly expert at 12."[57] After hats made by local weavers were displayed in the 1903 Osaka trade exhibition and large orders poured in, the mat weavers switched to making panama hats for export.[58]

Contrary to the handicraft hypotheses, the proportions ever-bound in 1915 for the three townships that Davidson identifies as the center of the industry are all below the all-Taiwan average rate for Hoklo of 56.8%. In Yuanli, whose population was 32% Hakka, only 17.6% of Hoklo were ever-bound. In Dajia and Da'an, both solidly Hoklo (93% and 99%, respectively), only 43.9% and 50.7%, respectively, were ever-bound.[59]

Like their Hoklo neighbors, Hakka women were responsible for producing the clothing worn by family members, and Hakka women were as skilled as Hoklo in producing handwoven cloth.[60] Given their greater role in field agricultural tasks, it is possible that Hakka women were less likely than Hoklo women to produce cloth for market. But in Taiwan, neither group was involved in textile production for the market, yet Hoklo continued to bind when Hakka did not, a difference that economics alone cannot explain.

In sum, the absence of textile handicrafts in Taiwan and Chahar had no effect on women's propensity to bind, and the reasons for the abandonment of footbinding in Liaoning are unrelated to the absence of textile handicrafts. In Jiangbei, additional examples of high rates of binding but no textile industry and textile-producing areas with little binding show no correlation between footbinding and textile production. Elevated rates of footbinding in high-Qing Yangzhou are explained not by household cloth production (which was absent, with textiles being imported from Jiangnan) but by the city's role as a marketplace for concubines and site of an elite merchant culture that prized footbinding.[61] Both Tongzhou and Haimen, districts that lie next to each other on the north bank of the Yangzi River, are areas of cotton production and women's household spinning and weaving, but footbinding was common only in Tongzhou and not in Haimen. That Haimen was settled by Wu speakers from Chongming Island, where natural-footed practices dominated, suggests that cultural traditions were more important than the nature of women's labor in determining footbinding rates in Haimen.[62]

HANDICRAFTS IN HEBEI

The handicraft hypothesis predicts that rates of footbinding would be highest where girls' production of handicraft commodities made significant contributions to family income.[63] Historically, the spatial distribution of handicraft production was not stagnant but changed over time as different lines of handicraft production waxed and waned in response to changing economic conditions. This was particularly true of cotton textile handicrafts as they met the challenge of competition from factory-produced yarn (and later cloth) beginning in the last decades of the nineteenth century. Following this logic, where handicrafts lost value, and families redeployed the labor of young girls to non-sedentary employments, then binding would be abandoned. (Note, however, the several counterexamples cited where women were regularly employed in non-sedentary fieldwork despite being bound-footed.) Where sedentary handicrafts continued to contribute important income to family budgets, footbinding would be maintained. Thus according to the handicraft hypothesis, the fate of sedentary handicraft production determined the fate of the footbinding practice.

Changes in Cotton Cloth Production

Hebei had emerged as an important cotton-growing area and as a producer of handmade cotton textiles in the seventeenth and eighteenth centuries.[64] Up until the late nineteenth century, yarn produced by hand spinning was woven into cloth on a wooden loom. Because as many as four hours of spinning were required to produce the yarn for one hour's weaving, the slow rate of yarn output prevented increases in cloth production.[65] Typically, young girls were assigned the low-skill job of spinning, while older girls and women worked the looms. In this period, home handicraft cotton cloth production for market was primarily concentrated in cotton-growing districts with access to ample supplies of raw cotton.[66] In Hebei, three areas (Xihe, Yuhe, and Dongbeihe) emerged as the major cotton-producing districts. The largest and most productive was Xihe, the piedmont area east of the Taihang Mountains in south-central Hebei. This area enjoyed the drainage, irrigation, and climatic conditions most favorable to cotton cultivation, and its output accounted for 60%–70% of the province's cotton.[67] Families in the counties outside these areas were able to grow or purchase only enough raw cotton to produce yarn and cloth sufficient to clothe their own family members. And in yet other areas, families specialized in more profitable lines of production and bought cloth imported from weaving centers in the cotton-growing districts.[68] According to the handicraft hypothesis, the highest rates of binding among cloth-producing families should occur in cotton-growing areas, where, it follows, the women picking cotton (a female task) should also be bound-footed.[69] In these areas, families whose budgets relied on cloth production for the market were under great pressure to maximize young girl's yarn production and thus, according to the hypothesis, to bind daughters' feet.[70] If this is true, lower rates of binding should be found in areas where cloth was produced only for family consumption, and not for markets, and in areas where cloth was purchased in the market and not produced at home. This assumes that no other home handicrafts demanded of young girls the kind of intense sedentary labor required by spinning.

Beginning in the late nineteenth century, machine-spun yarn (at first produced abroad, but then increasingly by mills within China) entered the Chinese market at competitive prices, and the expanded supply of yarn made possible increases in cloth production. An advantage of machine-spun yarn was that its greater tensile strength made longer warps possible, which, by reducing the time spent preparing warps, increased weavers' output.[71] However, because cloth made wholly of machine yarns lacked the warmth, weight, and durability of cloth made from the heavier homespun yarns, machine-spun yarn did not replace hand-spun.[72] In time, consumers came to appreciate cloth made from machine-spun warps and hand-spun weft that combined the advantages of both types of yarn.[73] Thus, despite the competition from machine-spun yarns, hand-spun yarn production persisted. Another consequence of the availability of supplies of machine-spun yarn was that weaving spread to non-cotton-growing areas that had not previously produced their own cloth.[74]

In the early decades of the twentieth century, improvements in loom technologies and increasing supplies of machine-spun yarn contributed to large increases in handloom cloth production. The improved looms, the fly-ing shuttle or pulling loom and the iron-gear treadle loom, had faster shuttle speeds that greatly increased handloom productivity. Gamble noted these advantages in Ding County: "A weaver could make one piece of cloth per day on the clumsy loom [old-style wooden loom], two on the pulling loom, and four on the iron loom."[75] The substantial increase in productivity made possible by the newer handlooms enabled handwoven cloth to continue to compete with machine-woven cloth.[76] And because much of the market for handloom cloth continued to prefer cloth that combined hand-spun weft with machine warps, the demand for hand-spun yarn only gradually declined.[77] The counties of Hebei differed greatly in the impact these changes had on local handicraft production. Some areas quickly adopted the new looms and took advantage of expanding markets, while others fell behind.

Two Hebei weaving districts were early adopters of the most efficient of the new looms, the iron-gear treadle loom, beginning around 1910. The Baodi weaving district included the counties of Baodi and Yutian.[78] The larger Gaoyang weaving district included five counties, Gaoyang, Qingyuan, Anxin, Renqiu, and Li.[79] Unlike the traditional centers of cotton textile handicrafts, Baodi and Gaoyang were not located in major cotton-growing districts; instead, they depended on supplies of factory yarn coming from Tianjin. Both districts also had access to transport lines that connected them to important markets for the cloth they produced. And both districts had poor soils subject to flooding, leaving considerable numbers of underemployed farmers seeking secondary employments to supplement meager family incomes. This conver-gence of factors made possible a rapid expansion of cloth production using iron-gear looms.[80] Baodi, at its high point in 1923, had 11,387 looms operating, and Gaoyang in 1929 had over 29,000.[81] The seven counties in the Baodi and Gaoyang weaving districts accounted for 32% of Hebei's total cloth produc-tion in 1928.[82] Baodi and Gaoyang weavers preferred machine-spun yarn for use in their iron-gear looms, for reasons both technical (the greater tensile strength of machine yarn could withstand the greater strain put on warps by iron-gear looms, and machine warps could be longer, saving time spent reset-ting warps) and supply-related (hand spinning was too inefficient to meet the demand for yarn from the more efficient iron-gear looms).[83] Recogniz-ing the earnings possible from the highly productive iron-gear looms, men took up weaving full-time in Gaoyang and Baodi; in Gaoyang, men consti-tuted one-third of the weaving labor force.[84] Given the strong preference for machine-spun yarn in iron-gear looms, hand spinning of yarn was no doubt abandoned and the labor of young girls in these advanced weaving districts redeployed to more useful employments.[85]

In the cloth-producing counties outside the advanced weaving districts of Baodi and Gaoyang, the less productive loom types accounted for a greater proportion of the weaving output, and hand spinning continued to provide a portion of the yarn supply at least for weft.[86] As returns to hand spinning declined due to price competition with machine-spun yarn, families sought to reallocate the labor of young girls to more profitable lines of handicraft production, which included weaving, if they were skilled enough.[87] If these more profitable alternatives were less demanding of long hours of tedious sedentary labor, the handicraft hypothesis predicts declining proportions bound. But if families redeployed girls' labor to handicrafts that resembled spinning in requiring long hours of sedentary labor, for example, plaiting a variety of fibers to make rush mats and straw goods, or, failing to find alternatives, kept girls spinning despite declining returns, they might continue to bind daughters' feet.[88] It is likely that spinning persisted longest in cotton-growing areas, where cash outlays were not necessary to obtain the raw material.[89]

A lacuna in the formulation of the handicraft hypothesis is the absence of discussion of class differentials. Students of handicrafts in rural China have often noted that "the poorer the peasant, the greater he relied on non-farm subsidiary employments to get by."[90] Evidence of this pattern comes from the cloth-producing district of Ding County in Hebei. In studies of textile handicraft production in four Ding County villages, the less farmland a household possessed, the greater was the proportion of its female members engaged in home handicraft production, and the greater the number of hours women spent in such production.[91] And in the cloth-producing district of Nantong, Jiangsu, it was found that "very few of the households having more than two mou [one-sixth of an acre] of available land per person of working age engaged in weaving activities and only families below that critical point produced significant amounts of cloth."[92] Although footbinding was "common among the landless as well as landowners," footbinding among the better-off for whom handicraft income was unimportant cannot be explained by the handicraft hypothesis.[93] Unfortunately, the county-level measures used in the analysis below do not allow the issue of class differences in binding to be pursued.

Table 7.2 is a schematic account of the various modes of yarn and cloth production experienced by localities in the late nineteenth and early twentieth centuries. Long before the changes initiated by the introduction of machine-spun yarn in the nineteenth century, the counties of Hebei varied in

TABLE 7.2. Stages in the transformation of hand spinning and weaving, late nineteenth and early twentieth centuries

Stage	Fate of hand-spun yarn	CLOTH PRODUCTION		
		Material cloth made of	Weaving centers	Loom types
I	Traditional hand spinning	Hand-spun yarn	Cotton-growing areas	Old-style wooden looms
IIa	Hand spinning persists as machine-spun yarn supplies increase	Machine-spun and hand-spun yarns	Cotton-growing areas	Old-style wooden looms
IIb	Hand spinning persists in cotton-growing areas, declines in others	Machine-spun and hand-spun yarns	Cotton- and non-cotton-growing areas	Improved pulling loom (flying shuttle)
IIc	Hand spinning persists primarily in cotton-growing areas among the poor	Machine-spun yarn; declining use of hand-spun yarn	Many outside cotton-growing areas	Iron gear treadle looms
III	Hand spinning for home consumption survives in the poorest areas having no better uses for girls' labor	Machine-spun yarn	Industrial cities	Power looms

their degree of participation in cotton growing and the production of cotton textiles. By 1928 (the date of the footbinding survey data), changes in local economic strategies and locational advantages with respect to access to labor, materials, and consumer markets had differentially affected counties across Hebei. Thus by 1928, Hebei's counties will be distributed among all the modes of yarn and cloth production represented in Table 7.2. With each new stage in Table 7.2, hand spinning declines, but the rate of decline is slowed by the growth in handwoven cloth production and the preference of consumers for cloth woven with hand-spun weft.[94]

By 1928, the population of women living in any one county would be composed of cohorts of women who grew up under similar or different conditions, depending on how many of the stages outlined in Table 7.2 their county had experienced in the lifetimes of the oldest cohorts. The oldest women (aged sixty to seventy) in 1928 would have grown up in traditional circumstances, and if their feet were bound, the binding would have taken place in the 1860s and 1870s. Younger women (aged twenty to thirty) grew up in the first decades of the twentieth century when the cotton textile industry was changing under the impact of machine yarn and improved looms; depending on the circumstances of their county (and family), these women may or may not have been put to work spinning yarn, and they may or may not have had their feet bound when they reached binding age. Younger women who lived in counties that had gone through several stages by 1928 experienced circumstances in childhood that likely reduced the importance of hand spinning and, according to the handicraft hypothesis, the chances of being bound-footed. Such counties would have lower overall proportions bound than counties that had gone through fewer stages. The predicted effect might be moderated in a particular county if plaiting other fibers for mats, wicker wares, and straw items was important, as these industries were less affected than hand spinning by the competition of factory production.[95]

Note that the samples of women interviewed in recent surveys show only small differences in proportions ever-bound between groups involved in handwork and those not. In the Sichuan cohorts born before 1920, 93% of textile worker women were ever-bound, compared to 78% of women who did not make textiles.[96] Thus textile work explains at most a 15% increase in binding. In the eight provinces surveys, the differential is smaller; for women born in the 1920s, the probability of being ever-bound was 0.956 for those who had done handwork for income and 0.911 for those who had not.[97] The high rates of binding among women not involved in handwork suggests they were employed in types of work less compatible with binding, where binding reduced their productivity rather than enhanced it. The high prevalence of binding among these women indicates that very many families were willing to pay the costs in lost labor to maintain their and their daughters' respectability.

Note that the ever-bound proportion when applied to a sample of elderly interviewees includes women who once bound, or have unbound their feet at some time in the past, but no girls under the age of binding (it is thus comparable to the Taiwan census ever-bound measure restricted to adult women only, but not comparable to the ever-bound measure applied to women of all ages). The 1928 footbinding data use a different measure, the proportion of women of all ages *currently* bound. The proportion of ever-bound women when applied to a sample that excludes young girls from the denominator will always be higher than the proportion of those currently bound in a population that includes women of all ages.

The 1928 county-level measures of the proportion of females currently bound averages the diverse rates of binding experienced by all the living cohorts of women, young and old. Assuming (in accord with Hebei's reputation) that most Hebei counties started at a high level of binding, a baseline level of binding circa 1890 of 70%–85% of the female population currently bound is plausible; this allows 15%–30% for the girls under the age of binding who have yet to be bound and a small number of women who never bound.[98] If counties in 1928 show proportions currently bound significantly lower than 70%–85%, what factors explain the difference? The handicraft hypothesis predicts that declines will be greatest in counties abandoning intense handwork for young girls and that rates will remain high where handicraft work maintained its importance. But there are other factors that could explain lower proportions bound: variations in proportions bound that predated twentieth-century changes in yarn and cloth production (contradicting any assumption of a uniform baseline) and the revolutionary changes in culture and politics that accompanied the turbulent decades surrounding the collapse of the Qing dynasty in 1911.[99] The available data, although inadequate to assess all these factors, can be used to assess the relation between footbinding and home handicraft industries in 1928.

Handicraft Industries in Hebei Counties

In 1928, the Hebei Province secretariat produced a large statistical compilation of county-level administrative and economic indicators, *Administrative Statistics of the Province of Hebei for the Year 1928* (Hebei sheng shengzheng tongji gaiyao, Minguo shiqi niandu). The compilation included, in addition to the 1928 census report of women currently bound, a table describing the home handicraft industries in every county (*jiating shougongye fenlei tongji biao*).[100] The significance of the handicraft data was recognized in 1933, when the *Nankai Weekly Statistical Service* published an analysis under the title "Home Industries in Hopei, 1928" and the prominent economist H. D. Fong used them in his survey of rural industries in Hebei.[101]

The entries in the home handicraft industries table provide output quantities and average values by county for each product type, as well as data concerning the source of the raw materials consumed in production. The most important product type documented was textile spinning and weaving (ninety-two counties, including four counties that also produced yarn and thread), which alone accounted for 77.5% of the total dollar value produced by home handicrafts in the province. Three categories, willow, bramble, and mulberry plaiting (thirty-three counties), rush mat weaving (thirty-eight counties), and plaiting straw wares including hats (fifteen counties), accounted for 10.5% of the total value.[102] Two categories that accounted for an additional 9.7% of the total value were concentrated in a small number of counties; these were fireworks (four counties) and fur and leather products (one county). The remaining categories, accounting for less than 3% of the total value, included felt carpets (four counties), hardware (three counties), paper (eight counties), rush-leaf fans and bags (six counties), and thirteen additional miscellaneous products spread over nineteen counties. At least fifty-three counties reported producing two or more handicraft product types. The production of handicraft commodities by value was highly concentrated; twenty-one counties producing over 1 million dollars' worth of handicraft products accounted for 78% of the total value of home handicrafts.[103] Many counties produced very little of value in any of these handicraft lines.

In all, 127 of Hebei's 129 counties were surveyed in the home handicraft industries table (Tianjin and Laiyuan Counties were not included). Almost all of these home handicraft industries employed significant amounts of female labor, even when men were also involved in various stages of production. The bulk of the total value is accounted for by cloth production (77.5%) and the plaiting of various fibers (10.5%), occupations for which female labor was heavily employed.[104] Three measures derived from the home handicraft industries table (the value of handicraft production per female, the number of bolts of cloth produced per female, and the exclusive use of hand-spun yarn in cloth production) can be used to assess the relationship between footbinding and the intensity of home handicraft production.

The first test of the relationship uses the overall dollar value of handicraft production per county, a measure that indicates the importance for family budgets of handicraft production for the market. Because the measures of output vary by product type (e.g., cloth by bolts [*pi*], yarn by weight [*jin*], mats and plaited wares by piece, straw goods by *jin*), they can be made comparable by converting each line of production into dollar values. For every product line in a county, the home handicraft industries table provides the quantity produced and the average price per unit; thus it is possible to compute a total dollar value for all the handicraft products in each county (as was done by the *Nankai Weekly Statistical Service* in its "Home Industries" analysis). To control for variable population size per county, the dollar value of home handicrafts in each county is divided by its female population as reported in 1928. This yields a dollar value per female, with higher dollar values indicating more intense female employment in handicrafts. The female population is used as the denominator rather than the total population, because of the important labor contribution of female family members to household handicraft production. This measure inflates the female per capita value because it ignores the male labor contribution, but it also deflates the value because the number of females is not restricted to those who did handicraft work (and is thus not a measure of the productivity of handicraft workers). Overall the dollar value per female should give a good measure of variation in the intensity of female handicraft labor across the counties. Note, however, that the handicrafts measures do not include many products that are also the result of female labor, such as the processing of food crops and the raising of pigs and chickens, which may have been less sedentary than the major handicrafts requiring long hours weaving and plaiting. These activities, not included in the home handicrafts table, along with work in the fields, were important female employments especially in counties where handicraft values are low.

In analyzing the relationship between footbinding and handicraft values, it is appropriate to treat the seven counties in the Baodi and Gaoyang weaving districts separately. Because of their use of highly efficient iron-gear looms and machine yarns, these counties produced very large quantities of cloth. These weaving districts alone accounted for 48% of the total dollar value produced by home handicrafts (Baodi District 7%, Gaoyang District 41%). The handicraft hypothesis predicts that both hand spinning and footbinding will be abandoned in such advanced weaving districts. The shift to iron-gear looms also brought a shift to male weaving in these districts.[105] Thus on several dimensions (technology, economics, gender), these advanced weaving districts experienced conditions shaping the use of female household labor very unlike the conditions affecting the majority of counties. Therefore the consequences for footbinding in the advanced weaving districts are examined separately from the remaining districts experiencing different conditions.

Both measures of handicraft values per female and proportions of females bound-footed are available for 118 of Hebei's 129 counties (excluding the 7 Baodi and Gaoyang counties treated separately and 4 counties for which one of the two variables is missing).[106] These 118 counties include the counties where mixtures of new and old-style looms and machine- and hand-spun yarns were common. As can be seen in the scattergram in Figure 7.1, there is no evidence of any relationship between footbinding and the value of handicraft production across the counties of Hebei.

Figure 7.1 shows how widely footbinding varied, without regard to the value of handicraft production per female.[107] The 31% of counties (37) that produced

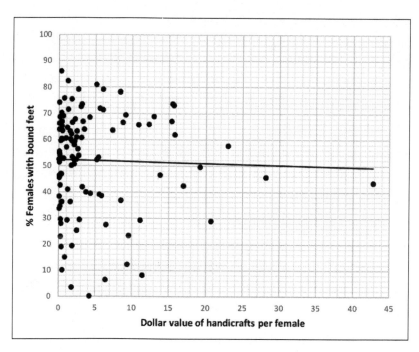

FIGURE 7.1. Proportions of females with bound feet by dollar value of handicrafts per female, 1928 (118 counties, Hebei; $r = -0.024$). *Sources*: Proportions bound-footed and female population: *Neizheng gongbao* 1929, vol. 2.7; *Hebei 1928* 1930: *minzhenglei* 36–39. Handicraft values: *Hebei 1928* 1930: *gongshanglei* 9–35; *Nankai Weekly Statistical Service* 1933: table 3.

the highest values per female (greater than $4) had both very high and very low rates of footbinding, with an overall average proportion bound of 49.2%, virtually indistinguishable from the 118-county average of 51%. These are the counties where women were heavily involved in the tedious work of plaiting, spinning, and weaving for market. The 81 counties with lower values of handicrafts also varied widely in the proportions bound-footed and had a slightly higher overall average of 52.4% bound. The correlation coefficient at −0.024 is extremely weak. The handicraft hypothesis, in its narrow focus linking footbinding to female labor in handicraft commodity production, fails to explain the binding of women's feet in the many counties where handicrafts were economically unimportant. There is no evidence here that would confirm any relation between footbinding and the presence of intense home handicraft production for the market. Note also that the many counties having minimal handicraft values, and presumably employing female labor in food processing and other agricultural activities not included in the home handicrafts table, also vary widely in the proportions bound-footed. For these counties as well, there is no simple relation between female employments and footbinding.

The results for the Baodi ($26 per female) and Gaoyang ($82 per female) weaving districts also raise doubts about economic determinants of footbinding. The handicraft hypothesis predicts that more efficient looms and the use of machine yarn reduce the pressure on young girls to spend long hours spinning yarn and thus "loosened the commitment to footbinding."[108] The proportion bound-footed in the Baodi district counties was an above-average 60% and in the Gaoyang district counties 34%. Conceivably, the Gaoyang district counties' below-average proportions bound fit the expectations of the handicraft hypothesis for an advanced weaving district, but the Baodi district counties' high proportions bound do not. Despite the similar factors at work in Baodi and Gaoyang—neither were major cotton producers and both were early adopters of iron-gear looms and machine-spun yarns—and the high dollar values produced per female, the rates of footbinding in the two weaving districts are highly divergent. Clearly, explaining the divergent rates of binding in the two advanced weaving districts requires factors beyond the economic.

The handicraft hypothesis maintains that bound feet make it easier to sustain long hours devoted to sedentary tasks. Because it is quite possible that long hours invested in some handicraft work produce goods of only small market value, it can be argued that using market values measured in dollars does not fairly represent all the hours devoted to different lines of handcraft production. There is no feasible way of equating the hours needed to produce a bolt of cloth, a reed mat, a straw hat or braid, or other plaited wares to create a measure of work hours that would include all the major handicraft types.[109] The central role of cotton textile production in the formulation of the handicraft hypothesis makes it appropriate to narrow the focus to the number of bolts of cloth produced per female. This gives a direct measure of quantities produced for the home handicraft industry that is the most significant by dollar value (77.5% of the handicrafts total). Of course, depending on loom type, the number of hours needed to produce a bolt of cloth can vary significantly. To moderate this effect, the Baodi and Gaoyang weaving districts using high proportions of the efficient iron-gear looms are excluded from the sample. Of necessity, the entire female population is used in the denominator (not the number of women actually weaving) to measure the importance of the weaving industry to the local economy, not to measure the productivity in bolts per weaver.

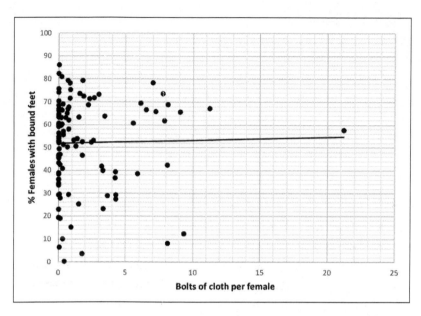

FIGURE 7.2. Proportions of females with bound feet by bolts of cloth produced per female, 1928 (118 counties, Hebei; *r* = 0.024). *Sources*: Proportions bound-footed and female population: *Neizheng gongbao* 1929, vol. 2.7; *Hebei* 1928 1930: *minzhenglei* 36–39. Bolts of cloth: *Hebei* 1928 1930: *gongshanglei* 9–35; *Nankai Weekly Statistical Service* 1933: table 2.

The results of the second test of the handicraft hypothesis comparing the numbers of bolts of cloth produced per female to the proportions bound-footed in each county are displayed in Figure 7.2. Again, these data provide no support for a relationship between footbinding and the number of bolts of cloth produced per female.

Counties that produced no cloth, as well as counties that produced large quantities per female, appear in Figure 7.2 in both the high and low ranges of footbinding.[110] The 24 counties that produced the highest numbers of bolts of cloth per female (greater than three) had an overall average proportion bound of 46%, somewhat lower than the average proportion bound of 52.4% for the 94 counties with very low or no production of cloth. Computing the proportion bound for the 15 counties producing five or more bolts of cloth per female raises the average bound-footed to 55.5%, but this is still not much different from the average bound for the remaining 103 counties of 51.1%. The correlation coefficient at 0.0236 is extremely weak. There is no evidence based on the bolts of cloth produced per female that would confirm any positive relation between footbinding and intense home handicraft production.

The tests of the handicraft hypothesis up to this point have examined the relation between proportions bound-footed and a single variable (dollar value of handicraft production, bolts of cloth) across all the counties of Hebei. The next approach, by comparing subsets of counties according to their use of hand-spun versus machine yarn makes it possible to test the close connection between hand spinning and footbinding posited by the handicraft hypothesis. The economist Li Feng reports that of 89 cloth-producing counties surveyed in Hebei in 1928, 45 used only hand-spun yarn, 23 used both hand-spun and machine-spun yarn, and 21 used only machine-spun yarn.[111] Although Li does not identify the counties, he cites as his source the 1928 Hebei provincial statistics on industry. It appears that he used the table on home handicrafts and based his categorization on the columns specifying the source of raw materials used in cloth production. These columns report the nature of the raw materials (e.g., machine yarn, homespun), the quantity, and the source (e.g., "this locality" for homespun, "Tianjin" for machine yarn). Li's analysis has been closely replicated, identifying 46 counties using only hand-spun yarn, 24 using both hand-spun and machine yarn, and 19 counties using only machine yarn (Baodi and Gaoyang included), for a total of 89 cloth-producing counties. Two of the 89 counties lack data on footbinding, leaving for analysis 87 cloth-producing counties.

Data for the cloth-producing subsets of counties are available on yarn use, cloth production, dollar value of handicrafts, cotton production, and footbinding (Table 7.3). Also available for analysis is a fourth subset of forty non-cloth-producing counties, which can be compared on the value of handicrafts, cotton production, and footbinding. Comparing the counties on these variables reveals that the subsets are distinguished not just by yarn use but by a number of related characteristics. First, note that the counties using only hand-spun yarn accounted for 32.6% of the province's total cloth production, compared to the 36.8% produced by counties using only machine yarn and 30.6% by counties using both types of yarn. That 32.6% of total cloth production came from the counties using only hand-spun yarns testifies to the continuing importance of the market for traditional handwoven cloth. However, counties using only hand-spun yarn averaged only 1.8 bolts of cloth per female, compared to 3.8 bolts per female for the subset using only machine yarn, and 3.2 bolts per female for the subset using both types of yarn. Not surprisingly, counties using

TABLE 7.3. Hebei counties classified by cloth production and yarn type, 1928

Counties	Number	Handicrafts $ value per female [total $ value] (%)	Bolts of cloth per female [total bolts] (%)	Cotton in *jin* per capita [total in *piculs*] (%)	% females bound
Cloth-producing counties using only hand-spun yarns	45	3.63 [15,206,784] (15.0)	1.8 [7,556,170] (32.6)	12.3 [1,077,348] (46.7)	44.8
Cloth-producing counties using both hand-spun and machine yarns	23	6.81 [14,973,518] (14.8)	3.2 [7,099,570] (30.6)	7.5 [357,592] (15.5)	58.6
Cloth-producing counties using only machine yarns	19	25.91 [58,184,474] (57.3)	3.8 [8,526,065] (36.8)	5.2 [256,517] (11.1)	53.7
Non-cloth-producing counties	40	3.49 [13,119,626] (12.9)	—	7.2 [617,286] (26.7)	50.6

Sources: Proportions bound-footed and female population: *Neizheng gongbao* 1929, vol. 2.7; *Hebei 1928* 1930: *minzhenglei* 36–39. Bolts of cloth and values of handicrafts: *Hebei 1928* 1930: *gongshanglei* 9–35; *Nankai Weekly Statistical Service* 1933: tables 2 and 3. Cotton per capita: Kraus 1980: app. B. Population 1931: *Neizheng nianjian* 1936, vol. 2: C.437–440.

Note: 1 picul = 100 *jin* (catties). Amounts in brackets are the aggregate amounts produced, followed by the percentages of the provincial total they represent.

at least some machine-spun yarn, unconstrained by limited supplies of hand-spun, and using higher proportions of improved looms, produced more per female than the counties relying on hand-spun exclusively. With respect to the dollar value of home handicrafts produced, the counties using only hand-spun yarn averaged $3.63 per female, compared to $25.91 per female for the subset using only machine yarn and $6.81 for the subset using both types of yarn. The higher production per female, combined with the higher value of cloth using machine yarns, contributed to the much higher values for those counties using machine yarns rather than hand-spun. The forty non-cloth-producing counties averaged the lowest handicraft values, at $3.49 per female.

Before the penetration of machine-spun yarn, traditional hand spinning and hand weaving of cotton yarn and cloth were concentrated in cotton-producing counties, where supplies of raw cotton were readily available. Families in cotton-producing districts could at minimal cost employ family labor to convert raw cotton into yarn and cloth for themselves and for the market.[112] Even when machine-spun yarn had become widely available at low prices, traditional hand spinning survived in areas that grew cotton.[113] The new weaving centers relying on machine-spun yarn tended to locate outside cotton-growing areas.[114] These patterns can be examined using cotton production figures reported by the Chinese Cotton Millowners Association, for 1932–36.[115] Counties using only hand-spun yarn accounted for 46.7% of the total cotton produced in the province, compared to 11.1% produced by counties using only machine yarn, 15.5% by counties using both types of yarn, and 26.7% by counties producing no cloth. Counties using only hand-spun yarn grew an average of 12.3 *jin* of cotton per capita (100 *jin* equal 1 *picul*), compared to 5.2 *jin* grown by the subset using only machine yarn, 7.5 *jin* by the subset using both types of yarn, and 7.2 *jin* by the subset producing no cloth. The high proportion of the total cotton crop, and the high production per capita in the counties using only hand-spun yarn in locally produced cloth, confirms that easy access to supplies of cotton encouraged the persistence of hand spinning in cotton-growing areas. However, cotton cultivation alone does not predict hand spinning; the substantial amount of the cotton crop grown in counties producing no local cloth suggests that some counties found it more profitable to sell their cotton and purchase cloth from elsewhere. That counties using only machine-spun yarn in cloth production accounted for the smallest proportion of the provincial cotton crop, and grew the smallest amount of cotton per capita, confirms that access to supplies of machine yarn, labor, and markets was more important to the location of the new weaving centers than proximity to supplies of raw cotton.

The values with respect to cloth production, handicraft work, and cotton cultivation characterizing the subsets of counties defined by yarn type are consistent with the economic and historical analyses of cotton textile production in early twentieth-century China. This confirms that the subsets identify four groups of counties that have adopted distinctive strategies adapting to the changing economics of cotton textile production.

The labor discipline version of the handicraft hypothesis puts particular stress on the tedium of hand spinning, a job relegated to unskilled young girls, and the need to bind their feet to keep them at work. The subset of counties producing cloth using only locally sourced hand-spun yarn, however, did not have higher than average rates of footbinding. The average proportion of females bound in counties using only hand-spun yarn was 44.8%, compared to 58.6% among counties using both hand-spun and machine yarn and 53.7% in counties using only machine yarn. Women in the four counties identified as producing hand-spun yarn for market (Ding County was the largest producer) averaged 50.2% bound. The forty counties that did not produce yarn or cloth for market averaged 50.6% bound. That the lowest average proportion bound is found in counties producing cloth only from locally sourced hand-spun yarns controverts the claim that hand spinning dictates footbinding. Even the counties producing hand-spun yarn for market had only average proportions bound. The counties using only machine yarn, where the handicraft hypothesis predicts that both the tedious work of young girls in hand spinning and footbinding were no longer needed, had higher, not lower, than average proportions bound, also contradicting the hypothesis.[116] These findings again point away from economic determinants of footbinding.

CONCLUSION

The rich data sources available for Hebei Province have been used to compare the proportions of women bound-footed to three different indicators of handicraft production: the total dollar value of home handicrafts per female, bolts of cloth per female, and type of yarn used in cloth production. Table 7.4 provides a summary view of the findings. None of the findings detected any correlation between female footbinding and handicrafts that would give support to the handicraft hypothesis.

Production indicators for the Baodi and Gaoyang weaving district counties are not included in Table 7.4. The population of the Baodi weaving district averaged 3.2 *jin* of cotton per capita, 7.3 bolts of cloth per female, handicrafts valued at $26 per female, and 60% of females bound-footed. The population of the Gaoyang weaving district averaged 5.8 *jin* of cotton per capita, 10.6 bolts of cloth per female, handicrafts valued at $82 per female, and 34% of females bound-footed. The averages for the 118 counties are 8.8 *jin* of cotton per capita, 1.34 bolts of cloth per female, handicrafts valued at $4.42 per female, and 51% bound.

The summary measure of footbinding, the proportion currently bound in 1928, by combining rather than distinguishing the birth cohorts, does not enable a reconstruction of the history of footbinding in a county. Nevertheless, incorporating data from all the counties of the province (all of which practiced footbinding to some degree) has provided a comprehensive test of the handicraft hypothesis. By 1928, rates of binding in Hebei had almost certainly declined from higher levels at the beginning of the century. The handicraft hypothesis predicts that in counties practicing intense home handicrafts, particularly those still using homespun yarn, footbinding will have remained

TABLE 7.4. Proportions of females with bound feet in Hebei counties classified by indicators of handicraft production, 1928

Counties	Number of counties	% females bound
Baodi weaving district	2	60.1
Gaoyang weaving district	5	34.4
Counties with high values of handicraft production (>$4 per female)	37	49.2
Counties with low values of handicraft production (<$4 per female)	81	52.4
Counties with high cloth production (>3 bolts per female)	24	46.0
Counties with low cloth production (<3 bolts per female)	94	52.4
Cloth producing counties using only hand-spun yarns	45	44.8
Cloth-producing counties using both hand-spun and machine yarns	23	58.6
Cloth-producing counties using only machine yarns	19	53.7
Non-cloth-producing counties	40	50.6

Sources: Proportions bound-footed and female population: *Neizheng gongbao* 1929, vol. 2.7; *Hebei 1928* 1930: *minzhenglei* 36–39. Values of handicrafts, bolts of cloth, and types of yarn: *Hebei 1928* 1930: *gongshanglei* 9–35.

Note: Average proportions bound for each group of counties are calculated by summing the numbers bound and the female populations and then calculating the proportion bound.

at higher levels and declined the least.[117] The evidence shows that centers of intense home handicraft production were no more likely to bind women's feet than counties where agricultural processing was more important than home handicrafts. These findings controvert claims that footbinding was an economic adaptation that enhanced the exploitation of female labor in sedentary handicrafts. And if handicraft work does not explain footbinding in the first place, then neither can declines in handicrafts explain declines in footbinding. Explaining variation in the rates of footbinding requires considering more than economic factors; the importance of local conventions that define the status of bound feet must also be taken into consideration.

The economic activities of women were not, however, irrelevant to the decisions families made when binding daughters' feet. Families were aware of the *losses* in productivity caused by hobbling a daughter by footbinding. Only if they judged that the loss could not be borne would they resist the cultural pressure to bind a daughter's feet. There are many reports that the poorest women in a community were not bound because they needed to earn money by doing menial tasks, many non-sedentary.[118] Because failure to bind feet put one's respectability in question, many families felt pressured to absorb the losses in women's productivity caused by footbinding.

Families encountering new circumstances in the twentieth century discovered that the work girls had customarily been assigned had lost value (e.g., spinning); in response, they had to redeploy the labor of daughters to new tasks. In this environment, families could no longer be certain what the costs of hobbling a daughter might be for the girl's natal or marital family. Nor, given the changing cultural trends, could they be certain that the economic losses incurred because of binding would be outweighed by a gain in status and respectability, whether in girlhood or in married life.

Data measuring the intensity of handicraft industries fail to account for the county-level variations in proportions bound-footed in Hebei. Unfortunately, no other indicators that could refine knowledge of the pre-twentieth-century baseline proportions of the bound-footed, as well as the role and the degree to which the many twentieth-century changes in economics, politics, and culture played in changing those proportions, have been identified.

A number of factors and patterns, however, are documented. There is a tendency for proportions currently bound to be considerably below the provincial average of 50.6% in Hebei's major cities, Beijing (11.6%) and Tianjin (22.6%), and in the counties where the major cities of Baoding (Qingyuan, 26.5%), Shimen (Shijiazhuang) (Huolu, 33.6%), and Handan (Handan, 23%) are located. The exception is Tangshan (Luan, 55.6%), at 5 percentage points above the provincial average.[119] The abandonment of the footbinding fashion in the early decades of the twentieth century by progressive elements of society, especially urbanites exposed to modern education and cultural trends, and often of elite status, undermined the hegemonic status of footbinding. Families preparing to bind the feet of daughters could no longer point with certainty to social elites as models upholding the fashion or to a marriage market valuing women with bound feet. These cultural shifts were accompanied by economic and political changes that also destabilized assumptions about the roles to be played by daughters.

In sum, the cases documented here demonstrate no systematic connection between intense handicraft labor by women and footbinding. High rates of footbinding exist in areas lacking textile handicraft industries in Taiwan,

Chahar, and Yangzhou and in many counties of Hebei. Seen from a distance, Hebei's high rates of binding, its dry fields, and its textile handicrafts fit the patterns predicted by both the agricultural and the handicraft hypotheses. But examined up close at the county level, the intensity of handicrafts fails to predict higher rates of binding in Hebei counties. Taiwan's Hoklo, with equally high rates of binding in both wet and dry field areas and no textile handicrafts, violate both predicted patterns. And Chahar and Liaoning, both with very little by way of textile handicrafts, have completely divergent rates of binding.

The power of the footbinding convention shows little regard for economic factors that would make hobbling women more compatible with the work they do in agriculture or in handicrafts. Where society dictated adherence to the fashion, and cast shame on those who did not conform, women suffered binding without regard to the work they did.

CHAPTER 8

Bannerwomen and Civilian Women in the Northeast

T HE 1928 census reveals surprisingly low proportions of women with currently bound feet in the northeastern province of Liaoning (8.1%) and the city of Beijing (11.6%) (see Table 7.1). Han civilians constituted large majorities in both areas, although significant banner populations resided in each. How did it come about that so few bound their feet in areas where a majority of women hailed from the high-binding provinces of Hebei and Shandong and where bannerwomen must have been constantly exposed to the footbinding fashion?

BANNERWOMEN'S FASHIONS

Contrary to reports of low proportions bound in Liaoning and Beijing, it has been common to claim that the prestige of footbinding fashions among civilian Han populations of China proper exerted a powerful allure among bannerwomen and led them to adopt styles imitating bound-footed women. The standard accounts suggest that preventing the adoption of Han fashions among bannerwomen required Qing rulers' constant vigilance, and despite repeated bans and threats of punishment, some bannerwomen still bound their feet.[1] This view is largely based on an incident in 1804 when nineteen Hanjun women of the bordered yellow banner who had bound their feet (to what degree is unknown) were presented for the palace service draft.[2] This caused the Jiaqing emperor to worry that the practice had spread to other banners, and he took steps to see the regulations enforced and parents and banner officers held accountable. In doing so, he spoke of the "bad customs of the Han" (*Hanren xiqi*) and of their "contaminating" (*ran*) effect. The other edicts regulating bannerwomen's dress collected in the same section of the Qing regulations and precedents address deviations in costume, earrings, and wide sleeves, but not bound feet.[3] Bannerwomen were not immune to the Han fashions they were exposed to in China proper, but these cases show only limited changes in the direction of footbinding and provide no basis for exaggerating the significance of the 1804 case.

Other accounts stress the styles, short of binding, that bannerwomen adopted to create the appearance of small feet. Early twentieth-century reports described a practice among bannerwomen of compressing the feet to achieve a narrow, knife-like effect (*daotiao*), also referred to as "willow branch feet" (*liutiao jiao*) or "loose binding." This did not involve breaking toe and arch bones and might last only a month, compared to the many years of binding begun in childhood required to achieve the bowed foot. It is unknown how many bannerwomen may have adopted this practice, which one source suggests was widespread in the late Qing. Although the narrowing effect differs from the bowed bound foot, most discussions of *daotiao* see it as bannerwomen's way of achieving a compromise between the prohibition on binding and the allure of the small foot fashion.[4]

Some suggest that bannerwomen found it easier to adopt platform shoes to hide big, natural feet under long robes, create an "illusion of smallness," and produce a gait that mimicked that of bound-footed women.[5] These accounts, reflecting Han-centric perspectives, leave the impression that bannerwomen could not resist the powerful influence of the Han footbinding fashion.

The interpretation of Manchu platform shoes as signs of the influence of Han footbinding styles has been repeated frequently and uncritically.[6] Mongolian origins, a desire to enhance stature, and utilitarian concerns to keep feet dry are explanations for the style as likely as a desire to adopt the short-stepped gait of the bound-footed.[7] Two platform shoe styles were common in the late nineteenth century. Horse-hoof platforms (*mati di xie*) raised the flat sole of the shoe several inches by means of a wooden block with concave sides attached at the center of the sole; these stilt-like shoes were the most clumsy to walk on. Flower basin shoes (*huapen di xie*) had thick soles tapered at the toe and heel.[8] Several kinds of evidence, including photographs, Manchu legends, and testimony of Western observers, give views of platform shoes that challenge the received accounts.

Inspection of photographs of bannerwomen raise doubts that low platforms could hide natural feet or that high platforms, with their large square or horse-hoof bases, could create an "illusion of smallness." Most early photographs of bannerwomen show them holding motionless poses required for long film exposures. Whether standing, sitting, or astride a steed, feet and clogs often show below the hems of dresses, and no attempt is made to pull the feet back beyond the gaze of the camera.[9] Portraits of Empress Dowager Cixi show her proudly displaying her elaborately decorated, horse-hoof-style, high platforms.[10] Faster film speeds made it possible to photograph elaborately coiffed and dressed bannerwomen strolling along city streets in an erect posture and making no effort to hide feet shod in flower basin (keel-shaped) platforms and flats or to mimic the gait of bound-footed women.[11]

Manchu traditions provide several explanations for the origin of platform shoes (none of which suggest Han influence). One view sees them as practical adaptations to living conditions in the northeast. Wooden clogs kept feet dry and prevented long, banner-style robes (qipao; see Figures 8.1 and 8.2) touching the ground in rough and muddy terrain. Platform shoes also provided protection from snakes and insects for women gathering produce in the hills.[12] Rigid-soled shoes for men and women were appropriate for horse-riding (and necessary to allow mounted archers to stand in stirrups).[13] A Manchu folktale gives to platform shoes a special cultural significance. This legend traces the origin of platform shoes to the heroic invention of Princess Duoluo Ganzhu (Doro Ganju), who had taken refuge in a remote village after being driven from her capital by an invader whose proposals of marriage she had spurned. Because the capital was surrounded on three sides by swamp, and the only access was along a road heavily guarded by the occupying army, her forces could not muster the numbers required for a frontal assault to retake the capital. One day, in deep despair, Duoluo Ganzhu was gazing out over the marshes when she noticed that the long legs and webbed feet of white Manchurian cranes enabled them to stand in water for hours without sinking in the mud. Inspired by what she had observed, the princess ordered her soldiers to equip themselves with wooden stilts. They then launched a surprise attack across marshy ground and retook the capital. To commemorate this legendary victory, Manchu women ever since have worn stilt-like platform shoes.[14] This delightful origin myth links the platform shoe style to assertive and heroic womanhood and to the beauty of the long-legged Manchurian crane.[15] Manchu folksongs also expressed pride in the beauty of natural feet, celebrated the freedom of movement they afforded, and poked fun at the clumsiness of bound feet.[16] None of these traditions betray any sense that Manchu fashions were inferior to Han.

Following the Qing conquest and the court's move to Beijing, the trend of banner elite fashion saw the platform soles grow thicker and higher and embroidered decoration grow more elaborate; it is likely the shoe styles changed from reign to reign as did hairstyles.[17] An account of British statesman George Macartney's mission in 1793 to the court of the Qianlong emperor includes a description of "Tartar" ladies: "Their feet were not cramped, like those of the Chinese; and their shoes with broad toes and soles above an inch in thickness, were as clumsy as those of the original Chinese ladies were diminutive."[18] A drawing of a banner lady by Pu-Qua dated 1799 shows her inch-thick-soled shoes.[19] Alexander Hosie, based on his many years of service as British consul in Manchuria beginning in 1894, observed: "There can be no mistake about a Manchu lady. Her erect carriage, due, no doubt to her natural feet, her distinctive coiffure and dress at once mark her as non-Chinese. Notwithstanding her erect carriage, however, her gait is slovenly, and is due to the thick inelastic soles of her shoes . . . but I have always been struck by the independent bearing and sprightliness of the Manchu lady."[20] Hosie annotated his comments with a long quotation from the *Illustrated Catalogue of the Chinese Collection of Exhibits for the International Health Exhibition, London, 1884* that distinguished between women's shoes with flat soles ("much like men's ordinary shoes") and soles of four or six inches worn by ladies when they go out in a chair or cart: "In use they are exceedingly inconvenient, but . . . they show the well-to-do position of the wearer."[21] The tallest horse-hoof platforms, worn by high-status women on formal occasions, forced their wearers to take slow deliberate steps and adopt a dignified pace.[22] Those who went about on foot were more likely to wear flower basin platforms and flats.

Dramatic coiffures, long single-piece gowns, and elevated clogs accentuated the tall stature of Manchu women and made for a striking appearance.[23] Bannerwomen wearing platform shoes and loose flowing *qipao* dress assumed an erect posture and a confident gait that was considered graceful and dignified (Figure 8.1).[24] Compare the walk of a bound-footed women as described in the *Chinese Repository* of 1835: "In walking, the body is bent forwards, at a considerable inclination, in order to place the centre of gravity over the feet; and the great muscular exertion required for preserving the balance is evinced by the rapid motion of the arms, and the hobbling shortness of the steps."[25] Adele Fielde describes the walk of the bound-footed: "Her dainty feet toddle and clump, and her gait is exactly that of one walking on the points of the

FIGURE 8.1. Manchu ladies strolling. *Source*: Okinawa Sobu 2013.

heels."[26] The result was a swaying motion in the walk of bound-footed women: "The tottering gait of the poor women as they hobble along upon the heel of the foot, they compare to the waving of a willow agitated by the breeze."[27] It is hard to imagine a contrast greater than that between the erect posture and gait of bannerwomen and the short, toddling steps of the bound-footed, who were forced to "stump about on their heels" and whose crippled feet often kept them confined close to home (Figure 8.2).[28] The standard accounts thus misinterpret bannerwomen's platform shoes and gait and greatly exaggerate the influence of the Han footbinding fashion. As Shengfang Chou points out,

FIGURE 8.2. Walking on platform shoes (*left*) and bound feet (*right*). *Sources*: Photograph (*left*) by William W. Chapin (1910), courtesy of National Geographic Creative. Photograph (*right*) Bettmann Archive, courtesy of Getty Images.

Manchu women "brought an alternative standard for feminine beauty that contrasted with the bodily aesthetic of Han Chinese women."[29]

The contrast in gender cultures between the Manchu banners and the Han extended well beyond standards of beauty and footwear styles. John Barrow, secretary to Macartney on the embassy to China in 1793, compared the Manchu women to the Chinese: "Women in Pekin were commonly seen among the crowd, or walking in the narrow streets, or riding on horseback, which they crossed in the same manner as the men; but they were all Tartars . . . their shoes appeared to be as much above the common size as those of the Chinese are under it. . . . The Chinese women are more scrupulously confined to the house in the capital than elsewhere. Young girls were sometimes seen smoking their pipes in the doors of their houses, but they always retired on the approach of the men."[30] Commentators noted as early as the seventeenth century the comparative social freedom and ease of manners of Manchu women in mixed-sex company.[31]

Owen Lattimore, who traveled extensively in the northeast in the early 1930s, found Manchu women "going about, joining in general conversation when men are present."[32] The missionary John Hedley noted they "mix with the populace much more freely than do the Chinese women." When visiting a Manchu village, Hedley reports being "inspected and interviewed by almost all the Manchu ladies of the settlement. Their freedom of manners ... were in marked contrast to the general conduct of Chinese women. ... They ... swarm[ed] into my room all the time I was there, asking questions and making the freest remarks."[33] Such unrestrained behavior contrasts with both the stricter separation of the sexes expected by orthodox Han norms and the restrictions on movement imposed by bound feet. Footbinding was incompatible with the duties expected of banner wives as well as with the free movement they enjoyed outside the home.[34] These sources show that Manchu women maintained their distinctive gender culture throughout the Qing.

THE ABANDONMENT OF FOOTBINDING IN BEIJING

Several accounts of the prevalence of footbinding in Beijing also contradict the impression that Han footbinding fashions had a powerful and irresistible influence. According to physician William Lockhart, a medical missionary who first arrived in China in 1838 and who worked in Beijing in 1861–64, the direction of influence ran from Manchu to Han: "The Tartar women never have their feet bound or compressed, as the Chinese women have had theirs ...; but, in Peking, great numbers of the Chinese women are seen with the feet of their natural size like the Tartar women; and, even in the most respectable families both of officers and civilians, the female children are not subjected to this painful proceeding. In Peking, it is not necessary to follow this foolish fashion; but in the other cities of the province, as in all other parts of the empire, the women's feet are compressed into the usual small size."[35]

Fu-ge, a nineteenth-century official and Han bannerman attached to the Imperial Household Department, reported that despite the craze for bound feet, bannerwomen did not bind, nor did 50%–60% of non-banner civilian women in the inner city of the capital (neicheng minnü) and 30%–40% of women in the nearby countryside.[36] Thus there is evidence that in the imperial capital the direction of influence was reversed and that many Chinese women in Beijing kept natural feet. Physician John Dudgeon, a long-term resident of Beijing writing in 1869, testifies that the Manchu influence in Beijing reduced not only the numbers binding but also the severity of binding among those who did bind:

> The Tartar women do not wear small feet but shoes with a large square piece of wood in the middle of the sole. These likewise appear very inconvenient; but in wet weather or muddy streets, they raise the finely embroidered satin slipper above danger. In Peking, the Tartar element is so strong, that small feet are less frequently seen than in the South. The small foot, too, is much larger here. A milder form of compression, especially among the country people, exists, the four toes being bound under the foot without changing the direction of the heel very much. Ladies in the South desire a three inch foot; here they are content with a seven inch.[37]

In Beijing, bannerwomen referred to bound feet, perhaps derogatorily, as "southerners' feet" (*manzi jiaor*), while unbound feet were referred to as "banner flats" (*qi ban*).[38]

The 1928 census reports that only 11.6% of Beijing females of all ages had bound feet (see Table 8.1), confirming the impressions of Lockhart, Fu-ge, and Dudgeon that binding was practiced by only a minority of women in Beijing. The professionalism and diligence of the Beijing police conducting the censuses provide assurance that the Beijing reports are of good quality.[39]

Disaggregating the Beijing figures reveals the variation among the three large areas into which the city was divided: the inner city (northern or "Tartar" city), the outer city (southern or Chinese city), and the suburban districts outside the city walls. The 1910 census figures report the presence of the banner and non-banner populations within these districts; although these reports were made nineteen years earlier than the footbinding census, it is likely, given Beijing's stagnant population, that the ethnic distribution in 1928 had not greatly diverged from the pattern that existed in 1910.[40] As shown in Table 8.1, the proportions bound in the inner city and the suburbs are extremely low, reflecting both the presence of considerable numbers of natural-footed bannerwomen and the influence of banner fashions on the non-banner (Han civilian) proportion of the population. The proportion bound in the outer city, where banner influence was reduced, was much higher, but at 20.8% it was still strikingly lower than the proportions bound in the surrounding province of Hebei (50.6%) and in the Ding County sample (52.4%). Assuming that the 1910 non-banner proportion of the population (60.3%) is still valid for the whole

TABLE 8.1. Proportions of females with bound feet in districts of Beijing, 1928

District	Female population	Number bound	1928 % bound	1910 % banner population
Inner city	203,001	17,570	8.7	41.9
Outer city	125,740	26,111	20.8	—
Suburbs	196,628	17,468	8.9	73.3
Beijing total	525,369	61,149	11.6	39.7
Hebei Province	12,636,525	6,396,704	50.6	—
Ding County	1,736	909	52.4	—

Sources: Female population and number bound: Neizheng gongbao 1929, vol. 2.1 (Beiping), vol. 2.7 (Hebei); Gamble 1943 (Ding County). Banner proportion of population in 1910: Han Guanghui 1996: 120, 126, 128.

city in 1928, and allocating all those with bound feet in 1928 to an estimated non-banner population, the proportion bound among non-bannerwomen would be a low 19.3%. The Beijing data confirm both that bannerwomen did not bind their feet and that banner influences caused Han civilian women to bind much less.[41] When compared to the Ding County sample's 52.4% bound, where many young women had already abandoned footbinding and over 90% of older women were bound, proportions bound as low as 19.3% must reflect a pattern of natural feet among older civilian women born before 1900 that predates the anti-footbinding trends of the twentieth century.[42]

That, under the Qing, Manchu women would set the fashion in the capital is not surprising, given the presence of the emperor and the undeniable wealth, power, and prestige of the banner elite concentrated there.[43] The presence in the city of a large number of high-status women with natural feet undermined the pressures of conformity that forced many Han women to bind their feet in other areas of the empire. The low proportions bound in 1928 Beijing reflect the legacy of this pattern among women born before 1911.

THE ABANDONMENT OF FOOTBINDING
IN THE NORTHEAST

The usual accounts of the Manchu attempts to discourage footbinding among Han civilians conclude the policies were a complete failure, at least beyond Beijing.[44] But the situation in Manchuria provides another instructive counterexample. Given that Manchuria had experienced large influxes of Chinese from regions of North China where footbinding rates were very high throughout the nineteenth century, and Chinese had for decades been the great majority in the northeast, this may be surprising. Yet a series of late nineteenth-century Western travelers and missionaries observed the predominance of natural feet among the women of the Chinese majority in southern Manchuria. Alexander Michie, who traveled from Tianjin to Mukden (Shenyang) in 1861, noted: "The women nearly all wear large, that is, natural feet; the small cramped ones being only seen in or near the larger towns. The country women are, in fact, out of fashion. The women are not kept in seclusion, but perform long journeys on horseback; and we always found the female population come out and stare at us when passing through towns."[45] Alexander Williamson, who traveled in Manchuria in the late 1860s, reports:

> The bulk of the people are Chinese immigrants, or descendants of immigrants, from the northern provinces. . . . The Manchus are in the minority. Moreover, there is some difficulty in distinguishing between them and their invaders. Those who live in the central province [Jilin] have settled down to agriculture or other definite pursuits; and in dress, manners, customs, and language follow the Chinese. . . . In general, it is only by inquiry that you can learn to which people they belong. The Manchu women have large feet, but this is not always a sign of Manchu origin, for many of the "celestials" have got sense enough, when removed from the restraints of fashion, to discard the atrocious custom of cramping their feet.[46]

Chinese immigrants arriving in the northeast entered a region where the footbinding fashion no longer held hegemonic sway.

The term *Manchu* is often used by these late nineteenth-century Western authors to refer to all bannermen (*qiren*), regardless of ethnic origin, in contrast to immigrant Chinese civilians (*minren* or *manzi*). This is confirmed by the Englishman H. E. M. James, who spent several months in 1886 traveling throughout Manchuria and gives the following account of the local ethnic categories he found in use among his informants:

> The Chinese of Manchuria mostly come, as their ancestors did, from the two northern provinces of Chihli and Shantung. But if you ask a man what nationality he belongs to, he will not call himself a Chinaman. He will either say, "I am a Min-jen"—i.e. a civilian—as distinct from the military, or, more frequently, he will call himself a Man-tzu, or a Southerner. This, a term of reproach in South China, where it is applied to the so-called barbarous aborigines of

Hainan or Formosa, is used without opprobrium in Manchuria. . . . In Manchuria, anyhow, the Chinese use it of themselves. Similarly, a Manchu will not call himself a Man-chou-jen, or Manchu, but a Ch'i-jen, or Bannerman, a term which would include Mongols and Chinese without the Wall.[47]

In contrast to China proper, in the northeast, the Manchus and the banners were the native population, and the incoming Chinese "southerners" were the invading outsiders. The prestige hierarchy of local society reflected this reversal of roles.

Chapter 7 considered whether Liaoning's status as a cloth-importing rather than cloth-producing region, because it freed immigrant women from Hebei and Shandong of textile handicraft work, had enabled them to abandon footbinding in their new homes. Like Liaoning, Chahar was a cloth importer, not a cloth producer, and a recipient of immigrants from high-binding regions, but high proportions of women in Chahar continued to bind while women in Liaoning did not. What made Liaoning society distinctive (and what Chahar lacked) was a social hierarchy headed by a non-binding elite.

In the late nineteenth century, landless Chinese immigrants poured into the northeast and steadily reduced the banner proportion of its population.[48] Despite their increasingly minority status demographically (bannermen were still a significant 24% of the Fengtian population in 1908), as "masters of the soil" the banners (or at least the banner elites) controlled many of the resources that attracted the immigrants. Banner land occupied a considerable proportion of all cultivated land in Fengtian Province (as Liaoning was known prior to 1928), and large areas were rented out to immigrant tenants. Banner elites (whether of Han or Manchu origin) served as managers of official lands and controlled considerable wealth; it was this strata that occupied the higher reaches of the status hierarchy in local society, rather than a native Han civilian literati or gentry elite.[49] Given that the local structure of power and status was banner dominated, it is not surprising for B. L. Putnam Weale, who toured Manchuria in 1903, to note that "it is more *chic* to be known as a Manchu than as a common Chinaman." Of women's costume, he comments: "Their dress is very distinctive, and in Manchuria as in other countries, it is fashionable for the women to follow the lead of the upper ten in the North by being Manchus if they can possibly manage it. . . . The women's headdress is very fantastic, and their feet are shod in long high-soled shoes of very peculiar design." Putnam Weale draws attention to the importance of banner elite leadership in fashion ("the upper ten") and the desires of the non-elite to emulate high-status banner fashions.[50]

The medical missionary Dugald Christie began a thirty-year residence in Mukden (Shenyang, the Qing capital in Fengtian) in 1883. Based on his long experience, Christie considered that "Manchu, Bannerman, and Chinaman are practically indistinguishable" in the northeast. Christie noted that although much of Manchuria's Chinese population originated in the provinces of Shandong and Hebei, where footbinding was nearly universal among adult women, a marked change in attitudes toward footbinding occurred when the immigrants settled in the northeast.[51] As Christie recollects:

> To the superficial observer it seems untrue that Manchuria is really Chinese, for wherever he goes he is struck with the curious, picturesque, and typically Manchu head-dress of the women, with its sparkling silver, gilt, or enameled ornaments. They wear the long Manchu robe, too, instead of the jacket and skirt of the Chinese woman, and they walk on their own natural feet, not on crippled and crushed deformities. How can the people be Chinese when the women are so evidently Manchu? The truth is that they are not Manchu but Manchurian. . . .
>
> Every year they are still crowding in from Shantung, Chihli, and other provinces. The woman who in her old home opposed tooth and nail the loosening by the fraction of an inch her little girl's foot-bandages, follows her husband to far Manchuria and settles down among her large-footed, rosy-cheeked sisters of the north. In a few years there are other little girls growing up in the home, with natural feet and Manchu dress, and in time they will marry and put up their hair in Manchu style. They have become Manchurian. The removal of these people from their ancient ancestral homes, and the gathering together of families from various provinces, result in a marked lessening of their conservatism, prejudices, and superstitions.[52]

Thus when Han civilians entered regions where the footbinding fashion no longer carried the prestige of elite associations, and conformist pressures shifted to favor natural feet, the footbinding practice quickly gave way. Second and later generations of immigrants from North China increasingly abandoned footbinding for the natural foot fashions of Manchuria.

Noting that Manchus and Chinese (both Han banner [Hanjun] families and civilian Chinese) intermixed freely in the city of Mukden (Shenyang),

John Ross, whose mission work in Manchuria stretched from the 1870s to the first decade of the twentieth century, corroborates Christie's observation:

> Moukden is a small edition of Peking. . . . It began as a purely Manchu city. The Manchus were exceeded in number at a later period by the Han-chun. But, unlike Peking, Manchus and Chinese lived promiscuously together. Partly from the larger numbers and greater social influence of the Man and Han [banner] people, partly from the smaller number of the ordinary Chinese with cramped feet, and their weaker influence, it became fashionable in Moukden for women to go about with natural feet. The result was that pure Chinese living in the city abstained from cramping the feet of their girls. Now, when a Chinese family comes into the city, the young women have their feet unbound. The feet of little girls are never bound — except those of the families of Chinese officials who are here only temporarily. Here, again, fashion is supreme, and compels the growth of natural feet.[53]

Chinese writers have also reported the low prevalence of footbinding in the northeast. Xu Ke, writing in 1914, noted the predominance of unbound feet in Manchuria, attributing it to the cultural amalgamation resulting from the intermixed settlement of Han, Manchus, and Mongols.[54] Ding Yizhuang interviewed an elderly woman in 1999 who had grown up in Shenyang in the early Republican period and whose recollections match Christie's and Ross's observations. Ms. Jing's parents were a bannerwoman and a civilian Han and she had grown up among her mother's banner relatives. Ms. Jing remembered that not only banner but also Han women wore the *batou* hairstyle and shoes with flower basin soles (*huapendi*).[55] Ding notes that intermarriage was frequent between the two groups; one of her interviewees reports that Han women marrying into banner families were required to adopt banner styles in headdress and footwear and to release bindings.[56] The historian Shao Dan points out that the intermixing of bannermen and Han civilians in the northeast contrasts with the demarcation between the two groups in China proper. The separation of banner garrisons from Han civilians administratively, residentially, and by occupation in China proper was absent in the northeast, where the populations were interspersed, and many bannermen, like the immigrants, were farmers.[57]

The ethnographic observations of Christie, Ross, and the others are corroborated by the 1928 census reports of the numbers of bound-footed women in the province of Liaoning, the southernmost of the three northeastern

TABLE 8.2. Proportions of females with bound feet in counties of Liaoning, 1928

Number of counties	Female population	Number bound	% bound	% of total females
11 counties >20% bound	875,655	299,097	34.2	13.1
40 counties <20% bound	5,162,553	192,071	3.7	77.1
7 counties not reporting	658,044	—	—	9.8
51 reporting counties	6,038,208	491,168	8.1	90.2

Source: Neizheng gongbao 1929, vol. 3.1

Manchurian provinces. The quality of Liaoning's census machinery benefited from the early investment in a modern police force in the province, dating from the administration of Xu Shichang (1907–9).[58] During the ensuing warlord era, the province enjoyed a period of stability from 1917 to 1928 when the able administration of a key civil official, Wang Yongjiang, strengthened local government.[59] The Fengtian police force during the 1920s commanded substantial manpower in every county, enjoyed significant budgetary support, and benefited from a police academy founded in 1926. Police maintenance of population records in the years prior to 1928 is evidenced by reports of two censuses of the population in 1924 and 1927.[60] Thus the Liaoning police had the experience and the machinery in place when asked to gather the information included in the 1928 census report.

In 1928, Liaoning was divided into fifty-eight counties, of which seven failed to report the numbers bound-footed. Overall, the proportion bound in Liaoning's fifty-one reporting counties in 1928 was only 8.1%, one of the lowest proportions reported for any province in 1928.[61] As shown in Table 8.2, the footbinding population was concentrated in eleven counties that represented only 13.1% of the total female population but 60.9% of those reported bound. In the remaining forty reporting counties containing 77.1% of the total female population, only 3.7% of the female population was bound.

The census figures from 1908–9 report the presence of the banner and non-banner populations in forty-seven reporting counties (missing data and boundary changes following 1908 reduce the comparability of counties between 1908 and 1928).[62] While these reports were made twenty years earlier than the footbinding reports, and despite constant immigration of Han in the intervening years, the ethnic distribution in 1908 gives important clues to the location of the banner populations in 1928.[63] Overall, the Fengtian female population in 1908 was 75% civilian Han and 24.6% banner. Of the banner females, 74% were Hanjun and the rest Manchu and Mongol. The banner

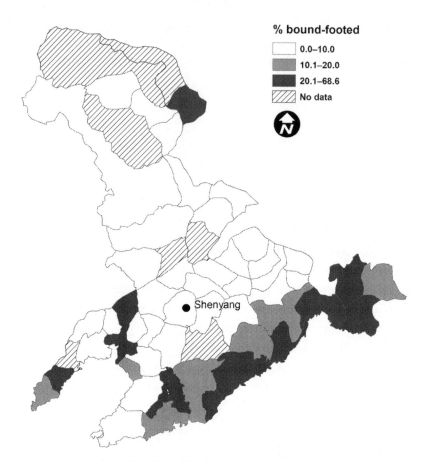

MAP 8.1. Proportions of females with bound feet by county, Liaoning, 1928. Liaoning County base map courtesy of Fan I-chun and the Center for Geographic Information Science, Academia Sinica, Taiwan. *Source: Neizheng gongbao* 1929, vol. 3.1.

population was concentrated in the densely settled core area of Fengtian in the Liao River plain.[64] As shown in Maps 8.1 and 8.2, the large areas of low binding in the core area coincides with a strong banner presence, reflecting the impact of banner fashions on the more numerous Han population.

The spatial distribution of the eleven counties having greater than 20% bound is shown in Map 8.1. Seven of these counties lie in a band in southeastern Liaoning along its Yalu River boundary with Korea. These counties lie outside the willow palisade that marked the boundary of the long-settled core, where the banner presence was strongest. The Qing government opened this eastern hilly region to settlement and established government offices there

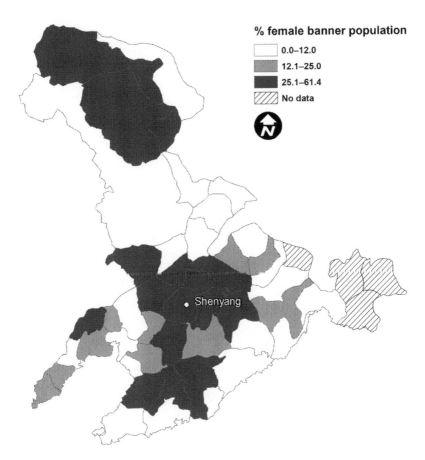

% female banner population

☐ 0.0–12.0
▨ 12.1–25.0
■ 25.1–61.4
▨ No data

Shenyang

MAP 8.2. Proportions of banner females by county, Liaoning (Fengtian), 1908–9. *Source: Manshū chihōshi: Sōkō* (1912), vols. 1–4.

beginning in the late nineteenth century. Thus these counties were recently settled by immigrants from Shandong and Hebei; C. Walter Young mentions an influx to the Yalu River zone of settlement by refugees fleeing Shandong floods and famines as late as 1911.[65] Since four of these southeastern counties have less than 12% banner populations, banner influence was weak and had had little time to affect the recent arrivals (there are no data on banner presence for two of the seven southeastern counties). The three counties that have proportions bound greater than 50% (Ji'an, Linjiang, and Changbai) are among the southeastern group and border the river as it makes it bend to the east.[66] Three of the four counties located in other parts of Liaoning and having greater than 20% bound are also counties that have less than 12% banner populations. There are two anomalous counties with high proportions bound but substantial banner presence. These are Xingcheng, with 48.6% bound and a population that is 22.9% banner, and Xiuyan (a southeastern county), with 24.3% bound and a population that is 30.1% banner. Why footbinding remained strong despite substantial banner influence in these two counties remains a mystery.[67]

In sum, of the nine counties having greater than 20% bound for which there are data on banner presence, seven were in counties having less than 12% banner females, where banner influence was weak, and the predominance of a Han binding population was able to recreate some of the hegemony of the footbinding fashion known in their home counties. But of the twenty counties having less than 12% banner populations in 1908, thirteen have proportions bound less than 20%, suggesting that in many cases even where banner presence was diluted, the footbinding custom was still weakened. It is likely the Han populations of these counties had a history of settlement in Liaoning longer than recent immigrants to the Yalu area counties and thus a longer exposure to the non-binding ethos of the banner-dominated society of Liaoning.

Note that the average proportion bound in the eleven high-binding counties is only 34.2%, much lower than Hebei's 50.6% and the Ding County sample's 52.4% (see Table 8.1). Even in Liaoning's high-binding counties, a rate of 34.2% suggests that the footbinding custom no longer held an unchallenged position and that the Manchurian influence was having an effect. Assuming that the 1908–9 non-banner proportion of the population (75%) is still valid for the whole province in 1928 (given constant immigration of Han, this is certainly an underestimate of the non-banner proportion), and allocating all those bound in 1928 to the estimated non-banner population of the reporting counties, the proportion bound would be a low 10.8%. The Liaoning data confirm both that bannerwomen did not bind their feet and that banner influences caused Han civilian women to bind much less than women in their provinces of origin.

The abandonment of footbinding by Han civilians in Manchuria resulted from emulation of a banner elite considered status superiors (and the shift to a region where custom and conformist pressures favored natural, not bound, feet), but this was not part of a broad spectrum, one-way transfer of cultural characteristics. It was the Manchus who adopted aspects of Chinese culture, agriculture, and language, as Williamson reported in the late 1860s, and whose martial skills declined, as the Qing emperors complained. The long-term cultural interchange between the banner and civilian groups is best understood as a case of mutual influence and acculturation, rather than a unidirectional adoption by one group of the customs and fashions of the other.[68] Taiwan presents a case of similar complexity; it was the Hakka who learned the Hoklo language, but, where their influence was strong, the Hakka example of natural feet undermined the hold of footbinding over the Hoklo. In each case it is necessary to understand how specific historical contexts shape prestige hierarchies and the direction of influence, a point underlined by the next example.

Owen Lattimore confirms that footbinding was readily given up in Chinese-dominated areas of Manchuria well beyond Shenyang, but he points out an important exception: "Chinese living in contact with the Manchus in Manchuria began very early to abandon the practice of binding women's feet. . . . There is a curious contrast in the readiness with which Chinese abandoned foot binding in Manchuria, and the tenacity of the practice along the Mongol frontier. I am inclined to attribute this to the ready amalgamation between Chinese and Manchus, as contrasted with the profound cleavage between Chinese and Mongols. . . . The Chinese population in Manchuria, identifying itself politically with the Manchus, took on Manchu characteristics to a surprising extent."[69]

Where Manchu influence was strong, both the Mongols and the Chinese followed the Manchu lead in fashions and culture, which meant for Mongols abandonment of their language and for Chinese abandonment of footbinding. But, Lattimore explains, where "there was less Manchu influence and the Mongols were in direct contact with the Chinese . . . the traditional antagonism between Mongols and Chinese was more effective." This cultural antagonism reinforced each group's commitment to its traditional customs, so that the Mongols "retained their language and national character with really extraordinary tenacity," and the Chinese retained footbinding.[70] The Mongols, who felt they were losing out to the Chinese economically, adopted a culturally defensive posture, leading them to preserve Mongol dress and language.[71] Lattimore notes that Mongol pastoral communities in the valley areas northeast of Kalgan (Zhangjiakou), having become surrounded by Chinese agricultural colonists, adopted agriculture and Chinese language, but retained their own traditions, including "the unbound feet of the women and their way of doing up the hair."[72] In the competition between Mongols and Han, each side looked down on the customs of the other. The Mongols considered themselves lords of the soil and resented Chinese intruders, and the Chinese disdained natural-footed Mongol women and continued footbinding.[73] In these areas, identity politics made footbinding into an ethnic marker that the Han preserved as a mark of their superiority, while in mixed Chinese-Manchu areas Han immigrants, freed from the hegemonic power of the footbinding fashion, emulated the natural-foot customs of the banner upper class.

Each ethnic situation in which footbinding Chinese confront non-binding groups—for example, banner populations, Mongols, and Hakka—must be examined closely for factors that affect the fate of the footbinding custom. Analyses imposing preconceived notions about ethnic identity markers and boundary maintenance distort the understanding of specific cases. In nineteenth-century Manchuria, where civilian Han and banner peoples inter-mixed, the result was not a heightening of ethnic differences through foot-binding by the Han, but an adoption of Manchu styles, including women's flower basin platform shoes and hairstyles. The result was that the Qing-enforced ban on footbinding among the banners spread through emulation into the civilian population. The cultural prestige of the footbinding fashion, hegemonic among Han elites and commoners in so much of China, was not unassailable but vulnerable to shifts in the prestige hierarchy.[74]

Somewhat surprising are reports that Manchu clogs were becoming fash-ionable in the port cities of coastal China in the early twentieth century. The theater and costume expert A. C. Scott noted that "Chinese women had also begun to adopt this style of shoe at the end of the nineteenth and beginning of the twentieth century" and that "as far south as Hong Kong fashionable middle class Cantonese women wore the Manchu sole."[75] According to Mrs. Archibald Little: "At Canton the women with natural feet wear what is called the boat shoe. . . . It is only at Canton that bound feet are in any sense a mark of gentility, though in Shanghai and many other parts they are a sign of respectability. The more distinguished ladies in Hong Kong or Canton who do not bind, wear the other—the clog-like—Manchu shoe with a very high heel quite in the center of the foot."[76] An unusual example of the influ-ence of Manchu fashions is the bowed shoe for bound feet placed on top of a Manchu-style horse-hoof sole pictured in the *Fourth Collection of Gathered Fragrances* (Caifeilu siji).[77] These examples suggest that Manchu fashions had an influence well beyond Beijing and the northeast.

CONCLUSION

The dramatic case of nineteen bound-footed bannerwomen appearing in the palace service draft in 1804 that unsettled the emperor and interpretations of bannerwomen's foot fashions as mimicking those of the bound-footed have led students of Qing history to exaggerate the influence of the footbinding fashion on banner females. Some have even assumed that bannerwomen were gradually adopting footbinding.[78] Ethnographic testimony of travelers and missionaries and the evidence of county-level data from the 1928 survey of footbinding contradict this view. In Beijing and the northeast, banner populations, despite Chinese cultural influence from more numerous Han immigrants, maintained a superior status and cultural self-confidence that strengthened adherence to the prohibition on footbinding by bannerwomen. The presence of the high-status banner example undermined the hegemony of the footbinding fashion among the immigrants from areas where binding predominated. The result was a significant influence of Manchu fashions on civilian Han, in Beijing and in the northeast, that led to the diminution of footbinding in those areas.[79] Rather than a contest of ethnic identities between bannermen and Han immigrants leading to the entrenchment of footbinding among the Han, a gradual process of acculturation led to its demise.

The emphasis on boundary maintenance and ethnic markers in the process of ethnic group formation in modern studies of ethnicity can be traced to the influential work of Fredrik Barth. Barth's work shifted the focus of studies of ethnicity away from the cultural features distinctive to particular ethnic groups (the "cultural content") to the boundaries between groups and the processes by which groups asserted their differences and maintained their integrity ("boundary maintenance"). It should be noted that in his analysis of cases, Barth was careful to specify the particular conditions in which the boundary dynamic did and did not apply.[80] Students of footbinding have been less careful, and too quick, to assume trends in footbinding customs are the result of identity politics and ethnic boundary maintenance. This can only be established by investigating the specifics of ethnic interaction case by case.[81] The boundary maintenance and ethnic marker hypothesis, noticing only the overall sharp divide in footbinding customs between Hoklo and Hakka in Taiwan, wrongly predicts that the presence of Hakka should cause the Hoklo to increase both the prevalence and severity of binding, when the opposite was the case. The boundary maintenance theory makes the same error with respect to Han and banner populations in Manchuria. With respect to seventeenth-century China during the Ming-Qing transition, indiscriminate use of the boundary maintenance hypothesis leads to the assumption, without evidence, that conflicts over adoption of the queue generalized to footbinding. In situations where conflicts escalate, social groups polarize, and identities become politically charged, the boundary maintenance hypothesis has greater relevance (e.g., the Mongol-Chinese frontier), but even then there is no guarantee that a particular trait, such as footbinding, will be swept into the mix.

Conclusion

The Tyranny of Fashion

I N their attempts to invent deeper meaning for and confer broad cultural significance on footbinding or to reduce footbinding to economic strategies,
recent theorists have discounted both the voices of Qing literati critical of
the practice and the reporting of many nineteenth-century observers of footbinding in its heyday, especially those who interviewed commoner women
about the practice.[1] These Chinese and Western observers saw footbinding
as nothing more than fashion, which in many places attained nearly universal prevalence not because of "deep cultural meanings" rooted in Confucian
gender ideology, anti-Manchu sentiments, or economic advantages, but as a
standard of beauty and an arbitrary fashion (with mean origins) that won
adherence because it was enforced by fear of ridicule and desire for status.
Adopted at first by a small elite, the fashion spread over centuries through
status emulation until it became in many places the norm, not the exception.
The great majority of Chinese women confronted the footbinding fashion as a
cruel and unavoidable social mandate, not as an optional adornment.

The case studies presented here stress the importance of local status hierarchies and pressures to conform as the means by which the practice maintained its hold. Several of them stand in opposition to notions that footbinding
served to mark ethnic identity. In an era of heightened ethno-nationalism
and identity-obsessed politics, many social science and historical analyses
seem to assume that competition between ethnic groups leads automatically
to an enhanced cultural differentiation in which selective cultural traits are
exaggerated and become politically charged as distinctive markers of group

identity. The deployment of these identity markers is presumed to occur in its most intense form along the boundaries of contact between competing groups. This leads to the assumption that distinctive cultural traits (wherever they are found) result from a process of group competition leading to heightened ethnic differentiation. Relying on what appears to be a solid theorem, incautious analysts explain ethnic differences as a result of identity politics, without producing detailed evidence demonstrating that such a process has in fact taken place. These analyses fail to consider the emergence of cultural differences in distinctive histories and internal group social dynamics, only some of which have to do with contact between ethnic groups, and when they do they are as likely to involve borrowing as they are identity-driven differentiation. The analysis of footbinding in Taiwan is a case in point, in which intra-ethnic status competition was most important to maintenance of the convention and the effects of cross-ethnic contact led to the weakening of footbinding, not its identity-driven enhancement. So, too, did the movement of North Chinese immigrants into the banner territory of Liaoning lead to the abandonment of binding, not its intensification. Nor did the contact between Manchus and Han during the conquest make binding into a badge of Han identity. The operation of identity politics in the creation of ethnic differences cannot be assumed; it must be established through evidence and analysis that tests alternative hypotheses.

THE CURIOUS BEAUTY OF BOUND FEET

The hegemonic power of the footbinding fashion is referred to repeatedly by bound-footed women, who in interviews explained their conformity in terms of beauty, marriage prospects, and social pressures. Some theorists have discounted Howard Levy's Taiwan interviews from the 1960s for perpetuating views linking footbinding to "sexuality, beauty, and marriage" and not to the labor of young girls.[2] Contrary to these claims, Levy's informants make no allusions to sex but many to beauty and prospects of marriage and also to social pressure and fear of derision if not bound. Despite suggestions that aesthetic appeal is "an elite rationale for footbinding" somehow incompatible with recognition of women's labor, Levy's informants' references to women's work, especially the work of non-binding lower-class women, link binding feet to both prestige and the kinds of labor women were expected to perform.[3] Notions of beauty were inseparable from the qualities of bound feet that preserved respectability and improved marriage chances. Bound feet served to distinguish a woman from the poorest and lowest class of women and the degrading work they did. Women who bound were often proud of the beautiful shapes their feet attained and their ability to tolerate the pain it took to bind them. For them, well-bound feet encased in embroidered shoes represented a personal accomplishment, a badge of pride, a demonstration of their diligence and craftsmanship.

Many of the women interviewed in Sichuan referred to the importance to them of having beautiful feet; the Sichuan life histories thus match closely the accounts in Levy's Taiwan interviews.[4] The women repeatedly mention social pressure, fear of being mocked, and pride in beautifully bound feet, as reasons for binding, not the labor they performed. Many of those interviewed let out their feet in order to do heavier work, in natal and marital families. For these women, work explained why they released their bindings, but beauty and status explained why they bound in the first place. The women regularly expressed regret that they had not been able to continue binding and preserve the shapes they had worked hard to attain. Coupled with these sentiments was a feeling of sorrow that their conditions of life had not enabled them to continue the binding that protected them from the scorn of others.

Girls' desires to have attractively bound feet should not be confused with erotic notions of bound feet as sexual appendages, which have been rightly debunked.[5] To have feet that both men and women found "beautiful" or "pretty" relates to concerns with status, dignity, and a desire to be attractive felt by even the poorest ranks of women. The poor fear ridicule as much as the rich. That women's small bound feet were considered by both males and females to be objects of beauty in late imperial Chinese culture is widely attested in the sources. Why that should have been is less easily answered, other than to point out that what constitutes "beauty" is culturally and historically relative, changing from society to society and generation to generation. The custom originated hundreds of years ago, became fashionable among elite sectors of society, and gradually spread as the lower ranks emulated the practice. Because small bound feet, whether erotic or not, were seen as objects of beauty and refinement by the rich and powerful, they conferred prestige and, at the least, immunized women from the scorn large feet would expose them to.

The same themes of beauty, marriage, and conformity to social expectations are memorably expressed by the elderly North Chinese women discussing footbinding in the celebrated documentary *Small Happiness*, which was filmed in the mid-1980s.[6] One woman reports: "In the old days, no one wanted to marry a woman with big feet. Blind or lame your feet had to be small." To the narrator's question "Were you willing to have your feet bound?" one informant replied: "How could we not be willing? Everyone else did it, people said tiny feet were good." And referring later to the suppression of binding: "If we were caught we'd be fined, so I let my feet out. Then I felt so ashamed of my big feet."

The interviews of women from all over China, and from periods ranging from the late nineteenth and the early twentieth centuries to the late twentieth century, repeat over and over again the desire to be respected, concern for beauty, and fear of ridicule.[7] The ethnography that emerges from these interviews is entirely consistent as well with Chinese historical texts from earlier centuries that document the importance of beauty, conformity to convention, and the shaming of the unfashionable natural-footed.[8] The nineteenth-century interviews, conducted in the heyday years of the fashion, are particularly valuable for two reasons. First, the missionaries conducting the interviews were fluent in local dialects and, as long-term residents of the same communities as the women they interviewed, had knowledge of the full context of their lives. And second, unlike those interviewed in the late twentieth century, the bound-footed women they interviewed had in turn bound the feet of their daughters and could provide both a mother's and a daughter's perspective. In these regions and periods, the footbinding fashion was firmly entrenched, its hegemonic status unchallenged, and those who resented the custom nevertheless felt pressured to conform.

If the economistic interpretation of footbinding is too dismissive of "aesthetic" claims and discounts the importance to women of beauty and its associated prestige, at the other extreme are views that inflate the cultural significance of footbinding and romanticize the women's culture of footbinding. These perspectives find evidence of women's agency in the making and decorating of shoes for bound feet, the rituals of binding, and gift exchanges of shoes.[9] Nowhere in the interviews are notions expressed that bound feet were signs of "modesty and morality" or "a celebration of women's work and motherhood," glosses for the custom that reflect at best the pretensions of the upper classes.[10] This social imaginary locates itself in the comfortable women's quarters of the elite. Not a word is spoken of the many servants who made possible the leisured lives of elite bound-footed women or the disdain the privileged expressed for the crudely bound feet of women of the lower classes. Criticism of the "discourse of shame" directed toward bound-footed women by twentieth-century anti-binding campaigns should not ignore the role of shaming that caused many lower-class women to bind in the first place.[11] The hegemony of the footbinding fashion trapped women in a status competition won by those who hobbled themselves. One of the most important achievements of the anti-binding campaigns was to deprive the bound-footed of the ability to denigrate the natural-footed.

Whatever role it may have appeared to play, footbinding was first and always a fashion that signaled status ranking. Eliminating footbinding did not eliminate patriarchy or other evils of the old society, but it did eliminate the particular pain and the particular prestige that the fashion created. It is important to recognize that the status hierarchy that incorporated the fashion of footbinding was a cultural dimension of class stratification that particularly burdened the poor.

THE COSTS OF FOOTBINDING

The footbinding fashion created tension between the work women needed to do and the scorn they suffered if their feet were not bound. This tension is highlighted by Fielde's account of one unfortunate woman: "She had so much work to do, that her feet were neglected, and got so large that they began to be a disgrace to the family before they were bound. She knew the pain would be dreadful, but it was more dreadful to have her neighbours say as she passed, 'There are two boats going by.' So she had them bound, and had to endure the pain until it ceased."[12]

Families evaluated the trade-offs between the status benefits of the footbinding fashion and the costs in lost mobility and productivity of the female members of the household whose feet were to be bound. Recognizing how the trade-offs differed among the social classes provides insight into the timing and motivation by which the practice spread through the social hierarchy. The first to adopt the practice were elite families for whom the status benefits were largest and the costs smallest. Elite standards of living did not depend on the work of female family members, whose leisure time was devoted to producing luxury goods. The fashion also spread easily among the merely wealthy who were anxious to improve their social standing and had the means to make up any losses in female productivity by substituting servant labor. As more and more families adopted footbinding, middling families with fewer resources felt the pressure to keep up with the fashionable and conform. For them, the balance of status benefit and economic costs grew closer, as their budgets depended on female economic contributions. But middling families could afford to absorb the economic costs that accompanied restricting their women to only sedentary employments compatible with bound feet. As yet more families felt pressured to adopt the fashion, not binding increasingly entailed a status loss that had to be avoided. The near universality of the practice among the respectable classes transformed natural feet into a sign, not just of low status, but of stigmatized status, deserving of ridicule and scorn. So yet poorer families adopted binding, less to enhance their lowly status than to preserve respectability and avoid ridicule. These lower-class families accommodated footbinding by adopting later and looser binding, making do with shoe styles that hid cucumber feet, and requiring their women to do all jobs required (not just sedentary or compatible jobs), including those that were painful and awkward for the bound-footed. The large size of the lower classes explains the findings that high levels of footbinding were not restricted to districts whose economies (agricultural or handicraft) provided female employments thought compatible with footbinding. Only the poorest, judging that tight family budgets could not sacrifice the maximum possible female labor contribution, resisted binding and suffered a loss of respectability as a consequence.[13]

Table C.1 provides a schematic summary of the trade-offs made by the different classes as they adopted footbinding. The perspective on costs and benefits in the table is that of family heads (overwhelmingly male). Therefore, while women may have benefited from status gains enjoyed by the whole family, the costs include only those accounted for in the family budget and thus do not include the pain and suffering endured by women due to binding.

Those who adopted footbinding did so because it preserved respectability and immunized them from scorn, not because they thought that bound feet were beautiful per se or that bound feet ensured a proper ordering of the genders. Far from celebrating binding as a means of self-expression within a women's culture, most disliked the custom for its cruelty and the disabling that made their lives harder, and they experienced it as something that society imposed.

The value of the status gain won by adopting binding diminished over time as the custom spread into the lower ranks. It was largest when only elites and wealthy bound, and at this early stage, the fashion was exclusive and most prestigious; it had the snob appeal of conspicuous consumption. But as the fashion spread into the lower classes, the status gain won by new adopters grew smaller. Binding, while still fashionable and status conferring, was no longer an exclusive sign of elite status. A bandwagon effect took over, and families adopted binding driven by the desire to be like others—by conforming

TABLE C.1. Schematic cost-benefit analysis of footbinding by class

Social class	Benefits	Costs	Female employments
Wealthy, elite	Status; look down on others, feel superior	Hire servants	Produce luxuries; severe binding
Middle classes	Status; look down on others	Loss of female labor productivity	Work compatible with bound feet
Lower classes	Avoid loss of respectability, escape ridicule	Loss of female labor productivity	Work often incompatible; later, looser binding
Poorest	Maintain full female labor productivity	Loss of respectability	Work of all kinds; reject binding

to the prevailing fashion. When footbinding became nearly universal, failure to bind risked a loss of status; to be different made one vulnerable to ridicule. Thus the footbinding fashion, once a comparatively voluntary move to enhance status, acquired coercive force, backed by intense social pressure and the threat of scorn. Fear of stigmatization as much as status emulation became the main force propelling the spread of the practice.

Why did the elites not adopt a new fashion and abandon footbinding if it was no longer exclusive? Instead of abandoning the practice, the elite response to the loss of exclusivity appears to have been to reclaim it by making the binding more extreme and by adding embellishments and stylistic modifications.[14] Elites could maintain their fashion edge by binding girls' feet earlier and more severely to attain smaller feet and by preferring brides with tiny feet for their sons. As binding became more severe, the crippling it caused could not be easily reversed to satisfy a different fashion trend. Elite families thus became committed to perpetuating the fashion and to preferring small-footed brides. So long as the top of the social hierarchy defined bound feet as desirable, footbinding would confer prestige on those who adopted the practice. Footbinding thus became enshrined in the prestige order as an essential (but not the only) attribute of status. Without it, one's respectability was put in question. Under these conditions, even elite families became trapped by fear that failure to bind would cause a loss of status.[15]

Table C.1 summarizes the processes by which the footbinding fashion could become nearly universal. Case studies of Hoklo in solidly Hoklo communities and of the counties of Hebei are examples of localities where the fashion was enshrined in status hierarchies and footbinding acquired hegemonic power. But footbinding was not immune to challenge. When Hoklo

Taiwanese came into contact with non-binding Hakka, and North Chinese immigrants entered banner territory in Liaoning, they came up against groups who were steadfast in their rejection of footbinding. The hegemonic power of the footbinding fashion weakened when confronted with alternatives given strength by groups positioned to maintain their own status hierarchies and confident of the superiority of their own customs. Given the two extremes of hegemonic domination and total rejection, how are reports of localities whose populations were split between binding elites and non-binding commoners to be explained?

In localities where binding penetrated the social ranks to become a nearly universal practice, a tipping point was crossed when large numbers of every rank adopted the fashion. Binding, no longer a sign of elegance, became the norm and not the exception. Marriageability came to depend on having bound feet. In these cases, the fashion was less an avenue of upward mobility than a prerequisite to respectability; not binding put one in the lowest ranks, subject to ridicule, mocking, and contempt. This is the situation found among Hoklo in Taiwan and in Hebei.

But there were some localities where the tipping point appears not to have been crossed, and binding remained an affectation of the elite. Nineteenth-century sources indicate that binding was prevalent in the southern cities of Guangzhou, Fuzhou, Suzhou, and Yangzhou but rare in their rural hinterlands.[16] But most of these reports lack specificity. Are they referring only to the wealthiest classes in these cities or to entire urban populations? How greatly did the prevalence of binding among urban commoners differ from that among their rural neighbors? Despite the claims of an urban-rural gap in Suzhou, reports of bound-footed women working in the cotton fields outside Suzhou contradict claims of a sharp divide.[17] In the case of Guangzhou, binding appears to have been widely adopted by merchants and the well-to-do but not by urban laborers and farmers.[18] That no urban-rural gap was evident in Taiwan casts suspicion on these claims. Unfortunately, the footbinding surveys in 1928 did not include regions containing these southern cities, and thus it is not possible to confirm the degree to which the prevalence of binding truly diverged between these cities and their rural areas. If real, is this an elite-commoner dichotomy or an urban-rural one?

It seems safe to assume in these southern provinces where lower rates of binding overall are widely reported that at the very least there was a sharp difference between an elite strata binding at high rates and a commoner strata binding very little.[19] What historical processes could have brought the downward diffusion of the footbinding fashion to a halt in these cases? Did families outside the cities rely too much on the productivity of female members to sacrifice those contributions on the altar of status? Would the economic hypotheses tested in chapters 6 and 7 find in these regions the confirmation that they failed to receive from the data on Taiwan and Hebei? What social cleavages worked to create the split between urban and rural or elite and commoner footbinding cultures? Did the rural classes resist the spread of the fashion; if so, what immunized them from the pressures to conform that was so strong in other regions? Did the urban classes (perhaps landlords ordering tenants?) discourage adoption of the fashion by those it deemed unworthy and on whose labor they depended? Zhang Qu, writing in 1738 on Guangdong, noted that the derision heaped on lower-class women who dared to bind their feet served to maintain the distinction between the classes.[20] Too little is known about how the social structures in these regions might have given rise to a bifurcated practice of footbinding and how they differed from the northern provinces (and Taiwan's Hoklo), where footbinding became nearly universal. Beijing represents an inverse of these cases: high binding in the surrounding counties of Hebei, but low rates of binding in the urban core dominated by the banner and Manchu elite. In Beijing's case, a clear political and cultural divide in the status hierarchies between urban and rural discouraged footbinding in the city but condoned it in the counties. But no comparable division is known to have existed between the southern cities in question and the societies of their hinterlands. Finding solid evidence on which to build an explanation of these differences remains unfinished business for future researchers.

THE DEMISE OF FOOTBINDING

The purpose of this work has been to probe the social forces that made footbinding an essential prerequisite of respectability in late imperial Chinese society. Thus the focus has been on the fashion in its heyday and not its decline in the twentieth century. A brief review of the forces that brought footbinding (but not patriarchy or the exploitation of women) to an end underlines its dependence on the nature of the status hierarchies that dominated local societies. In territories where there were no centers of nonconformity (e.g., Hakka, banners), the footbinding custom persisted because no one dared to be the first to abandon footbinding; the risk of ridicule and humiliation was too great. And who would marry a daughter with natural feet? Footbinding continued not because families liked it or were unaware of its faults, but because, trapped by a status convention, they did not know how to stop. When anti-footbinding societies began to proliferate in the 1880s and 1890s, they recognized that to escape the convention required mutual pledges from family heads to stop binding daughters' feet and to select natural-footed brides for sons. Only in this way could marriages for natural-footed daughters be guaranteed. Elite men were only inclined to make such pledges when they became aware that the custom was ridiculed as a sign of backwardness in the Western and Japanese circles with whom they were in increasing contact. In these primarily urban and elite circles, footbinding caused a loss of status, not a gain. Anti-footbinding tracts broadcast objections to the custom that were often not new but had been rarely voiced publicly. The tracts decried the cruelty of the custom, the economic wastefulness, and the harm to women's health and began to undermine the hegemonic hold of the fashion. Linking the custom to China's degraded status vis-à-vis the foreign powers wedded the anti-footbinding campaigns to the rising tide of nationalism. Footbinding became a source of humiliation on the international stage, and rejecting binding an act of patriotism.[21] Many city dwellers and especially those of the younger generations, male and female, were persuaded by these arguments and rejected the custom. With the downfall of the Qing dynasty in 1911, and the rise of a new Republican elite committed to reforms, footbinding went into rapid decline in the urbanized areas of the country.[22] Bound feet became shameful, and natural feet, no longer stigmatized, were declared beautiful.[23] Brides with bound feet were no longer favored in the marriage choices of educated families.[24] In the cities, footbinding was dislodged from its privileged place in the status hierarchy surprisingly quickly. However, in the countryside, commoner men and women, much less exposed than elite men and urbanites to these new cultural currents, remained determined to fulfill their duties to daughters and make them marriageable by binding their feet. So the progress of the anti-footbinding societies in the wider society was slow.

When society ridiculed women who released their bindings, convincing individuals of footbinding's harms was not enough to eliminate the practice. Reformers, frustrated by the difficulty of winning families' voluntary cooperation, sought government intervention. In the early nineteenth century (and quite independently of the foreign influences current at the end of the century), Qian Yong called on local officials to prohibit binding and on prominent families to take the lead; if they did so, he predicted, within ten years the whole society would follow suit and abandon footbinding.[25] Responding to increasing anti-binding sentiments among progressives, leading reformers such as Kang Youwei and Liang Qichao proposed official bans at the end of the nineteenth century.[26] Local authorities proposed bans as well, as noted in the case of Taiwan gentry seeking to use agricultural associations to enforce prohibitions. According to Edward Alsworth Ross: "One Fokien village petitioned the Viceroy to *command* them to unbind their daughters' feet. All disapproved of the cruel custom but no one had the courage to lead the way."[27]

In 1902, when Empress Dowager Cixi issued a decree lifting the ban on marriage between Manchu and Han, she also lamented the harm done by footbinding. She called on the literati to enlighten the populace and work toward gradual elimination of the practice, but did not forbid the practice for fear that officials would abuse such authority and cause disturbances.[28] Following the proclamation of the empress's edict, numerous governors-general became official sponsors of anti-footbinding efforts, published anti-binding views, and supported natural foot societies.[29] Republican governments after 1911, and Japanese colonial authorities in Taiwan, more sure of public support and of their own authority, issued prohibitions.[30]

The new, rising generations of political leaders and educated youth were firmly opposed to footbinding and often saw its perpetuation as a matter of national disgrace. Both the Nationalist and the Communist Parties supported actions against footbinding. However, official prohibition was less effective especially in rural areas where the populace was not yet convinced of the need to abandon an age-old custom and where natural-footed women were still laughingstocks.

The Nanjing government prohibition on footbinding of 1928 set out regulations imposing a graduated set of pressures to stop the practice.[31] If three months of persuasion were unsuccessful, coercive action by a female foot inspector in coordination with local police was to follow. Girls under age fifteen if bound were ordered to be immediately unbound; if at the end of the period of persuasion the family head had failed to comply, he would be fined; if after a month the girl in question was still bound, then the fine was doubled and a female foot inspector could force the unbinding. A less severe set of pressures was applied to women aged fifteen to thirty, and only persuasion could be used against women over thirty.[32] Where willing compliance was not forthcoming, beleaguered Republican regimes were often unable to sustain enforcement efforts.

Revolutionaries used a campaign strategy to mobilize bursts of opposition to footbinding. The importance of collective action to the dismantling of the footbinding convention is illustrated in the following account by the journalist Anna Louise Strong. During the Northern Expedition in 1927, a leftist government came to power in Wuhan that mobilized strong support from student and labor organizations.[33] In this period of revolutionary fervor, the Hankou Women's Union launched an anti-footbinding campaign among urban cotton-mill workers. Strong relates the account of the campaign given her by union representatives:

> "We started our work against foot-binding in the cotton mills," they told me. These women stand all day on their feet; they realize that they did wrong to bind them. For many of them it is too late to change, but they are willing to save their daughters. Formerly a daughter was more profitable if she had "golden lilies," for they could get a better marriage price for her. But now she is more profitable for work in cotton mills if she has normal feet. Economic pressure is against foot-binding. Nevertheless it took the sudden blast of Revolution to destroy established custom. Once the drive starts against foot-binding, thousands of women join. There was such enthusiasm against foot-binding in one cotton mill in the British Concession that the streets were littered with bandages which the women tore off. Those who were convinced tore off first their own bandages and then compelled others to do likewise.[34]

Despite having to work on their feet for long shifts, mill workers were still afraid to risk the ridicule of others that would come with unbinding on their own. The Women's Union campaign allowed the mill workers to share their pain and to unbind in an environment where they would enjoy the solidarity and support of comrades acting together. Collective political action was able to break the hegemony of the footbinding custom that individual decisions taken in isolation could not achieve.

During the anti-Japanese war, the Communist governments of revolutionary base areas soon learned that policies that were too aggressive in combating footbinding (and other "feudal" practices affecting women) stirred up opposition from husbands and mothers-in-law.[35] The party gave priority to mobilizing women's labor for production, and education against footbinding was only stressed when it directly hindered production.[36] By the time the People's Republic was proclaimed in 1949, there were only a few places where the anti-footbinding campaigns of previous decades as well as recent wartime experiences had not convinced parents that footbinding should be abandoned and that there was no advantage for either daughters or daughters-in-law to have bound feet. The new government condemned footbinding as feudal and mobilized local authorities and the women's associations to stand in opposition to the practice. In 1949, the youngest generation of women was growing up without bound feet, but there were also many women who had been bound in the intervening decades who were now able to let out their bindings. Bereft of elite associations and opposed by the authorities, footbinding had at last lost both its cachet and the force of convention.

Chinese Character Glossary

Non-Chinese terms are designated as follows:

H Hokkien
J Japanese
K Korean

ba gu 八股
ban Guanyin 半觀音
bango (J) 蕃語
baojia 保甲
baoweituan 保衛團
batou 把頭
Beh-ke chiah pak-kha (H) 要嫁即縛腳
benchao 本朝
bendaoren 本島人
bian fa 辮髮
binu 婢女

ca-bo-kan-a (H) 查某嫺仔
chang yong yu 常用語
chanzu 纏足
chanzuzhe 纏足者
Chaozhou 潮州
Chaozhou shi xinfu gongxie 潮州式新婦
    弓鞋
chen min 臣民
cong bixia 從陛下

dajiao manpo 大腳蠻婆
daotiao 刀條
Duoluo Ganzhu 多罗甘珠

erxin 二心

fan Hanren guanmin nannü 凡漢人官民
    男女
fandi 番地
fang jiao 放腳
fang zu 放足
fengsu gailiang hui 風俗改良會
fu jiao 縛腳
fu ti 復剃

geta (J) 下駄
gong'an ju 公安局
gongxie 弓鞋
guo su 國俗
guozu 裹足
Guozu zi ci chi jin 裹足自此弛禁

Hakka 客家
Hanjun 漢軍
Hanren xiqi 漢人習氣
Hanren zhi louxi 漢人之陋習
hoan-a (H) 番仔
Hokkien 福建
Hoklo (H) 福佬, 河洛, 鶴佬, and 學佬
hokō (J) 保甲
hontōjin (J) 本島人
Hou you ding Shunzhi ernian yihou
    suosheng nüzi jin guozu, Kangxi
    liunian chi qi jin 後又定順治二年以
    後所生女子禁裹足,康熙六年弛其禁

Hu Yinglin 胡應麟
Huang Ji 黃機
huapen di xie 花盆底鞋

jie 街
jie chanzu hui 解纏足會
Jiechan Hui 解纏會
jiechanzuzhe 解纏足者
jizi 屐子
jōyōgo (J) 常用語
jun 軍
juxing guozu huishang quanti 俱行裹足
　毀傷全體

kaitensokusha (J) 解纏足者
kuan minjian nüzi guozu zhi jin 寬民間女
　子裹足之禁

Li Ruolin 李若琳
Li Yu 李漁
Liu Rushi 柳如是
liutiao jiao 柳條腳
"Lun nü xue" 論女學

maiko 舞妓
Man zhuang 滿裝
Manzhou fengsu 滿洲風俗
Manzhou jiufeng 滿洲舊風
Manzhou qiren 滿洲旗人
Manzhou shiyang 滿洲式樣
manzi 蠻子
manzi jiaor 蠻子腳兒
mati di xie 馬蹄底鞋
Min ji 閩籍
Ming yimin 明遺民
minjian funü 民間婦女
Minnan 閩南
minren 民人
mokgeuk (K) 木履

Nan xiang nü bu xiang 男降女不降
nanren buxu chuan daling daxiu, dai
　rongmao, ge yao shuyao 男人不許穿
　大領大袖, 戴絨帽, 各要束腰

neicheng minnü 內城民女
neige da ku dang'an 內閣大庫檔案
Neizheng gongbao 內政公報
nü zhuang 女裝
nüren buxu shutou, chanjiao 女人不許梳
　頭, 纏腳

pak-kha (H) 縛腳
pingjiao sao 平腳嫂

qi ban 旗板
Qian Muzhai 錢牧齋
Qian Qianyi 錢謙益
Qian Yong 錢泳
Qiangnan zhi tou buru ruonü zhi zu 強男
　之頭不如弱女之足
qiji 旗髻
qing bianfa ru guo su 請辮髮如國俗
qing ju da bai 輕裾大擺
qipao 旗袍
qiren 旗人
qu 區

ran 染
Ruo you xiao taguo yimao ji ling furen
　shufa guozuzhe, shi shen zai benchao
　er xin zai taguo ye. Zijin yihou fanzhe
　ju jia zhongzui 若有效他國衣帽及令
　婦人束髮裹足者, 是身在本朝而心在
　他國也。自近以後犯著俱加重罪

san cun di 三寸底
sandai heifū (J) 三大弊風
sandai rōshū (J) 三大陋習
shang benzhi hui quanti 傷本質毀全體
Shantou 汕頭
shi 市
shō (J) 庄
shufa guozu 束髮裹足
shuimian 水面
Shunzhi ernian jin guozu 順治二年禁裹足
Shunzhi shiba nian yiqian minjian zhi nü
　wei jin guozu 順治十八年以前民間之
　女未禁裹足

Si Lang tan mu 四郎探母

sim-pua (H) 媳婦仔

Souwen xubi 搜聞續筆 (*Further Essays in Search of Hearsay*)

Souwen xubi 謏聞續筆 (*Further Essays on Rumors*)

Sun Zhixie 孫之獬

taguo 他國

Taibei Tianran Zu Hui 臺北天然足會

Taiwan Dōkakai (J) 台灣同化會

Taiwan Tonghua Hui 台灣同化會

Tao Zongyi 陶宗儀

tensokusha (J) 纏足者

Teochew 潮州

Teochiu 潮州

tianxia yijia, neiwai fengsu buke youyi 天下一家, 內外風俗不可有異

tifa chuibian 薙髮垂辮

tifa ling 薙髮令

Wang Bu 王逋

Wang Shizhen 王士禎

Wang Xi 王熙

wangguo 亡國

wangguo louxi 亡國陋習

Wochao yiguan 我朝衣冠

xiangying mian jinzhi ke ye 相應免禁止可也

Xie Qian 謝遷

Yao jia ji fu jiao 要嫁即縛腳

Ye Mengzhu 葉夢珠

yimao zhuangshu 衣帽裝束

yizhisi yuanwailang 儀制司員外郎

Youxiao taguo yiguan shufa guozu zhe, zhong zhi qi zui 有效他國衣冠束髮裹足者, 重治其罪

Yu Huai 余懷

Yu Zhengxie 俞正燮

Yuan Mei 袁枚

Yue ji 粵籍

Zhang Qu 張渠

zhuang 庄

zhuofu jiuzhang 酌復舊章

"Zi chuan xing" 淄川行

zi jing guobian jianku beichang shi zhi chanzu zhi hai 自經國變艱苦備嘗始知纏足之害

zi Kangxi yuannian yilai suosheng nüzi yingting qi guozu zhe 自康熙元年以來所生女子應停其裹足著

Zichuan 淄川

Notes

INTRODUCTION: SEEKING STATUS, AVOIDING SHAME

1   Ebrey (1990: 216–18; 1999), Ropp (1981: chap. 4), and Lin Yutang ([1935] 1991) review many of these tropes in both Chinese and Western literatures.

2   See Mackie (1996) for a useful model of self-enforcing conventions applied to footbinding.

3   Ebrey (1993: 41; 1990: 220–21) speculates that as the scholarly ideal came to dominate Song notions of elite masculinity, exaggerating feminine characteristics through footbinding prevented literati from seeming effeminate (a notion that seems to reflect Western ideas about gender differences). She links this trend to a desire to differentiate Chinese from northern steppe cultures. This interpretation shares the tendency to link footbinding to identity vis-à-vis an outside group (women, steppe peoples), rather than to status competition within the ruling classes.

4   Ebrey 1990: 216–17; 1993: 37–43; Ko 2005: 111ff.; Mann 1997: 167–68.

5   Ebrey 1993: 37–43; Tao Zongyi 1936: 158.

6   See "Conclusion" in chapter 2 for a discussion of this process as it took place on the southeast coast of Fujian.

7   Ko 2005: 128; Hu Yinglin 1964: 147.

8   Manchu military power was based on a system of multiethnic fighting forces organized into large civil-military units called banners. Manchu, Mongol, and Chinese (Hanjun) banner armies were instrumental in the conquest of China and became the Qing state's elite military force. Banner households were granted land and income and formed a hereditary military caste (Rawski 1998: 61).

9   Ko 2005: 131–32. See also Qian Yong's early nineteenth-century comments on regional variations, in Ko (2005: 139–40).

10 Mann 1997: 26–28, 56, 167–68; Ko 2005: 131–32, 266n49.

11 For historical studies, see Ko (2005) and Ebrey (1990, 1993). On the material culture of footbinding, see Jackson (1997); Ke (1995, 1998, 2003); Ko (2001); and Li, Feng, and Ke (2005). For ethnographic accounts, see Turner (1997), Bossen (2002), Gates (2015), and Bossen and Gates (2017).

12 E.g., Doolittle 1865; Fielde 1887; Little 1908.

13 Gates 2015; Bossen and Gates 2017.

14 Levy 1967; Blake 1994; Mann 1997; Turner 1997; Ebrey 1999; Gates 2001; Ko 2005.

15 E.g., Blake 1994: 699; Turner 1997; Ko 2005: 2.

16 Large parts of Hebei were devastated by the Mongol campaigns in the early twelfth century and were resettled by immigrants from Shanxi only in the early Ming. By the eighteenth century, Hebei was the most densely settled of the northern provinces (Huang 1985: 114–16; Shepherd 1993: 430).

17 Ho Ping-ti 1962: 229.

CHAPTER 1: THE QING CONQUEST AND FOOTBINDING

1   A version of this chapter was previously published in *Frontiers of History in China* 11.2 (2016): 279–322.

2   Ko 1997: 22; 1998: 41–42; Mann 2002: 436–39; Wang Ping 2002: 33–34; Gao 2007: 32; Rowe 2009: 109; Blake 1994: 690n13, 706; Theiss 2004: 225n9.

3   Ko 1998: 42; 2001: 12; 2005: 251, 266; Mann 2002: 437–38; Lu 2010: 148; Ma 2010: 22.

4   Adopting the queue required both shaving the pate and braiding the hair left at the back of the head (*tifa chuibian*).

5   Crossley 1999: 179–80; Roth 1979: 6–7, 9. References to the practice of shaving the head and submitting (*tifa guixiang*) from 1621 can be found in *Manbun rōtō* (1955, vol. 1: 293, 295), and *Manzhou shilu* (1985: 330 [*juan 7*, Tianming 6.3.21]), where shaving the head is rendered in Manchu as *uju fusifi*.

6   Roth 1979: 29–31; Wakeman 1985: 60.

7   The 1636 and 1637 decrees are found in *Taizong shilu* (1985: 404 [*juan 32*, Chongde 1.11 *guichou*] and 446 [*juan 34*, Chongde 2.4 *dingyou*]). A Manchu-language version of the 1636 text is in *Manbun rōtō* (1963, vol. 7: 1438–41; see also Roth Li 2010: 287–91). For historical context, see Roth (1979: 29–31), Wakeman (1985: 208–9), Rawski (1998: 40), and Chen Shengxi (1985: 71).

8   The 1636 regulations are included in *Qing Taizong shilu gaoben* (1978: *juan 14*, 7). A description of Ming men's hats can be found in Wakeman (1985: 648).

9   The 1638 ban appears in *Taizong shilu* (1985: 554 [*juan 42*, Chongde 3.7 *dingchou*]): "Ruo you xiao taguo yimao ji ling furen shufa guozuzhe, shi shen zai benchao er xin zai taguo ye. Zijin yihou fanzhe ju jia zhongzui." Unless otherwise noted, all English translations are mine.

10 The original 1638 Manchu text is transliterated in Kawachi (2010: 441–42). A modified version of the Manchu text is found in Imanishi (1969: *juan 7*-458, 164). I thank Mark Elliott for pointing me to the Kawachi volumes. *Qingchu neiguo shiyuan manwen dang'an yibian* (1986, vol. 1: 332 [Chongde 3.7.16]) translates the Manchu into Chinese and gives *guozu* for the Manchu term for "binding feet," *bethe bohire*. Bound feet are referred to by the Manchu words for "small feet," *ajige bethe*, in Imanishi (1969: 164).

11 The truncated version of the 1638 order, "Youxiao taguo yiguan shufa guozu zhe, zhong zhi qi zui," is found in *Donghua lu* (1968, vol. 1: *juan 3*, Chongde 3.7 *dingchou*, 135a). A nearly identical version is included in *Qing shi gao* ([1927] 1977: *juan 3*, 64). The *Donghua lu* collected abstracts of selected memorials, many of which were included in the Veritable Records (Biggerstaff 1939).

12 "Banner people" (*qiren*) were distinguished from the rest of the Qing population, most of whom were "civilians" (*minren*) and who were overwhelmingly Han.

13 Ko 1997: 16, 19–22; 1998: 41–42; 2001: 12; 2004: 70; 2005; 132, 251n61, 266n49; Mann 1997: 27; 2002: 437–38; Wang Ping 2002: 33–36. Rowe (2009: 109) cites Ko (2005) in making a similar claim.

14 Structuralist expectations, that where "A" is important to one ethnic group's identity, then "not-A" will be important to a competing group's, are a misleading guide to political reality. Barth's (1969) concepts of boundary maintenance and ethnic identity markers have been widely misused by those ignoring the many contextual factors necessary to the operation of those principles.

15 Claims of multiple bans can be found in Levy (1967: 66–67), Chang and Chang (1998b: 82, 85), Harrison (2000: 73), Elliott (2001: 470), Mann (2002: 437), Spence (2002: 127), Feng Erkang (1986: 336), Feng and Chang (2002: 339), Nagao (1942: 828), Gao (2007: 32), and Rowe (2009: 109).

16 *Shizu shilu* 1985: 57, 60 (*juan* 5, Shunzhi 1.5 *gengyin* and *xinhai*); Wakeman 1985: 421–22, 646; Struve 1984: 47, 58–61. Surrendering military (*jun*) were not exempted.

17 *Shizu shilu* 1985: 151 (*juan* 17, Shunzhi 2.6 *bingyin*). For a translation of the key sections, see Kuhn (1990: 54–55). The edict uses "yimao zhuangshu" to refer to male dress, as opposed to the shaving, regulations. The edict orders the immediate transmission of the decree to all the provinces.

18 Wakeman 1985: 646–50; Struve 1984: 60–61.

19 Yu [1833] 1965: 504; Qian [ca. 1838] 1979: 630.

20 Wang Bu 1974: 6485; 1995: 578.

21 *Ming Qing shiliao, ding bian* [1951] 1972: 749b.

22 On the assembly, see S. Wu (1970: 10–19ff.) and Oxnam (1975: 70ff.).

23 The damage to the body caused by footbinding is also the theme of Mao Zhibin's call on an upright government to ban footbinding, "Jin chan zu biao." Mao's undated manifesto is included in a late seventeenth-century collection (see Mao 1973: 8 *ji, juan* 4, 10a–b, 3591). Ko (2002: 164–65) provides a partial translation.

24 Zeng 2007: 37–39.

25 Wang Bu 1974: 6485.

26 Wang Bu 1974: 6485. Variant translations of the punishments are given by Levy (1967: 66) and Spence (2002: 127). Both drew their accounts from secondary sources. Levy cites Nagao (1942: 828), who does not cite a source for the punishments. Spence based his translation on Feng Erkang (1986: 336), who in turn cites Qian Yong ([ca. 1838] 1979: 629). Wang Xi uses the possibility of false accusations as an argument against the prohibition; whether that was a hypothetical, or an argument from experience, is unknown, but it might be clarified by the search of the legal archives for pertinent cases, an endeavor that lies beyond the scope of this research. None of the sources reviewed here cites any such case.

27 Wang Bu 1974: 6485; for background, see Oxnam (1975: 85–86). The role of the Chinese scholar-official Wei Yijie, who advocated eliminating the eight-legged essay in 1663, is documented in Struve (2004: 1–32).

28 Wang Shizhen 1992: 26.

29 Wang Shizhen [1691] 1982, vol. 1: 55; 1992: 29. Wang's position was as *yizhisi yuanwailang*.

30 Wang Shizhen [1691] 1982, vol. 1: sec. 128, "Bagu."

31 In 1665, Huang Ji, then junior vice president of the Board of Rites, had submitted a memorial complaining that the new exam format had lowered standards and calling for restoration of the previous format. See *Shengzu shilu* 1985: 221 (*juan* 14, Kangxi 4.3 *renyin*).

32 Wang Shizhen [1691] 1982, vol. 1: 55. For details regarding changes in the exam format and the use of the eight-legged essay, see Oxnam (1975: 86) and Elman (1994: 119).

33 Wang Shizhen 1992: 29.

34 See Ko's claim associating footbinding with Confucian culture (1997: 27n34).

35 The regents are referred to in the historical literature as the "Oboi regents," named after the influential regent Aobai.

36 Oxnam 1973: 285; 1975: 85–86, 193–95; Wakeman 1985: 1067–69; Spence 2002: 125–33.

37 Lynn Struve (2004: 3) rightly points out Chinese officials might take either side in debates over these policies and warns against reducing them solely to questions of the extent of Manchu dominance. In this connection, Struve cites the role of the Chinese official Wei Yijie, who articulated long-standing literati complaints against the eight-legged essay format in the examination system that matched the regents' own views.

38 For critiques of footbinding dating from earlier centuries, see Ebrey (1990: 216–17). And see Mao Zhibin's call to ban footbinding, which likely dates from the seventeenth century (Mao 1973; Ko 2002: 164–65).

39 Wang Xi [1707] 2009: 116–17 (*Gong ji, juan* 1, 1a–3a); 446 (*Nianpu*, 37b, entry for 1668). See also *Qing shi gao* [1927] 1977: *juan* 250, 9694. Wang's memorial on restoring old precedents complains of the proliferation of rules and regulations without regard to significance and calls for respecting Shunzhi precedents. Struve (2004: 22) suspected that Wang Xi's pursuit of the program of restoring old precedents likely lay behind the rescission of the examination reforms, but she was unaware of Wang Xi's memorial targeting both the ban on footbinding and the exam reforms, known only through Wang Bu's transcription.

40 Oxnam 1975: 77, 85–86, 193–95; Spence 2002: 129–33. Wang Xi, *jinshi* of 1647 and thus a Qing "new man," rather than a Ming remnant, was also fluent in Manchu and became a confidant of the Shunzhi emperor, who summoned him to record his will (which is said to have been destroyed by the regents and replaced by a forgery). Restoring Shunzhi-era precedents must have had particular meaning to him (see Hummel 1943–44, vol. 2: 819; Wakeman 1985: 1008). Spence (2002: 129) reports that Huang Ji played a key role in arranging the sudden accession of the boy emperor Kangxi to personal rule in 1667.

41 See, on the elimination of the eight-legged essay, *Shengzu shilu* 1985: 154 (*juan* 9, Kangxi 2.8 *guimao*) and, on its restoration, *Shengzu shilu* 1985: 365 (*juan* 26, Kangxi 7.7 *renyin*).

42 Ye Mengzhu records that in "early Kangxi" footbinding by civilian women was prohibited and in the eighth year of Kangxi (rather than the seventh) the prohibition was rescinded. Ye observes that so entrenched a custom as footbinding could not be

quickly changed (Ye Mengzhu 2007: 206–7). Ye makes no mention of a 1645 ban, and Ye's brief note has not been cited by other scholars.

43 Zhao [ca. 1790] 1957: 654–56.

44 Chen Dongyuan [1937] 1984: 232; Nagao 1942; Levy 1967; Feng Erkang 1986; Feng and Chang 2002; Gao 2007; Ko 1997; Mann 2002: 437; Spence 2002: 127.

45 Yu [1833] 1965: 504. On Yu's anti-footbinding views, see Lin Yutang ([1935] 1992: 39–41) and Ropp (1981: 144–46).

46 Yu [1833] 1965: 504.

47 Qian [ca. 1838] 1979: 630. See also Ko 2005: 141.

48 Qian [ca. 1838] 1979: 630.

49 Works by Fu-ge ([1860] 1984), Wu Zhenyu (2005), Qiu Weixuan ([1914] 1991), Duyiwotuishi ([1930] 1973), Jia Shen (1929), and Li Rongmei ([1936] 1998) are discussed in Shepherd (2016). Although most of these works cite no sources, they repeat accounts of the bans that first appeared in Yu and Qian. Jia Shen introduces a new date, Shunzhi 17 (1660), in addition to 1662, for a ban on footbinding, which likely came from essays by Kang Youwei (2007, vol. 1: 4) and Liang Qichao (1999, vol. 1: 80), neither of whom cites any source. Sow-Theng Leong (1997: 36, 78–79) relies on a reference drawn from Qian Yong when he reads into an account on Hakka history their supposed compliance with Qing bans (see Shepherd 2016: 300). Mann (2002: 437) relies on Leong's interpretive reading.

50 Biggerstaff 1939: 103. The publication history of the *Donghua lu* volumes covering the early reigns is unclear. The earliest printed editions Biggerstaff was able to locate date from the Daoguang reign (1821–50), although he cites an undocumented source that states copies "circulated in manuscript, many years before it was printed" (1939: 103–5).

51 Chen Shengxi 1985: 77. Women wearing Jurchen costume and hairstyles may have been a trope of transition-period literature. In an allegorical scene depicting the fall of Yangzhou to the Jurchens in 1133 in his 1661 novel, Ding Yaokang contrasts among a large body of female captives the willing nature of women who have adopted Jurchen costume and hairstyles to the virtuous women who mourn and weep (Wai-yee Li 2014: 493).

52 See Gu Yanwu's poem "Zi chuan xing" (1983: 169–71), celebrating the attack on Zichuan by the rebel Xie Qian. Zichuan was also the home of Pu Songling; for references to the Xie Qian attack in Pu's work, see Xie Guozhen (1982).

53 Ko 1997: 21–22.

54 Loyalist sources characterize Sun as currying favor by advocating the resumption of the tonsure (*fu ti*), arguing that it is China (Zhongguo) that should follow the emperor's lead (*cong bixia*), not the reverse, and advocating that the queue become the national custom (*qing bianfa ru guo su*) (see Table 1.2).

55 Wakeman 1985: 868–70; Chen Shengxi 1985: 76–77; Ko 1997: 20–21, 27.

56 Shi 1959: 71–72. The passage appears under a heading for Qian Muzhai, that is, the scholar-poet Qian Qianyi, and refers to Qian's joke about his shaven head.

57 Tan 1960: 354–55. It is unclear what form of braiding was thought appropriate to Manchu women; perhaps the reference is to buns on the crown of the head, in the style

common to bannerwomen (*qiji*) (see Sun Wenliang 1990: 834). Tan Qian also reported that Sun and Li Ruolin (d. 1651) requested the queue become the national custom (*guo su*). Sun and Li, both of whom were twice-serving officials and vice presidents of the Board of Rites, were members of a group of officials who had voluntarily shaved their heads (Wakeman 1985: 426–27, 441, 460–61, 863, 868–70). Ying Zhang (2017: 158–64) discusses the factional politics involving Sun and Li at this time.

58 *Yantang jianwen zaji* 1968: 23–24. This source reports that Sun memorialized saying that the new rulers, having pacified China, should establish their own regulations, and in matters of hair and dress, China should follow "your majesty's" lead (*cong bixia*). *Souwen xubi* 1974: *juan* 1, 9b. This source reports that the reimposition of the head-shaving command (*fu ti*) in 1645 resulted from a memorial of Sun and Li Ruolin.

59 *Shizu shilu* 1985: 177 (*juan* 20, Shunzhi 2.8 *bingshen*); *Donghua lu* 1968, vol. 2: Shunzhi 2.8 *bingshen*; *Qingshi liezhuan* 1962, vol. 10: *juan* 79.25a–26b; *Qing shi gao* [1927] 1977: 9631, 9633 (*juan* 245, *liezhuan* 32).

60 According to Ko (1997: 17), the term for "female attire" (*nü zhuang*), when used as a subheading in encyclopedias, included footbinding.

61 See Rawski (1998: 41) and Elliott (2001: 246–51) for descriptions of items of Manchu female dress.

62 In addition to Chen Shengxi (1985: 76–77), Ko (1997) cites *Qingchao yeshi daguan* (1921, vol. 3: *juan* 3, 6–7). There are also accounts in the well-known works of Xu Ke ([1928] 1966, vol. 46: sec. 91, *fushi*: 61) and Gu Cheng (1997: 211).

63 Ko 1997: 22.

64 Ko 1998: 42; see also the more extensive account in Ko 1994: 274–82.

65 Although Liu was bound-footed, and said to be proud of her small feet, it did not prevent her from traveling in male disguise and fooling her future husband, Qian Qianyi, when they first met (K. S. Chang 1991: 15). Reports of Liu Rushi riding horses and donkeys also make one wonder how tightly bound her feet may have been (see Wai-yee Li 1999: 390–91).

66 After Qian died in 1664, the widowed Liu committed suicide, not as a martyr to Ming loyalism, but because of a dispute over rights to Qian family property (K. S. Chang 1991: xx; Ko 1994: 274; Wakeman 1985: 878–79). Qian's own reputation remained high until the Qianlong emperor targeted him in the literary inquisition (see K. S. Chang 2006: 199–218; see also Wakeman 1985: 1096–97).

67 Wai-yee Li 1999: 394–412.

68 K. S. Chang 1991: 10–17.

69 Wai-yee Li 1999: 390; see also 363–64, 383.

70 K. S. Chang 1991: 15–18; Wai-yee Li 1999: 394–412.

71 Wai-yee Li 1999, 2005; Xia 2004.

72 Wai-yee Li 2014: 487–93.

73 On late-imperial women's literature, see Widmer and Chang (1997), G. Fong (2008), and Fong and Widmer (2010). On literature in the transition, see Struve (1993), Wang and Shang (2005), and Idema, Li, and Widmer (2006). In her introduction to *Trauma and Transcendence*, Wai-yee Li (2006: 25) does mention the purported ban in a nod to Ko's ethnic marker thesis, but she muddles the dates (1644–48, instead of 1664–68)

and provides no evidence for a ban's existence or of reaction to it. There is no entry for "footbinding" or "bound feet" in the extensive index to Li's massive *Women and National Trauma* (Wai-yee Li 2014).

74   G. Fong 2010: 29; Ko 1994: 168–71; Mann 1997: 56.

75   Li Yu and Yu Huai are discussed later in this chapter; on Yuan Mei and footbinding, see Schmidt (2008).

76   Wai-yee Li 2010: 206 and passim; see also Hu Siao-chen 2010: 249. In both cases, the reference to bound feet is made metonymically by referring to bowed shoes, *gongxie*.

77   Chang and Chang 1998b: 82–85. For evidence of the bans, Chang and Chang cite a source drawing on Qian Yong's *Collected Works from Lüyuan*.

78   Wai-yee Li 1999: 395–96; 2014: 118–19, 169, 170, 366n133, 369–70.

79   Wiens 1969; Fisher 1977; Santangelo 1988.

80   Ko 2002: 157; 2005: 138.

81   On Yu Huai, see Lin Yutang (1960: 221–24), Levy (1966), and Wai-yee Li (2012: 339–42, 347–49). On Li Yu, see Eberhard (1971), Hanan (1988), and Chang and Chang (1998a).

82   Ko 2005: 251n61; see also Ko 1998: 42; Mann 2002: 437; see also Lu 2010: 48.

83   Typically, women bound the feet of young daughters, with the acquiescence, if not active encouragement, of their husbands. As daughters matured, they became responsible for maintaining their own bindings. When they married, their binding might be influenced by their husbands and in-laws.

84   Turner 1997; Wang Ping 2002: 34–35; Gao 2007: 36–46. On resistance to the queue, see Wakeman (1985: 647ff.).

85   Zhao [ca. 1790] 1957: 656; Qian [ca. 1838] 1979: 629; Ko 1994: 131–32, 139, and 20, 22 (for early twentieth-century observations). See also McLaren (2008: 56), on the rarity of binding in Nanhui, east of Shanghai, and Finnane (1998: 677–81), on variations in binding prevalences in the Jiangbei hinterlands of Yangzhou.

86   Gao 2007: 41–42.

87   Finnane 2004: 55–56; Gao 2007: 41. See also Wai-yee Li 2014: 489–93.

88   Population figures from Elliott (2001: 121, 369).

89   The low prevalence of footbinding in Beijing is discussed in chapter 8.

90   For a discussion of the criteria of Han identity in imperial China, see Ebrey (1996).

91   Shih 1967: 76–77; Jen Yu-wen 1973: 121, 361; Ono 1989: 11.

92   P. Cohen 1997: 204; Pruitt [1945] 1967: 51–52.

93   Mann (2002: 437) and Lu (2010: 148) assume the phrase was current in the early years of the Qing and use it as evidence that footbinding expressed resistance to the Qing conquest. Xia (2004: 119–20) provides a detailed examination of the history of this saying.

94   Liang 1999, vol. 1: 33.

95   Harrison 2000: 72–74. Compare Ko (1997: 11) and Levy (1967: 32), who discuss the fanciful proposal of a late-Ming scholar, Qu Jiusi, to weaken barbarians by convincing them to bind their women's feet so their men would be ensnared by feminine charm and lose their martial spirit (Shen 1997: 598–99). Qian Yong also drew a connection between footbinding and dynastic weakening (see Ko 2005: 142). Hill Gates debunks erotic notions of footbinding in her essay of 2008.

96 Gates 1997a: 182.

97 Rhoads 2000: 187–98, 204. There are no reports that Han working women whose feet were not bound were ever targeted.

98 Bannerwomen at the height of the anti-Manchu violence in late 1911 sought to save themselves by adopting Han dress and removing distinctive Manchu styles. See the striking set of cartoons reproduced in Rhoads (2000: 182ff.; discussion on 196, 204). Post-1911 photographs of bannerwomen wearing their distinctive costumes suggests that these were short-term measures that had limited effect. See, e.g., Perckhammer 1928; Sidney D. Gamble Photographs, *Manchu Woman—Walking*, roll no. 226: Peking, 1267, and *Devil Dance—Manchu Woman*, roll no. 67B: Peking Lama Temple, 728.

99 Ko 2005: 266; Mann 2002: 437. Seeing in footbinding a form of resistance (rather than conformity or victimhood) serves to magnify the importance of female agency and women's culture in the practice of footbinding, ideas important to Mann's and Ko's contribution to women's history.

100 Rawski 1985. No hard evidence has been cited to document a continued spread of footbinding in the Qing; Mann and Ko point to factors that suggest it did (Mann 1997: 26–28, 56, 167–68; Ko 2005: 131–32, 266n49). It is very likely that the numbers of women binding increased along with the population, but it is much harder to determine whether increasing *proportions* of women bound.

CHAPTER 2: THE TAIWAN CENSUS OF 1905

1 A confusing set of overlapping terms for these groups and their languages is found in the English-language literature on southeast coast society, Taiwan, and the overseas Chinese in Southeast Asia. Most of these terms are transliterations of endonyms as they were pronounced in the local dialects. The Taiwanese settlers from southern Fujian were speakers of dialects known as Minnan, or Hokkien. The people themselves are referred to as Hokkien or Hoklos. An additional group of Hoklos are located on the coastal plain of neighboring Guangdong Province, primarily in Chaozhou Prefecture. The Chaozhou Hoklos, because they are speakers of dialects closely related to Hokkien known as Teochiu, are also referred to as Teochiu or Teochew. The Hakka, who came primarily from the interior of northeast Guangdong, are known by a single term: both the people and the language are called Hakka (cf. Leong 1997: 3, 20, 41).

2 Shepherd 1993.

3 Pyle 1969: 157ff., 163ff.

4 Liu and Smith 1976: 269–73.

5 Lamley 1970.

6 Gotō 1909: 530–31.

7 Hayami 2001: chap. 3.

8 Peattie 1984: 84–85; Chang and Myers 1963; *SPCF 1905* 1909: 22.

9 The Japanese were not alone in perceiving these practices as backward; Chinese Republican reformers also targeted them for elimination (Harrison 2000; Ko 2005: 51).

10 Trans. Chang Lung-chih (2003: 166).

11 Takekoshi 1907: 156; Washizu 1940: 115; Wang Yigang 1960: 13. The three degenerate practices are referred to variously as *sandai heifū* (three major corrupt practices) and *sandai rōshū* (three major evil customs). These phrases also appear in early twentieth-century Chinese reformist literature.

12 Hastings 1993; Hirano 1993; Shibusawa 1958: 21–24, 35.

13 Jennings 1997: 18–28.

14 Takekoshi 1907: 156–57. Experience in Korea confirmed the need for more prudent policy. In late 1895, the pro-Japanese and pro-reform government of Korea ordered all Korean men to cut off their topknots. This overly zealous measure stirred up widespread unrest and attacks on Japanese interests and led to the downfall of the pro-reform group (Duus 1995: 115–18).

15 Wang Yigang 1960: 13–14; Wu Wenxing 1986: 70–74.

16 C. Tao 1994: 144; Broadwin 1997: 426.

17 Wang Yigang 1960: 14–17; Wu Wenxing 1986: 73–79.

18 Wang Yigang 1960: 16.

19 *Taiwan guanxi jishi* 1984, 3.12: 323.

20 The proportion reported released in Jiaobanian in 1915, following the official prohibition, is even below average.

21 *SPCF 1905* 1909: 1–2; Ch'en Ch'ing-ch'ih 1975; Wolf and Huang 1980: 16–27; Ts'ai 2009.

22 Li, Yang, and Chuang 2011: 351–52.

23 Areas in the mountains beyond effective government control, and populated by aboriginal groups not yet "pacified," were not included in the census area.

24 G. Barclay 1954: 140–45.

25 G. Barclay 1954: 10–11.

26 *SPCF 1905* 1909: 19; Wolf and Huang 1980: 18–24; Hong Rumao 2005: 36.

27 *SPCF1905* 1909: 10, 19.

28 Hong Rumao 2005: 35–37.

29 The unclear standard for reporting women as dependents or as having their own occupation, and the failure to report occupation by provenance in the general tables and by age and marital status in the footbinding tables, reduces the value of the occupational data for studies of footbinding (*SPCF 1905* 1909: 61–62, 72; G. Barclay 1954: 59, 77–78).

30 Qing administrative practice in Taiwan employed distinctions of provenance in immigration control, examination quotas, and local security (see, e.g., Shepherd 1993: 212). Native place defined by a hierarchy of encompassing administrative units was an important component of identity among Taiwanese; common origins provided the basis for establishing important social ties in the population. The Japanese government's imposition of order and the suppression of communal strife gradually reduced the political significance of provenance for the colonial administration, and the use of provenance declined in Japanese censuses and vital statistics in the 1930s.

31 Collingwood 1868: 143; Steere 1874: 317; 2002: 125, 133; Bax 1875: 26; T. Barclay 1890: 670; Mackay 1895: 101–2; Pickering 1898: 66–68; Davidson 1903: 581, 590–91; W. Campbell 1915: 55, 249; Lian Heng 1979: 604.

32 Dukes 1885: 111; Johnston and Johnston 1907: 84. Given these reports of widespread footbinding among Hoklo, it is surprising that the map purporting to show the prevalence of footbinding across China by Davin (1976: xii) puts southern Fujian and Taiwan in the "natural feet" zone. Turner's more detailed mapping gives a confusing picture of Taiwan (both "no binding" and "binding common") and Fujian ("binding uncommon"), although Xiamen is labeled "binding common" (1997: 447). Turner (1997: 454) finds reporting on footbinding in Taiwan to be contradictory but appears not to have consulted any of the sources on nineteenth-century Taiwan mentioned above. Gates (2001) reports interview data collected in 1991–92 that reveal variations in rates of binding in various south Fujian localities.

33 Cf. *SPCF 1905* 1909: 18, 95.

34 Cf. Leong 1997: 3, 20, 41.

35 A more extended discussion of footbinding and identity among the Zhanghua Guangdong women can be found in Shepherd (2015: 73–82).

36 Data on provenance are drawn from *Census of 1905, Kekka hyō* (1908: table 8, females only); data on proportions bound and released and on language in daily use are drawn from *Census of 1905, Shūkei gempyō, zentō no bu* (1907: tables 10, 22, 24) and *Census of 1905, Shūkei gempyō, chihō no bu* (1907: tables 18, 34, 36).

37 Leong 1997: 3, 41; Xu Jiaming 1973.

38 Fielde 1887: 30–32; Little 1908: 280–81.

39 Myron Cohen, personal communication, 2013.

40 Shepherd 1993: 386–87.

41 Shepherd 1993: 385–86.

42 Shepherd 1996. On the impact of blocked channels of mobility on patterns of acculturation, see Shepherd (1993: 376–77).

43 The immigration of Han males into Taiwan to take advantage of its unopened lands led to sexual imbalances on the frontier, which eased gradually over the course of the eighteenth century. Of the sojourners who remained in Taiwan, a few found wives in plains aborigine villages, but most brought over wives from their mainland homes (Shepherd 2004). Brown (2004: chap. 4) overestimates the numbers of early Han settlers who took plains aborigine wives. The plains aborigine population was too small to have provided wives for the much larger numbers of settlers, and even partially filling the demand would have severely constricted the reproduction of plains aborigine populations. As evidence of high rates of intermarriage at an early stage, Brown argues that a distinctive southern Hoklo culture developed that incorporated plains aborigine features ("short-route Han"). As evidence of such features, Brown (2004: 156–59) cites low rates of minor (little daughter-in-law) marriage and what she misinterprets as lower rates of footbinding among Hoklo in south Taiwan compared to those in the north; neither of these stand up to scrutiny. Several researchers have shown that regional variations in minor marriages in Taiwan are best understood as the result of marriage market demographics, not cultural differences (Shepherd 1991; Chuang and Wolf 1995; Wang, Kok, and Chuang 2008). As evidence of low rates of binding in south Taiwan, Brown cites statistics giving proportions of women footbinding without controlling for age; she misinterprets a footbinding rate of 68% of Hoklo

women of all ages as low, when in fact that rate corresponds to binding among over 90% of adult women, which leaves little room for influence from non-Han aversions to footbinding (Gates [1999: 309–10] also misinterprets these rates). Brown (2004: 156) also cites a lower rate of binding in Xinzhu compared to Haishan, which is explained herein as a result of the influence of Hakka, not plains aborigines. Evidence presented in chapter 5 shows that rates of binding among south Taiwan Hoklo were as high as those among Hoklo in the north. Where did the settlers obtain wives? The early waves of Han settlers were male sojourners, who returned frequently to mainland homes and families. Many men married in their home communities and, when traveling to Taiwan, left wives in their mainland-based parental families. Once they had established a more stable livelihood in Taiwan, they brought over wives and children. As the number of these families grew, high male sex ratios declined to moderate levels (Shepherd 2004; G. Barclay 1954: 212). Recent genetic studies of plains aborigines and Han also cast doubt on the notion that a large "short-route Han" population emerged in south Taiwan (Chen Shu-juo 2008).

44   Shepherd 1993: 386–87, 394, 527n134; 2003.

45   Gully and Denham 1844: 93.

46   Dukes 1885: 111; Johnston and Johnston 1907: 84.

47   Gamble 1943: 182.

48   Turner 1997: 448–51. See discussion in chapter 6.

49   Wolf 1995; Wolf and Chuang 1994; Shepherd et al. 2006; Shepherd 2011.

50   Constable 2000: 387–88; Blake 1981: 51–59; Xie Aijie 2002.

51   Ebrey 1990: 216–17; 1993: 37–43; Ko 2005: 111ff.; Mann 1997: 167–68.

52   An early, but ambiguous, reference to six-inch feet and clogs (*jizi*) occurs in a poem by the late Tang poet Han Wo (844–923), who spent the last years of his life in Fujian; see the discussion in Schafer (1954: 88) and Ko (2005: 111–12, 133, 261n4).

53   Chaffee (1985: 132–33) shows that Fujian ranked first among the circuits in the production of *jinshi* in both the Northern and Southern Song. On the imperial clan presence in Quanzhou, see Chaffee (2001).

54   Ebrey 1993: 38; Chaffee 2001: 40.

55   Chaffee 1985: 149–53, 197; Clark 2001.

56   P. Ho 1962: 227, 229.

57   P. Ho 1962: 238, 107.

58   For overviews of mercantile culture, see Rawski (1985) and Brook (1998). On the flourishing maritime trade of the southeast coast, see Clark (1991) on the Song, Rawski (1972: chap. 4) on the late Ming, and Ng (1983) on the early Qing.

59   Qu Tongzu 1965: 130–32; P. Ho 1962: 65–67; Clunas 1991: 151–54. The only restriction Qu mentions with respect to binding is the prohibition of binding by women of certain hereditary mean peoples, which presumably lapsed when they were made commoners in the Yongzheng reign.

60   T'ien 1988; P. Ho 1962: 73ff.; Clunas 1991: chap. 6; Finnane 2004: 55–56, 228–32. One need not endorse T'ien's theory of scholarly frustration to appreciate his documentation of these patterns, including widow suicides, and their intensity in late-Ming locales characterized by merchant wealth and academic success.

61 Clunas 1991; Brook 1998.
62 Ko 2005: 128, 193; Elvin 1999: 152–53.
63 P. Ho 1962: 234–35, 246, 249–51; Chaffee 1985: 149–51; Rawski 1972: chap. 4.
64 T'ien 1988: 82, 86–88.
65 Ng 1983. For high rates of binding in the Xiamen area, see Dukes (1885: 111) and Johnston and Johnston (1907: 84).
66 Hsieh 1929: 206; Gibson 1901: 135–36; Lechler 1878: 358–59; Chen Han-seng 1936: 106–7.
67 Xu Xuzeng [1815] 1965: 298. Sow-Theng Leong's reading of this passage (1997: 34–36, 78–79) misleadingly inserts a reference to Qing bans on footbinding (see Shepherd 2016: 300).

CHAPTER 3: THE 1915 PROHIBITION

1 Hong Minlin 1976: 148; Godley 1994.
2 Wu Wenxing 1986: 80–82, 88–89; Wang Yigang 1960: 19–22; Zhang Shuwen 2008: 76–80; Miao 2013.
3 Lamley 2007: 218; Tsurumi 1977: 65–68.
4 Wu Wenxing 1986: 87–90.
5 Wu Wenxing 1986: 89–91, 96; Lamley 2007: 219; Wang Yigang 1960: 17; Ts'ai 2009: 131.
6 Wu Wenxing 1986: 91–96. The three top essays, written in literary Chinese, were separately printed as *Chanzu zhi bihai ji jiuji* (1915), with a preface by the chief civil administrator, Uchida Kakichi.
7 *Taiwan aikoku fujin*, issues for 1914 and 1915.
8 Wu Wenxing 1986: 97–99; Wang Yigang 1960: 17–18; Ts'ai 2009: 130–31.
9 Wu Wenxing 1986: 98–99; Ts'ai 2009: 131. On the pain and the difficulty walking that women endured when unbinding, see Macgowan (1913: 83–86).
10 Levy 1967: 239, 276–79, 285, 323–26; see also Ts'ai 2009: 132. A. Wolf's informants from the late 1950s also confirmed the use of coercive measures by the police (1995: 53).
11 Wu Wenxing 1986: 99.
12 *SPCF 1905* 1909: 141.

CHAPTER 4: FOOTBINDING FOR MARRIAGE

1 *SPCF 1905* 1909: 132.
2 E.g., Gates 2015: 72; Levy 1967: 230; Wolf and Huang 1980: 85. Brown et al. (2012: 1038–39) report sayings from across China linking binding to good marriages. A sample Taiwanese expression is, "If you want to marry, bind your feet" (in Hokkien, *Beh-ke chiah pak-kha*; in standard Chinese [Mandarin], *Yao jia ji fu jiao*) (W. Campbell [1913] 1972: 526).
3 That bound feet were in fact deemed sexually attractive has been rightly questioned by Gates (2008). But note the observation that in Guangdong concubines were usually natural-footed: "The second and third wives are generally women of large feet and low origin, the first wives being almost invariably, excepting of course in the case of Tartar

ladies, women of small feet" (Gray 1878, vol. 1: 212). Natural-footed concubines were both less costly (in bride-price) and better able to perform domestic chores.

4   Wang Yigang 1960: 15–16; Hong Minlin 1976: 147; Turner 1997: 467.

5   In a pyramidal class structure, better-off families are fewer in number than families of lower status. If one assumes high proportions marrying, monogamy, and balanced sex ratios at marriage age, brides of equal and lower status will outnumber high-status grooms, and the opportunities for marrying up will be few. High rates of hypergamy would have to be balanced by high rates of hypogamy. If excess female mortality creates shortages of marriage-age women at all ranks, and men are allowed multiple wives, as in nineteenth-century China, the opportunities for women to marry up increase.

6   Gates 2015: 97.

7   Brown et al. 2012: 1051–52, 1056.

8   G. Barclay 1954: 215–16. For a case of a dowered older bride, see Brown et al. (2012: 1042–43).

9   Wolf and Huang 1980: 141–42; M. Wolf 1972: 94, 108ff.

10 Because the 1905 census does not provide data on marital status by both age and provenance for the population as a whole, it is only possible to calculate the mean ages at marriage for the ever-bound and the never-bound for the Taiwanese population (all ethnicities combined) in 1905, and not separately for Fujianese. The mean age at marriage for ever-bound Taiwanese accurately reflects the age at marriage of ever-bound Fujianese, because 99.6% of ever-bound Taiwanese women in 1905 were Fujianese. And a solid majority of 61.5% of the "never-bound" category was Fujianese, despite including the Hakka and plains aborigine minorities. Although the overall average age at marriage of Hakka in 1915 is higher than that of all Fujianese, it was lower in 1915 than that of the never-bound Fujianese. Thus including so many Hakka in the calculation for 1905 is likely to lower the mean age at marriage of the never-bound, not raise it. Therefore the Taiwanese measures in 1905 underestimate the substantial gap in mean ages at marriage that existed between the ever-bound and the never-bound Fujianese.

11 Johnston and Johnston 1907: 84, 157–66; Little 1901: 101; E. Ross 1914: 181.

12 G. Barclay 1954: 211–13.

13 G. Barclay 1954: 226.

14 This pattern agrees with Mackie's account of footbinding as a "self-enforcing convention" that is "maintained by interdependent expectations on the marriage market" (1996: 999). Missing from Mackie's account is any treatment of variations in the strength of the convention and measures thereof, which this study provides in the analysis of prefectural and township variation, in chapter 5.

15 Wolf and Huang 1980; Chuang and Wolf 1995; A. Wolf 1995.

16 A. Wolf (1995: 223 and passim) documents the resistance of the young to minor marriage.

17 Wolf and Huang 1980: 265; A. Wolf 1995: 283.

18 In the ten sites, the average proportions of bound-footed women in major, minor, and uxorilocal marriages were 87%, 86%, and 89%, respectively. A sample size of 3,039 marriages was analyzed.

19   Wolf and Huang 1980: 265.

20   Levy 1967: 225.

21   Levy 1967: 271.

22   Levy 1967: 272. Fielde also describes men inspecting the bride's feet at a wedding feast (1887: 37). Another example is described by Jung Chang in her memoir *Wild Swans*, cited by Broadwin (1997: 429).

23   Hinton and Gordon 1987.

24   E.g., Gates 2015: 71.

25   Fielde 1887: 30.

26   Hinton and Gordon 1987.

27   E. Ross 1914: 178–79.

28   The proportions of Taiwanese females twenty-one and older with currently bound feet, by age and marital status, in 1905 are calculated from *Census of 1905, Shūkei gempyō, zentō no bu* (1907: table 22) and *Census of 1915, Kijutsu hōbun* (1918: table 31).

29   Pruitt [1945] 1967: 22, 62–63.

30   Gates 2015: 75, 97.

CHAPTER 5: REGIONAL VARIATIONS AMONG THE HOKLO FUJIANESE

1   *Taiwan zaiseki kan'minzoku kyōkanbetsu chōsa* 1928: 4–5. The provenance survey data are reported by the township administrative units created in 1920. The percentages reported here are based on a regrouping of the township data to approximate the prefectural boundaries existing in 1905.

2   The strength of the relationship between the x and y variables in each scattergram is indicated by "r," the Pearson correlation coefficient.

3   Lamley 1981; Hsu 1980; Pasternak 1972: 142–46.

4   As stressed in anti-footbinding literature: Little (1901: 109), Chow (1896), and C. Tao (1994: 164–65).

5   Lin Hsin-yi 2011: chap. 4.

6   Hsu 1980: 99–100; Lamley 1977: 176–79, 186–92; 1981.

7   Hsu 1980: 100. Cf. DeGlopper's account (1995: 137), which tells a story of a Lugang husband ordering his wife to unbind to prepare to fight in lineage battles.

8   More detailed presentation of the data on bilinguals can be found in Shepherd (2015: 83–87).

9   The 1905 footbinding data are reported by age, provenance, and prefecture. The tables of the total population by age and prefecture are reported for Taiwanese but not by provenance; the proportion Fujianese of each prefecture has been used to estimate the number in each prefectural age-group.

10   Calculation of the singulate mean age at binding is done by using the same technique demographers use to calculate mean ages at first marriage from census reports of the proportions ever-married by age. The technique requires that the proportions ever-bound by age calculated from the 1905 census prefectural populations have not been changing in previous decades, and the data at the higher ages do show great stability in the rates ultimately attained. This condition enables one to infer the history of a

typical cohort from the 1905 age-group data for each prefecture. The use of the singulate mean age calculation also requires that the status "ever-bound," once attained, can never be lost; the data fulfill that condition because women who unbind their feet are reported as "released," not "never-bound." In these calculations, the proportions everbound in ages twenty-six to thirty serve as the proportion ultimately bound (Wachter 2006: 224–25).

11 Levy 1967: 229, 245, 258.

12 *SPCF 1905* 1909: 132; Ino 1905: 302; Levy 1967: 216, 267–70, 281; Hong Minlin 1976: 146; McNabb 1903: 22–23; Roberts and Steel 1997: 73,77; Ke 1998: 48–55. These sources include descriptions of the diseased flesh that accompanied the process, but which is left out here. Northerners, according to one source, achieved tiny feet without crushing the arch (Ko 2005: 170).

13 Little 1908: 280–81; Doolittle makes a similar observation (1865, vol. 2: 200).

14 Fielde 1887: 27.

15 Levy 1967: 284; see also 281.

16 Note that the calculation of the average age at binding takes into account only those who do ultimately bind; thus it is possible to have a low average age at binding when those who do bind are only a small minority of the local population. However, when binding is practiced by the majority and the average age at binding is low, there will be large numbers of the younger (and larger) age cohorts who will report being bound. These young binders would contribute large numbers to the usual measure of the prevalence of binding: "% Fujianese ever-bound at all ages." Thus to ensure that the measure of binding's prevalence among Fujianese is independent of the "age at binding" measure, those under age thirty are eliminated from the calculation of "% Fujianese ever-bound" and the correlation uses only the proportion of Fujianese women over thirty who ultimately bind.

17 The 1915 data for each of 2,961 cadastral areas (drawn from the *Census of 1915, Gairan hyō* [1917], have been aggregated into the larger 1920 townships (with average female populations of 5,640) set out in the *Census of 1920, Yōran hyō* (1922) volume. Seventeen townships with very small populations have been excluded from the sample.

18 The makeup of the Guangdongese in these townships is confirmed by the Hakka Affairs Council 2010–11 survey (2011: 36–39). The Hakka Affairs Council survey used a variety of criteria, including parentage, self-ascription, and language to define members of the Hakka ethnic group (2011: 26–27). Despite the gap of nearly a hundred years between the 1915 census and the 2010–11 survey, there is an impressive persistence of ethnic patterns, especially in the more rural areas.

19 For a more detailed discussion of Hoklorized Guangdongese in Zhanghua townships, see Shepherd (2015: 73–82).

20 Wen Lang Li 1967: 62–63, 66.

21 Three of the four townships that are not directly adjacent to Hakka-dominant townships are at one remove: adjacent to low-binding Fujian-dominant townships that are adjacent to Hakka townships. The fourth township, Huoshao (Green Island), on the east coast, lies closest to areas dominated by non-Han populations.

22 Hakka Affairs Council 2011: 36–39, A-33.

23 For an example of the use of adjacency or contiguity defined by the sharing of at least one common border point in the spatial analysis of innovation diffusion, see Goldstein and Klüsener's analysis of fertility decline in Prussia (2014: 505). For analyses of fertility change among Taiwan townships that take into account spatial diffusion processes, see Montgomery and Casterline (1993, 1996). For an analysis using spatial statistics to analyze the pattern of footbinding in Taiwan that makes findings similar to those presented here, see Ye Gaohua (2017).

24 The Taiwan Household Register Database is maintained by the Program for Historical Demography, Academia Sinica, Nankang, Taiwan. The Zhubei registers were collected by Chuang Ying-chang and have been analyzed in Chuang (1994), Chuang and Wolf (1995), and A. Wolf (1995).

25 The ethnic identification of the provenance groups is based on Chuang (1994).

26 See also A. Wolf 1995: 53.

27 Mackay 1895: 102; see also Steere 2002: 125.

28 Xu Ke [1928] 1966, vol. 16: sec. 42, *fengsu*: 31–32, 28; see also Xie Aijie 2002; Wolf and Chuang 1994: 427.

29 A. Wolf 1995: 53.

30 Bossen and Gates 2017: 187n12.

31 A. Wolf 1995: 53; Pasternak 1972: 131; cf. M. Cohen 2005: 94–95.

32 Pasternak 1983: 25–26; cf. Constable 2000: 387–88; Blake 1981: 51–59, cf. 121.

33 Wang Fuchang 1993: 57; cf. Blake 1981: 65–66.

34 The demonstration effect of Hakka adjacency is analogous to the social learning or pioneer effect "in which new information is diffused because people learn of its advantages by observing forerunners" (Goldstein and Klüsener 2014: 506), but the added effect of undermining peer pressure and hegemony is worth stressing in the case of the footbinding convention.

35 Smith [1899] 1970: 213.

36 *SPCF 1905* 1909: 139.

37 Stevens 1918: 84, 144, 172, 186. Fielde's depth of knowledge of the Teochiu is reflected in her publications on Teochiu language (1878, 1883) and society (1887, 1894).

38 See Leong 1997: 25; Hashimoto 1973; Fielde 1887: 132; Riddell 1901 (map).

39 G. Campbell 1888.

40 Fielde 1887: 31.

41 See Wolf and Chuang 1994: 427; Wang Fuchang 1993.

42 Wealthy households in Taiwan purchased young girls to be servant-slaves, or *binu* (H: *ca-bo-kan-a*), whose natural feet equipped them for tasks bound-footed family women could not do. Opinion differed on whether custom made their servitude lifelong or obligated masters to arrange their marriages. In 1839, the Taiwan intendant Yao Ying threatened masters with punishment if they did not arrange marriages for such girls by the time they reached age twenty-five (*Taiwan guanxi jishi* 1984, vol. 3.5: 254–55; Wolf and Huang 1980: 115–17).

43 Hong Minlin 1976: 145, 147. Many sources list derisive terms for unbound or poorly bound feet: Douglas ([1873] 1970: 257), Macgowan (1913: 70), Levy (1967: 110), Feng Jicai (1994: 197; 2004: 168), Zhang Shuwen (2008: 46), Chang Mo-chun (1992: 126–27),

Xie Aijie (2002: 573), and Ko (2005: 182–83). The goddess Guanyin is usually portrayed as having natural feet. To be mocked as "half Guanyin" is to have natural feet but to lack the virtues of the bodhisattva.

44 Macgowan 1913: 26. Doolittle also reports that large-footed women in Foochow (Fuzhou) wore dress and hair ornaments that distinguished them as a separate class (1865, vol. 2: 202). Zhang Qu reports of eighteenth-century Guangzhou that footbinding marked a class distinction that brought public shaming if violated ([1738] 1990: 52).

45 Wang Yigang 1960: 16.

46 Levy 1967: 247, 249. Gates's Sichuan life histories also make numerous references to fears of being ridiculed for poorly bound feet and to pride in the beauty of bound feet (2015: 30, 36, 43, 46).

47 Fielde 1887: 30.

48 Fielde 1887: 32.

49 Fielde 1887: 32.

50 Macgowan 1913: 27.

51 The impact of binding on the quality of mother-daughter relations has been the subject of retrospective speculation. Notions that binding might strengthen mother-daughter relationships should be questioned, given the equal likelihood that binding damaged trust between daughters and mothers and was experienced not as loving care but as cruel abuse (Broadwin 1997: cf. 428 and 422; Ma 2010: 54). This perspective suggests that psychologically, footbinding, inflicted by mothers who themselves had suffered binding, was more than just a lesson mothers taught daughters about their place in a male-ruled world (Blake 1994: 682; D. Wu 1981).

52 Levy 1967: 251.

53 Levy 1967: 239.

54 Levy 1967: 246.

55 J. Ross 1908: 213.

56 Johnston and Johnston 1907: 84, 157–66; Little 1901: 101; E. Ross 1914: 181.

57 Cf. the challenge to erotic motivations by Gates (2008).

58 Contra Ko (2001: 52, 63), Blake (1994), and Broadwin (1997).

CHAPTER 6: WOMEN'S LABOR IN AGRICULTURE

1 Levy 1967: 46, 274–75; Mann 1997: 55; Ko 1997; 2005: 182ff.

2 Cf. the "light labor hypothesis" stressing handicrafts, not field labor: Gates (2001); also Bossen (2002).

3 Cf. Doolittle 1865, vol. 2: 200–201; Fielde 1887: 27; Little 1908: 280–81; Levy 1967: 284.

4 Turner 1997: 449–51; Davin 1976: 118–20; J. Buck 1937: 292.

5 Qian Yong had made similar observations in the early nineteenth century (see Ko 2005: 139–40).

6 E. Ross 1914: 175, 294. For other North China examples where bound-footed women worked in the fields on their knees, see Franck (1923: 360), J. Buck (1937: 292), and M. Wolf (1985: 6). Walter Mallory's travels in North China led him to observe of bound-footed women: "Many of the women labor in the fields in spite of their

infirmity, and it is surprising that they are able to do so at all; but the amount of work which even the most active can accomplish is comparatively small especially in occupations which require walking or standing" (1926: 98).

7   On the outdoor work and rarity of footbinding among farm women in the Guangzhou area, see Zhang Qu ([1738] 1990: 52), Faure (2007: 246), E. Ross (1914: 175), and Chen Han-seng (1936: 104, 107–8). On traveling to Hunan, see Tong and Li (1979: 49). On traveling to Swatow, see Ball (1925: 718).

8   Davin 1976: 118–20; J. Buck 1937: 292.

9   Turner 1997: 448–51.

10 Finnane 1998: 678–81, 689. Finnane conducted interviews in these areas in the 1990s.

11 Huang 1990: 56, 51–52; Fortune 1847: 256–57.

12 On Ding County, see Gamble ([1954] 1968: 216–18). Women born before 1900 in this county were over 90% bound (Gamble 1943).

13 Pasternak 1972: 49, 81; Wolf and Chuang 1994: 427–28.

14 Sando 1981: 34. Levy's informants confirm that women with tiny feet could not work in wet fields (1967: 284).

15 Sando 1981: 114.

16 Steere 2002: 27.

17 Steere 1874: 318.

18 C. Liu 2005: 39–40, 184.

19 M. Cohen 1976: 148. See also the comments on northern Hakka in Wolf and Chuang (1994: 428).

20 Wang and Apthorpe 1974: 44; Wolf and Chuang 1994: 428.

21 Bossen 2002: 48–49, 61.

22 M. Wolf 1968: 41, 60, 78; Chuang 1994: 191–92. A. Wolf reports that it was still considered exceptional for a woman to work in paddy fields in the northern community of Haishan in the 1950s, and one Hoklo farmer suggested a woman working in a paddy field would pollute it (1995: 52).

23 Ts'ai 1990: 288; Davidson 1903: 381.

24 *Taiwan Sōtokufu tōkeisho* 1905: 518–31, 532–48, 569–80, 705–10.

25 *Nōgyō kihon chōsasho* 1923b. Wet crops include wet rice and some green manure; dry crops include upland rice, sugarcane, sweet potato, peanuts, beans, sesame, linseed, millets, wheat, barley, jute, ramie, tea, citrus, bananas, and some green manure.

26 G. Barclay 1954: 40–41.

27 *Nōgyō kihon chōsasho* (1923a) reports, in addition to crop areas, dry and wet field areas. The correlation for 280 townships of percent dry field area to percent everbound is a very weak 0.08.

28 Doolittle 1865, vol. 2: 201; Fielde 1887: 27; *SPCF 1905* 1909: 137; Little 1908: 280–81.

29 *Nōgyō kihon chōsasho* 1923a.

30 Doolittle 1865, vol. 2: 201. For details of Doolittle's life in Fuzhou and his writing, see Barnett (1985: 110, 197n48).

31 Fielde 1887: 31.

32 Ko 2005: 22, 131–32; Finnane 1998: 677–78.

33 *SPCF 1905* 1909: 137.

34   *SPCF 1905* 1909: 137–38, 89.

35   G. Barclay 1954: 116.

36   The 1915 village-level population data (*Census of 1915, Gairan hyō* 1917) have been regrouped into the 301 administrative districts created in 1920 (*Census of 1920, Yōran hyō* 1922). The 301 districts are classified according to their administrative label in 1920: 3 cities (*shi*), 36 towns (*jie*), and 262 rural districts (*zhuang* [rural townships], *fandi* [aborigine districts], and *shuimian* [boat dweller districts]). The three cities are Taipei, Taichung, and Tainan. There were twelve prefectural capitals in 1915; these include the three cities and nine towns. The three major port towns (Jilong, Lugang, and Gaoxiong) were not prefectural capitals in 1915, but were very important commercial centers. Taidong (both a town and a prefectural capital) is not included in the calculations because its female population was less than 80% Fujianese. Independent lists of urban centers by Davidson (1903: 598) and the listing of twenty-two towns with populations over five thousand in the *Statistical Summary of Taiwan* (1912: 80) confirm the importance of the larger centers identified in the 1920 administrative designations as "towns" and "cities."

37   Fielde 1887: 30–32; Doolittle 1865, vol. 2: 201; *SPCF 1905* 1909: 137–38, 89; Finnane 1998: 677–78; 2004: 55–56.

38   On the economic changes, see Myers (1972) and S. Ho (1978).

CHAPTER 7: WOMEN'S LABOR IN HANDICRAFTS

1   Ho Ping-ti 1959: 73ff.; Wang Shida 1932–33. The 1908–11 returns, where they have been preserved, provide valuable information on ethnicity and banner populations, which will be of use in the analysis of footbinding patterns in chapter 8. The quality of the 1908–11 returns suffered, however, because at that time several provinces had yet to establish the modern police departments charged with directing the census, and the local census machinery was often poorly funded and understaffed.

2   Aiming to reunify China, Nationalists, based in the southern province of Guangdong, launched military campaigns against northern warlord cliques in 1926. The campaigns met with a series of successes, internal splits, and setbacks, but finally achieved a reunification of China under a single Nationalist-led government in 1928 (Sheridan 1975: chap. 6).

3   *Neizheng nianjian* 1936, vol. 2: C.404; *Minguo shiqinian ge sheng shi hukou diaocha tongji baogao* 1931: 21. Detailed regulations governing the conduct of the 1928 census can be found in the *Hebei tongzhi gao* (1993, vol. 3: 2903–4) and in the discussion in N. Liu (1935: 109).

4   Lin Qiumin (1990: 118–19) identified eight provinces and four cities reporting on footbinding in the *Neizheng gongbao*. I have located reports from two more cities, Jinan and Qingdao (*Neizheng gongbao* 1930, vols. 3.3 and 3.4). It appears a number of the sixteen reporting provinces used a reporting format that did not call for enumeration of the bound-footed (see, e.g., Anhui, in *Neizheng gongbao* 1929, vol. 2.6). Only half of the sixteen provincial returns received are reproduced in the volumes of the *Neizheng gongbao* for 1929 and 1930. The reports from the five provinces not included in Table 7.1

have large proportions of non-reporting counties, which suggests low-quality reporting and less professionalized police. The Hebei report is also included in *Hebei 1928* (1930).

5   The Nanjing government Interior Ministry in 1928 ordered every county and city to include footbinding in its population schedule in order to establish baselines for carrying out a prohibition of the practice (Lin Qiumin 1990: 118–19, citing *Neizheng gongbao* 1928, vol. 1.4: 25–26; see also Zhang Ruohua 2014: 187).

Other categories enumerated in this format included gender, students, able-bodied men, men keeping the queue, Nationalist Party members, the employed and unemployed, religion (six kinds), the disabled, and felons (see, e.g., the Hebei returns, in *Neizheng gongbao* 1929, vol. 2.7). Note that standard census items such as age, marital status, and ethnicity are not included in these surveys. The absence of reports by both age and sex deprives demographers of a key tool used to assess the quality of enumerations.

6   P. Ho 1959: 79–83.

7   Zhili was renamed Hebei and Fengtian was renamed Liaoning in 1928 by the Nationalist government.

8   The Boxer rebellion was a popularly inspired anti-foreign uprising whose suppression resulted in the occupation of Beijing, Tianjin, and other cities in northern China by a coalition of military forces from Western nations and Japan in 1900 (Spence 1999: 230–33).

9   Reynolds 1993: 162, 167.

10   Reynolds 1993: 164, 168.

11   MacKinnon 1980: 155.

12   MacKinnon 1980: 156–60; Wang Jiajian 1984: 58–59. Gamble (1963: 64) relates the biography of a Hebei village leader who attended a police training course for one year, circa 1911, and served as a policeman for four years in Hebei's Wanping County.

13   Reynolds 1993: 164–69; MacKinnon 1980: 151–63. Zhili included large parts of Chahar and Jehol, before they were created as separate jurisdictions in 1914; see the map in MacKinnon (1980: 38).

14   As the basic unit of subcounty government by 1914, the ward played a key role in taxation, policing, and population registration for all the regimes that came to power in Hebei during and after the warlord era (Duara 1988: 61–63; H. Li 2005: 158, 214). Gamble distinguishes the ward (*qu*) as a supra-village level directed from above, from village-level units running their own affairs. He makes a similar distinction between county police funded by village taxes remitted to the county and village police and other guardsmen hired locally by crop-watching and other self-defense organizations (Gamble 1963: 1–2, 6, 114, 172, 207).

On Hebei's investment in policing, see Duara (1988: 80–83). Given the broad range of responsibilities assigned to the police, personnel and training remained the most important expenditure categories. Local government expenditures on police in each Hebei county are provided in *Hebei 1928* (1930: *minzhenglei* 78–83), but not the numbers of police. The *Hebei sheng gexian gaikuang yilan* provides information on numbers and/or expenditures on police and the militia (*baoweituan*) at the county level as of 1933. The *Hebei tongzhi gao* provides similar information on forty-one counties circa 1935 (1993, vol. 3: 1591–1603). Compared to twenty-three other provinces in 1934,

Hebei had the most counties with ward-level police offices (122 of 130), the most ward offices (516), and the most police (5,735) (Han Yanlong 1993: 579, 599–600).

15 Wang Jiajian 1984: 184, 201.

16 Duara 1988: 196, 67–70, 77–78. Huaiyin Li also notes instances when ward police were called on by the magistrate to prompt taxpaying (2005: 96, 117, 241).

17 MacKinnon 1980: 152.

18 *Tianjin renkou shi* 1990: 83–86, 88; Wang Jiajian 1984: 139–40.

19 The numbers report the ordinary population (*putong hukou*) figures and do not include special categories enumerated separately (e.g., people residing on boats, in temples, public facilities). City population figures cover areas under Chinese administration and do not include international concessions.

20 Levy 1967: 278–79; Gamble 1921: 98; Yang Xingmei 1998.

21 Gamble 1943.

22 Gates 2015: 11–12, 19. The survey was conducted in cooperation with the Sichuan Provincial Women's Federation.

23 Brown et al. 2012: 1046–47; Bossen and Gates 2017: 39.

24 Gates 2015: 17.

25 Bossen and Gates 2017: 42, 53, 75.

26 Mann 1997: 167–68; Ko 2001: 80–81; Gates 2001: 134–35. The timing of the expansion of cotton textile weaving into North China is thought to have been relatively late; Chao estimates it was only getting started at the beginning of the seventeenth century (1977: 21). The anti-footbinding policies adopted by the Manchu founders of the Qing state suggest that footbinding was an already well-established practice among the northern Chinese who had moved into the Liao basin in the early 1600s. It is unclear whether the footbinding witnessed by the Manchus at that time was a practice restricted to the elite or whether it was widespread among commoner Chinese. But it appears that footbinding among commoners may have predated, rather than followed, the spread of cotton textile handicrafts in the north.

27 Gates 2001: 135–36; 1997b: 121–22.

28 Gates 2015; Bossen and Gates 2017.

29 Gates 2015: 1–2, 76. According to Bossen and Gates, binding a daughter's feet "was an efficient way to make them stay seated and work with their hands" (2017: 8, 12).

30 Hindman 2009; Tuttle 1999.

31 Gates 2015: 38, 46, 75–76.

32 Cf. Bossen and Gates 2017: 15; Chao 1977: 174, 179–80.

33 Isett 2007: 216.

34 Isett 2007: 212.

35 Chao 1977: 181, 200; Isett 2007: 217–20.

36 *Customs Trade Reports*: A. MacPherson, Newchang (1867: 11); Geo. Hughes, Newchang (1878: 4); B. Russell, Newchang (1888: 2).

37 E. Ross 1914: 175. Kalgan is Zhangjiakou.

38 Cressey 1932: 286; K. Chang 1956: 107; Lattimore 1932a: 295. Buxton estimates the advance of Chinese agricultural settlement north of Kalgan (Zhangjiakou) at about one mile a year from 1872 to 1922 (1923: 396, 400).

39   Isett 2007: 216.

40   Kraus 1980: 9, table 1.2.

41   Gamble [1954] 1968: 308; Chao 1977: 197.

42   Christie 1914: 13–14; Lattimore 1932b: 269. The abandonment of footbinding by immigrants to the northeast is discussed in chapter 8.

43   K. Chang 1956: 219–20; Lattimore 1932a: 296; 1934: 85–86.

44   Chao 1977: 22–23; Rawski 1972: 66, 74–75.

45   Chao 1977: 23, 171, 181; *Customs Trade Reports*: George Hughes, Amoy (1870: 92); H. E. Hobson, Tamsui (1871–72: 157).

46   Kraus 1980: 9, table 1.2.

47   Ng 1983: 136, 165.

48   S. Ho 1978: 15. Import and export values for 1899–1902 from the Japanese colonial customs confirm these patterns of trade (Davidson 1903: 625–34).

49   *Customs Trade Reports*: H. Kopsch, Tamsui (1867: 74); George Hughes, Amoy (1870: 92); H. E. Hobson, Tamsui (1873: 92); James H. Hart, Takow (1873: 109).

50   Mackay 1895: 64.

51   Davidson 1903: 525–26, 628, 633.

52   Davidson 1903: 530, 535, 542, 633–34.

53   Davidson 1903: 543, 545, 532.

54   Davidson 1903: 529, 538.

55   *Yuanli zhenzhi* 2002: 454; *Dajia zhenzhi* 2009: 1259–60; *Danshui tingzhi* 1870: 298, 327.

56   Davidson 1903: 529.

57   Davidson 1903: 529.

58   *Yuanli zhenzhi* 2002: 951; *Dajia zhenzhi* 2009: 1261–62. Davidson (1903: 645) includes a brief notice of the recent developments. Tributes both lamenting and praising the hard work done by mat weavers are included in the *Miaoli xianzhi* (1893: 233) and the *Yuanli zhi* (1897: 115).

59   *Census of 1915, Gairan hyō* 1917: tables I.3, III.3; *Census of 1920, Yōran hyō* 1922: table I.3.

60   Chen Dongsheng 2015; Zhou and Zhang 2015.

61   Finnane 1998: 676–77, 681, 683.

62   Finnane 1998: 677, 680, 682, 684.

63   Bossen and Gates 2017: 8.

64   Chao 1977: 21, 23. See also note 26 above on speculations that footbinding spread along with cotton textile handicrafts.

65   Chao 1977: 179.

66   H. Fong 1936: 692; Chao 1977: 53, 173, 181, 186.

67   H. Fong 1934: 277–80; H. Li 2005: 27–29.

68   Chao 1977: 181, 197; Ma and Wright 2010: 1357–58; Isett 2007: 212.

69   Chu and Chin 1929: 8; Huang 1990: 51.

70   Bossen and Gates 2017: 139–40.

71   Chao 1977: 180.

72   Chao 1977: 170–71.

73   H. Fong [1932] 2014: 238; Feuerwerker 1969: 24–26.

74   Chao 1977: 180–81, 186; Ma and Wright 2010: 1359–60.

75 Gamble [1954] 1968: 302; Chao 1977: 183–84.

76 Chao 1977: 185.

77 Chao estimates, on a China-wide basis, that between 1905–9 and 1924–27 hand-spun yarn output declined by 25%, while handwoven cloth production increased by 50% (1977: 232–33).

78 H. Fong 1936; Li Feng 1934: 63.

79 H. Fong 1935: 77.

80 H. Fong 1935: 77–80; 1936: 695, 707, 710; Chao 1977: 186–87.

81 H. Fong 1935: 86; 1936: 735.

82 *Nankai Weekly Statistical Service* 1933: table 2.

83 Chao 1977: 180, 184.

84 H. Fong 1933: 58; Grove 1993; Chao 1977: 186.

85 Cf. Bossen and Gates 2017: 54.

86 E.g., Gamble [1954] 1968: 302–3.

87 Chao 1977: 176, 182, 185.

88 Girls plaited mats and straw goods, as suggested in Bossen and Gates (2017: 11, 13).

89 Chao 1977: 173, 181.

90 Kraus 1980: 138.

91 Zhang Shiwen [1936] 2009: 417–66; Gamble [1954] 1968: 94, 98.

92 Chao 1977: 177.

93 Bossen and Gates 2017: 16.

94 Chao 1977: 232–33.

95 Bossen and Gates 2017: 67.

96 Gates 2015: 171.

97 Bossen and Gates 2017: 144.

98 Multiple sources confirm the predominance of footbinding in Hebei. See Qian Yong's early nineteenth-century observations in Ko (2005: 139–40); also Gamble (1943: 181–83), Fairbank and Goldman (1998: 173), M. Cohen (2005: 94–95), Levy (1967: 228–30), and Turner (1997). Bossen and Gates's interview samples provide additional evidence of high rates of binding throughout North China (2017: 53, 75).

99 Although Hebei generally had a reputation for high rates of binding, there were certainly counties where binding was less common; see, for example, the non-binding population in Laishui County described by Ament (1899: 318, 326). Qian'an County, apparently due to its large banner population, also had low proportions bound; the Manchu autonomous county of Qinglong was created out of Qian'an (see note 41 in chapter 8).

100 *Hebei 1928* 1930: *gongshanglei* 9–35.

101 H. Fong 1933: 44–49; see also Li Feng 1934.

102 *Nankai Weekly Statistical Service* 1933: 105.

103 H. Fong 1933: 46.

104 H. Fong 1933: 26; Gamble [1954] 1968: 287, 318–19; Bossen and Gates 2017: 11, 13.

105 H. Fong [1932] 2014: 233; 1933: 58; Grove 1993: 97–98.

106 Two of the 129 Hebei counties, Xinle and Puyang, failed to report the proportions bound-footed.

107 In Figure 7.1, the outlier points are Shulu County at $42, where processing fur and leather goods generated considerable handicraft income, and Nanle at $28, where women plait straw goods for export. As H. Fong observed, "There are more people in the district who make their living by straw plaiting than by farming" (1933: 26).

108 Bossen and Gates 2017: 54.

109 Cf. Bossen and Gates 2017: 139.

110 In Figure 7.2, the outlier point, at 21.2 bolts per female, is Wan County, which lies to the west of Baoding (Qingyuan County) and has access to the Jinghan railroad. "Families in every village [in Wan County] weave as a by-employment, using machine yarn as the warp and hand-spun yarn as the weft" (*Hebei 1928* 1930: *gongshanglei* 43).

111 Li Feng 1934: 63, 76.

112 H. Fong 1936: 692; Chao 1977: 173, 186; Gamble [1954] 1968: 288, 301–3.

113 Chao 1977: 173, 181.

114 Chao 1977: 186–87.

115 Identifying counties that had high per capita production of raw cotton presents a number of challenges. The best county-level data available on cotton production in the relevant years are those collected by the Chinese Cotton Millowners Association, and the "best such survey" is that for Hebei in 1936, when 127 out of 129 counties were included (Kraus 1980: 19–20, 26; Chao 1977: 220; H. Fong 1934: 276–80). However, the areas devoted to cotton cultivation and the yields obtained varied greatly from year to year as prices and weather conditions fluctuated. Because of these fluctuations, identifying the major producing areas based on yields from a single year is risky. The number of Hebei counties included in the annual surveys reached 59 in 1932 and 75 by 1933; for these counties (the major cotton producers of interest to the Cotton Millowners Association), there are multiple-year reports (H. Fong 1934; Kraus 1980: 17, app. B). Those counties surveyed only in 1936 generally produced very little cotton. To limit as much as possible the effect of single-year fluctuations in production, the average production, 1932–36, is used for as many years as are reported for each county. The measure, *jin* (catty, 1.3 pounds) per capita of cotton per county, should provide a good indicator of supplies of cotton sufficient to support traditional yarn and cloth production. A per capita measure (including both males and females) provides an indicator of the extent to which cotton would be available for market production after satisfying family clothing requirements.

116 See Bossen and Gates (2017: 54) on the pattern predicted by the handicraft hypothesis.

117 Bossen and Gates 2017: 8.

118 Levy 1967: 272–73; Doolittle 1865, vol. 2: 201; Fielde 1887: 27; Little 1908: 280–81.

119 *Neizheng gongbao* 1929–30, vols. 2–3.

CHAPTER 8: BANNERWOMEN AND CIVILIAN WOMEN IN THE NORTHEAST

1 Levy 1967: 67; Wu Hong 1997: 354; Rawski 1998: 41; Gao 2007: 33–34. Citing only Ko (2005), Rowe's overview of Qing history concludes that "apparently declining numbers" of Manchu women rejected footbinding (2009: 109).

2   Gao Hongxing suggests that binding was a deliberate strategy Hanjun (bannermen of Han origin) took to disqualify daughters from the unpopular palace service draft, rather than a copying of Han styles (2007: 33). This claim has not been repeated elsewhere, and Gao provides no source or additional evidence for his claim. On the unpopularity of the service draft (which selected young women of banner families for service in the palace), despite monetary compensation, see Elliott (2001: 253–54).

3   Rawski 1998: 41; Wu Hong 1997: 354. Of the four edicts governing banner apparel that are commonly mentioned, only the 1804 edict was concerned with footbinding: on this occasion the Jiaqing emperor complained that bound feet (*chanzu*) were not in accord with the dynasty's prescribed dress (*Wochao yiguan*) (*Qing huidian shili* [1899] 1991, vol. 12: 82 [*juan* 1114, Jiaqing 9, p. 17b]). Three other edicts of 1759, 1775, and 1839 refer to Han costume, earrings, and robes with wide sleeves (but not footbinding) that violate Manchu customs (*Manzhou fengsu*, 1759, and *Manzhou jiufeng*, 1775) (*Qing huidian shili* [1899] 1991, vol. 12: 81, 83 [*juan* 1114, Qianlong 24 (1759), p. 15a; Qianlong 40 (1775), p. 15b; Daoguang 19 (1839), p. 20a]).

4   Gao 2007: 34–36. Most of the sources on *daotiao* can be traced back to Yao Lingxi's *Caifeilu* compendia (see Yan 1941). Ko (1998: 44–45) gives the most detailed synopsis in English of the passages. Yan Gui (1941) reports that girls aged ten to sixteen, desiring to enhance their beauty, adopted the style. See also Levy 1967: 67, 255. "Willow branch feet" (*liutiao jiao*) likely refers to the same practice (see *Beijing nübao*, no. 86 (November 14, 1905): 2–3; Rhoads 2000: 94). A related practice was the wearing of tight socks to narrow the feet (Zhou 2005: 98). Jackson (1997: 37) confuses "loose binding" with the Manchu practice of *daotiao*. Elliott confuses the narrow knife-blade style with the "cucumber" foot in which the toes but not the arch are broken (2001: 470n63).

5   Levy 1967: 67–68; Ko 1997: 19; Wang Ping 2002: 36; Mann 2002: 437; Elliott 2001: 247. The earliest source found making the claim that high platforms were intended to mimic the gait of the bound-footed women is that of H. E. M. James, writing in 1888, who says the "enormously high heels, placed almost in the centre of the sole, . . . communicate[s] to the whole figure that elegant tottering gait so much admired in those possessing the real 'Golden Lilies'" ([1888] 1968: 110–11). The flower basin plat-form shoes, as depicted in Sun Wenliang (1990: 291), correspond to the "boat shoe," with keel-shaped soles, referred to in Elliott (2001: 247–49). Shoberl reports (from an unidentified source) that Chinese called these platforms "in derision, *Tartar junks*, on account of their resemblance to the ordinary vessels of the country" (1823, vol. 38: 119). The most extreme heights were found in horse-hoof-style shoes, in which Empress Dowager Cixi was often pictured (Sun Wenliang 1990: 55–56). Several sources state that low-ranking bannerwomen ordinarily wore flats or low platforms, and high-fashion tall platforms were reserved for formal dress occasions and elite women (Zhou 2005: 98; Zhang Jiasheng 1999: 529; Jin 1989: 28; Han and Lin 1990: 70; Ding 1999: 14).

6   Levy 1967: 65–68; Garrett 1994: 60–61; Ko 1997: 19; Mann 1997: 27; Jackson 1997: 49; Harrison 2000: 73; Elliott 2001: 247; Wang Ping 2002: 36; Mann 2002: 437.

7   Scott 1958: 30.

8   Scott notes that the horse-hoof-style high platforms "induced a short tripping step which was the mark of the refined woman in old China" (1958: 30). See Scott (1958: 23) for a drawing showing the two styles of platform shoes.

9   See the examples in Putnam Weale (1904: 184), Bryan (1907: 103, 139), Boyd (1908: 79), Lucas (1990: 224), Fu Yuguang (2008: 3, 20, 186), and Cody and Terpak (2011: plate 54).

10   Der Ling 1914: 22; Garrett 1994: 59, Jackson 1997: 150; Arthur M. Sackler Gallery 2011. Carl explains how Cixi sat for a portrait: "Although not more than five feet tall, as she wears the Manchu shoes with six-inch-high stilt-like soles, to avoid throwing the knees up higher than the lap she must sit upon cushions" (1906: 9). Princess Der Ling describes the palace workshop maintained by the empress to craft her shoes (1933: 172–79).

11   See Chapin 1910: 924, 926; Holmes 1914: 184–85; Perckhammer 1928: 4; Hu Piyun 1995: 41; Okinawa Soba 2013; Gao 2007: 34; Fu Yuguang 2008: 186; Sidney D. Gamble Photographs, *Manchu Woman — Walking*, roll no. 226: Peking, 1267; *Devil Dance — Manchu Woman*, roll no. 67B: Peking Lama Temple, 728. Photographs of elite women standing in floor-length dresses that cover both feet and shoes were conforming to conventions of formal portraiture, not trying to hide natural feet or create an "illusion of smallness" (see, e.g., Conger 1909: 294, 348). Qing painters doing formal portraits of women followed long-held conventions that at most showed shoes peeking out from beneath long robes; these conventions did not apply to erotic paintings that displayed the bound feet of Han women in seductive poses (cf. Cahill 2010, 2013). Two unusual pre-twentieth-century Chinese paintings showing the shoes and feet of women in Manchu costume have been located. One is the portrait (of uncertain provenance) showing a woman on horseback with her feet in stirrups, reproduced in Jiang (1992: 10). The second is an erotic painting showing a woman standing in a long Manchu robe and flower basin shoes that dates from the mid-nineteenth century (see Bertholet 2011: 178). Late nineteenth-century photography appears to have opened the way to representation of women's feet in non-erotic contexts. I thank Jan Stewart for her helpful suggestions regarding these issues. Portrayal of women in Manchu shoes and costume in the Beijing opera dates only from the twentieth century. In the theater, costumes of different periods were mixed with no regard for historical accuracy; thus the role of the Song-period Mongol princess in the opera *Silang Visits His Mother* (Si Lang tan mu) was played wearing Manchu styles (Scott 1959: 24, 35, 72).

12   Scott 1958: 30; Han and Lin 1990: 70, Dudgeon 1869: 95; *Manzu minjian gushi xuan* 1983: 234.

13   Vollmer 1977: 27.

14   *Qicai shen huo* 1984: 99–100; *Manzu minjian gushi xuan* 1981–83, vol. 1: 184; Manzu minjian gushi xuan 1983: 234; a condensed English translation is at The Origins of Manchu Chopine (2013). All three Chinese versions are based on the story as recounted for folklore researchers by one Fu Delian, of Aihui (Aigun) District, Heilongjiang, which is the site of a Manchu ethnic village and the residence of a few remaining native Manchu speakers.

15   Platform shoes appear to have been common among Northeast Asian peoples, and the centrally placed Manchu platform sole bears a resemblance to Korean and Japanese clogs. Korean clogs (*mokgeuk* or *namaksin*), with centrally placed platform "heels," are

shown in Lee, Hong, and Chang (2005: 153, 175–78). The single-toothed Japanese *geta* and the *okobo* style worn by apprentice geisha (*maiko*), although different in their use of thong uppers, also resemble the Manchu sole. The suggestion that Manchu platform shoes took inspiration from Italian Renaissance chopines seems highly fanciful (Ko 2004: 70–71). Reflecting the footbinding perspective, Wadley in his rendition of the bannerman tale of "Suoluoyan guards the pass" mistranslates a reference to palace shoes with "three inch soles" (*san cun di*) as "less than three *cun* long" (1991: 88–89). Hidehiro Okada gives the correct translation as "three-inch-high-soled shoes" (1993: 172). Manchu *tahan* is defined as "clog," "wooden shoe," "wooden sole," and "horseshoe" in Norman (1978: 269).

16   Yang Xichun 1988: 133–34; Zhou 2005: 96–97.

17   Zhou 2005: 92–93, 97; e.g., Sun Wenliang 1990: 405.

18   Staunton 1798, vol. 2: 296; see also Davis 1836, vol. 1: 255. *Tartar* is commonly used in pre-twentieth-century Western writing on China to refer to Manchus.

19   Alexander and Mason 1988: 223. The portrait is labeled as that of a Tartar lady.

20   Hosie 1910: 24–25.

21   *Illustrated Catalogue of the Chinese Collection of Exhibits for the International Health Exhibition, London* 1884: 13–14.

22   Wang and Fu 1991: 14.

23   See photos in Chapin (1910: 924, 926), Holmes (1914: 184), Perckhammer (1928: 4), Okinawa Soba (2013), and Gao (2007: 34).

24   Zhou 2005: 84, 98; Fu-ge [1860] 1984: 160, "qing ju da bai"; Xu Ke [1928] 1966, vol. 46: sec. 91, *fushi*: 105–6; Chou 2009.

25   Anonymous 1835: 538. On the gait of the bound-footed, see Levy (1967: 52–53), Jackson (1997: 119), and Fairbank and Goldman (1998: 173). Ko notes the importance of shoe style to gait and the difference in gait produced by the level platform shoe and the high-heeled shoes sometimes worn by the bound-footed (2001: 60, 104; 2004: 70). Li Yu (1610–1680) and Yuan Mei (1716–1797) both warned that binding that created overly small feet came at the expense of gracefulness in carriage. For Li Yu's comments, see Eberhard (1971: 286–88), Du (2010: 139), and Chang and Chang (1998a: 70). For Yuan Mei's comments, see Levy (1967: 69), Jia (1929: 25), and Schmidt (2008).

26   Fielde 1887: 29.

27   Davis 1836, vol. 1: 256.

28   When walking on natural feet in platform shoes, the leading leg swings forward, and the trailing leg pushes off with the forefoot to propel the body forward. The bound-footed woman clomping along on her heels achieves forward motion by using thigh muscle to lift the leading leg to plant the bound foot heel first, then repeats the same motion with the trailing leg.

29   Chou 2009.

30   Barrow 1805: 66; see also Shoberl 1823, vol. 38: 118–21.

31   Wang Shuo 2006: 107.

32   Lattimore 1932b: 269–70.

33   Hedley 1910: 49, 89.

34   Ding 2004: 276.

35 Lockhart 1864: 473–74.

36 Fu-ge [1860] 1984: 156; Elliott 2001: 247. In the nineteenth century, the inner city still had a large banner and a small civilian population (see Naquin 2000: 376, 383). John Ross (1908: 215–16) considered footbinding to have maintained its preeminence in the outer or Chinese city, in contrast to the situation in Mukden, described below.

37 Dudgeon 1869: 95. Arthur H. Smith ([1899] 1970: 199) and the *Illustrated Catalogue of the Chinese Collection of Exhibits for the International Health Exhibition, London* (1884: 15) also noted the Manchu influence on footbinding in Beijing.

38 Xia 2004: 128; *Beijing nübao*, no. 218 (April 3, 1906): 2; Zhou 2005: 97. For more on the appellation *manzi*, see the discussion by H. E. M. James ([1888] 1968) below.

39 The Beijing report is found in *Neizheng gongbao* (1929, vol. 2.1 [January]); by 1928, Beijing had lost its status as the national capital and is more correctly referred to as "Beiping." The 1928 surveys were conducted by the Beijing city police (*gong'an ju*). The Beijing police were one of the most professional police forces in China during this period, benefiting from a police academy, a high ratio of police to population, and, after 1927, a budget supported by dedicated tax revenues (Gamble 1921: 75–80, 85; Duncan 1933: 2–8, 41–42; Strand 1989: 69–72, 95–96; Reynolds 1993: 171–72). In addition to usual policing functions, the police were charged with the maintenance of household registers and censuses (Gamble 1921: 91–94; Duncan 1933: 37–38). Strand notes reports of several police censuses of Beijing taken in the 1920s that preceded the 1928 report (1989: 297n37).

40 Gamble 1921: 56. Rapid population growth through immigration would have disrupted the ethnic composition, but Beijing's population saw little growth in the early decades of the twentieth century. The reported population in 1910 was 1,128,808; in 1922, 1,133,541; in 1928, 1,287,516; and in 1929, 1,329,602 (Han Guanghui 1996: 128; Strand 1989: 297n37; *Neizheng gongbao* 1929, vol. 2.1). Elliott (2001: 98ff.) provides historical background on the residential segregation of banner and Han civilian populations in Beijing.

41 There were additional concentrations of banner populations in the Hebei area outside of Beijing. Four Manchu autonomous counties having majority Manchu populations lie within the boundaries of modern Hebei Province (*Zhongguo minzu renkou ziliao* 1994: 203–4, 558–59). Many of those claiming "Manchu" identity today are the descendants of banner populations, which included Hanjun as well as Manchus. The territories of three of these counties (Fengning, Weichang, and Kuancheng [created in 1962]) in 1928 were in Jehol (Rehe) Province, for which no 1928 population and footbinding survey is available. The fourth Manchu autonomous county in modern Hebei, Qinglong, was created from Hebei's Qian'an County, along with parts of Funing and Linyu Counties in 1933. In the 1928 population survey of Hebei, only 857 of 338,741 women in Qian'an County are recorded as having bound feet (*Neizheng gongbao* 1929, vol. 2.7). The near absence of binding in Qian'an confirms the strong banner cultural influence in banner-dominated localities.

42 That women under age thirty constituted a lower proportion of Beijing's population (47.3%) than in the Ding County sample (59.4%) reinforces this conclusion. The 1917 police census of Beijing, which reports the population by age and sex, covered the

population in the inner and outer cities of Beijing but not the suburbs (Gamble 1921: 416). In the larger Ding County sample of 5,255 families (14,862 women), 56.4% of women were under thirty (Li Jinghan 1933: table 23). In the sample from the rural villages A and C (in Wanping County), in the vicinity of Beijing (839 women), 52.1% were under thirty (Gamble 1963: 321).

43 Manchu cultural influence in Beijing is not contradicted by the court's patronage of painters using Han women as standards of beauty (see Shan 1995: 58; Wu Hong 1997).

44 Levy 1967: 65–69; Mann 1997: 26–27; Wang Ping 2002: 33–36; Ko 1997; 2005: 266.

45 Michie 1863: 165.

46 Williamson 1870, vol. 2: 59–60. Williamson uses the contemptuous "celestials" to refer to the Chinese civilian population.

47 James [1888] 1968: 123–24.

48 The 1908 census of Fengtian, the southernmost of Manchuria's three provinces, records a population over 10 million, of which 75% was civilian Chinese (including recent immigrants) and 24% banner (4.7% Manchu, 1.6% Mongol, and 17.8% Han bannermen) (Enatsu 2004: 16). It is likely that similar proportions of the smaller populations of Jilin (5 million) and Heilongjiang (2 million) were banner (Wynne 1958: 17).

49 Enatsu 2004: 34–35, 39, 45. Shao Dan points out the absence of a native Han civilian gentry or literati elite in the northeast that might have competed for status with the banner elite (2011: 36).

50 Putnam Weale 1904: 271–72. For a photo of Manchu women wearing platform shoes in Manchuria, see Putnam Weale (1904: 184).

51 Multiple sources confirm the predominance of footbinding in Hebei and Shandong. See Qian Yong's early nineteenth-century observations in Ko (2005: 139–40); also Gamble (1943: 181–83), Johnston ([1910] 1977: 195), Atwell (1985: 76, 147, 265), M. Yang (1945: 63), Smith ([1899] 1970: 198–99), Fairbank and Goldman (1998: 173), M. Cohen (2005: 94–95), Levy (1967: 228–30), Turner (1997), and *Neizheng gongbao* (1929, vol. 2.7 [Hebei]). Women in the rural districts of Shandong's provincial capital, Jinan city (83,814 women) were 55.9% bound in 1928; David Buck considers police registration in Jinan to have produced relatively reliable census figures (*Neizheng gongbao* 1930, vol. 3.3; D. Buck 1978: 148, 227). Bossen and Gates's interview samples provide additional evidence of high rates of binding throughout North China (2017: 53, 75).

52 Christie 1914: 13–14.

53 J. Ross 1908: 216.

54 Xu Ke [1914] 1989: 369.

55 Ding 1999: 136, 143.

56 Ding 1999: 149, 102.

57 Shao 2011: 30–35. Shao also notes that the policy of expelling the Hanjun from the banners in China proper was not applied to banners in the northeast, where Hanjun constituted a preponderance of the banner population. Elliott discusses the policy of expulsion (2001: 337–41). The pattern of mixed communities of bannermen and civilians is also noted in Isett (2007: 58–59, 111–13).

58 Ping-ti Ho (1959: 76) suggests that due to the efforts of Xu Shichang, the census machinery in Fengtian alone of all the provinces in 1908–11 was capable of generating accurate

population data (see also Enatsu 2004: 85–88). The numbers of police stationed in each county circa 1908 are reported in *Manshū shi sōkō* ([1911] 2000, vol. 5: 44–48).

59 Suleski 2002: 37–38, 210–13.

60 Suleski 2002: 84, 241n6; Wang Jiajian 1984: 92–94, 248. The large numbers of police and *baojia* personnel stationed in each county in 1928 are reported in *Fengtian tongzhi* (1983, vol. 3: 3280–85 [*juan* 153 and 154]).

61 Lin Qiumin 1990: 118; *Neizheng gongbao* 1929, vol. 3.1.

62 The banner population is reported by county in the Fengtian volumes (1–4) of *Manshū chihōshi: Sōkō* (1912). Ding Yizhuang documents the history of the banner garrisons in the northeast (2002: 60ff.).

63 The reported population of Fengtian totaled 10,238,309 in 1908 and had grown to 14,807,354 in 1928 (Enatsu 2004: 16; *Neizheng gongbao* 1929, vol. 3.1).

64 James Reardon-Anderson reviews the history of settlement in the late seventeenth and eighteenth centuries in the Liao plain; lands were overwhelmingly allocated to banner garrisons and official estates, but reclaimed for agriculture primarily by Chinese migrant tenants and workers (2005: 37–41; Isett 2007). Liaoning's northwest finger of counties lies outside the core in what was originally Mongol territory; this hilly country remained sparsely settled until the twentieth century (Reardon-Anderson 2005: 41–45, 80–81).

65 Reardon-Anderson 2005: 75–77, 79–81; Young 1928: 297–98. Gottschang and Lary (2000) document the flows of immigrants into Manchuria from Shandong. As mentioned, Shandong's reputation is of a province having very high rates of footbinding, and in these decades very few of the immigrant women would have been affected by the anti-footbinding trends centered in the cities. Bossen and Gates document a very late beginning for declines in footbinding in rural Shandong (2017: 75).

66 Today these counties lie over the border from Liaoning in Jilin Province.

67 Both Xiuyan and Xingcheng (formerly Ningyuan) Counties were initially settled in the eighteenth century (Reardon-Anderson 2005: 38–39). Whether the pattern of binding had persisted since the initial settlement or was a result of a recent influx of footbinding immigrants remains uncertain. My reading on the histories of the two counties has yet to produce any suggestive possibilities (see *Manzu shehui lishi diaocha* [1985], on Xingcheng; Zhang Qizhuo [1984], on Xiuyan). The proportions banner in the 1908 populations of Xiuyan and Xingcheng closely match the proportions reported in the Japanese census of Manchuria in 1940 under the category "Manzhou qiren" (Xiuyan, 25.3%; Xingcheng 21.9%) (*Wei Manzhouguo zhengfu gongbao* 1990, vol. 91 [2439: 56; 2483: 400]).

68 Rhoads 2000: 52–63.

69 Lattimore 1932b: 269.

70 Lattimore 1934: 85–86.

71 E. Sun 1952: 202–6, 209.

72 Lattimore 1932a: 296.

73 Hedley's comments confirm the cultural antagonism between Chinese and Mongols (1910: 26–28, 33).

74 Yunnan Province in China's far southwest presents a wide range of contact situations between various non-Han indigenous and immigrant Han populations. In situations where Han obtained dominant positions, prestige hierarchies favoring binding emerged, and both Han families seeking to display refinement and non-Han elites seeking to assert a status equal to Han are reported adopting the binding fashion (Yang Xingmei 1998: 120–22; Bossen 2002: chap. 3). In other situations, indigenous elites remained dominant, and footbinding made no headway in indigenous communities (Giersch 2006: 205). The demographic, economic, and cultural reasons Taiwan's plains aborigines rejected footbinding, despite their adoption of much of Hoklo culture, are discussed in chapter 2. Brown has studied the interesting case of the Tujia, a highly Sinicized population in southwestern Hubei, who considered themselves Han until they were classified as a non-Han minority by the People's Republic. This was an area that experienced, over centuries, successive waves of Han immigration. Intermarriage with the local population followed, and by the nineteenth century, if not before, the local population was regarded as a local variety of Han (Brown 2004: 166). Brown found that footbinding had been adopted among the Tujia as "a sign of wealth and class, not ethnic identity." Better-off Tujia bound daughters' feet more severely, while commoner women made do with cucumber feet (Brown 2004: 177). None of these examples where two ethnic groups come into contact show enhancement of the footbinding fashion for the sake of heightening ethnic differences.

75 Scott 1958: 30, 47.

76 Little 1908: 282–83. The Manchu fashion is also mentioned in Ball (1925: 197).

77 Yao 1938. The caption reads: "Chaozhou style bride's bowed shoe" (*Chaozhou shi xinfu gongxie*).

78 Levy 1967: 67; Rowe 2009: 109.

79 Qing historical studies of the banners have emphasized the garrison populations in China proper and paid too little attention to the sizable banner populations in the northeast. Shao Dan (2011) helps correct this neglect.

80 Barth 1969: 9–38.

81 For examples of work that stresses contextual factors, see Banton (1983) and Patterson (1975: 305–49). Banton's chapters 6 and 7 make important analytic distinctions between group- and individual-based competition and hard and soft boundaries as factors determining whether "boundary maintenance" does or does not become salient in the interaction of ethnic groups. The sociolinguist Peter Trudgill also argues against axiomatic assumptions that concerns to mark identities motivate linguistic diffusion and dialect changes (2010: 186–92).

CONCLUSION: THE TYRANNY OF FASHION

1 For Qing literati critiques, see Ropp (1981: chap. 4) and Lin Yutang ([1935] 1992).

2 Brown et al. 2012: 1044. It has become fashionable to disparage a venerable and pathbreaking work on footbinding, Levy's 1967 *Chinese Footbinding: The History of a Curious Erotic Custom* (reissued in 1991 as *The Lotus Lovers: The Complete History of the*

Curious Erotic Custom of Footbinding in China). There is no denying Levy's interest in sexual practices in East Asian cultures, as a glance at the titles of his many books demonstrates. Nor did he hesitate to adopt suggestive titles as a marketing ploy. Readers who bought his footbinding book looking for prurient material were likely disappointed. Levy's work on footbinding is a rich compendium of information about the practice of footbinding in all its dimensions, including discussions sociological, ethnographic, and historical, as well as translations of Chinese literary sources, many drawn from Yao Lingxi's *Gathered Fragrances* collection. The multidimensional nature of Levy's approach to footbinding cannot be reduced and dismissed as one interested only (or even primarily) in sex. Only the second of three parts of the book is primarily concerned with the bedroom arts and is in many ways less explicit than Gates's (2008) scholarly article debunking the erotic attraction of bound feet for the masses of Chinese. In the third part of the book, Levy introduces ethnographic interviews he himself conducted in Taiwan in the early 1960s (none of which touch on sex). Ko's dismissive description of Levy's book as "fragmentary" and a "thinly veiled disguise of his fascination and longing" could equally apply to her own "rhetoric of disavowal" in her *Cinderella's Sisters* (2005: 231, xi).

3   Brown et al. 2012: 1044; Levy 1967: 274, 283, 284, and passim.

4   Gates 2015: 30, 36, 43, 46. Note that the insults hurled at the feet of women have to do with status ("slave-girl") and lack of beauty ("flat-foot") and not with skill in handicrafts or with diligence and laziness.

5   Gates 2008.

6   Ko (2005: 13) attempts to discount the reports of these women by erroneously claiming they explained the custom by calling it "feudal," using the Marxist term *fengjian* introduced by the Communists many years after the events they relate. In fact, it was not the women but an elderly man who, in a separate interview, used the term in reference to binding. The women were relating their personal experiences. Interviews, like texts produced by literati, must be contextualized, but that does not make them any less authentic or worthy of respect.

7   On the late nineteenth century, see, e.g., Macgowan (1913), Little (1908), Fielde (1887), and Mackay (1895). On the early twentieth, see *SPCF 1905* (1909); popular anti-footbinding literature (e.g., as reviewed by C. Tao [1994]); Pruitt ([1945] 1967); and Gamble (1943). On the late twentieth, see Levy (1967), Hinton and Gordon (1987), Brown et al. (2012), Gates (2015), and Bossen and Gates (2017).

8   Ko 2005: 128, 131; Ebrey 1993: 40.

9   Ko 2001: 54, 63–67, 69–72.

10 Ko 2001: 45, 52. No source citations accompany these claims.

11 Ko 2005: 59–68.

12 Fielde 1887: 101.

13 The situation confronted by plains aborigines in Taiwan (discussed in chapter 2) most resembles that of the poorest strata in the schematic, accompanied by the added impetus to reject binding coming from a non-Han cultural tradition valuing women's labor contribution.

14 Ko (2005: chap. 7, figs. 1–22) documents frequent changes in a variety of shoe styles and in particular the decreasing size of the bound foot and the introduction of the bulged arch and high heels in the sixteenth century (2005: 189, 191). Ko also identifies a variety of regional styles (2001: 110–28). Elvin refers to the spread of the "custom of competitive women's fashions" in the seventeenth century (1999: 152).

15 Fear of ridicule for not binding appears to have emerged among elites early in the process; see the comments (cited in the Introduction) from the fourteenth century by Tao Zongyi on shaming non-binders and the sixteenth-century comment of Hu Yinglin that people made fun of non-binders (Ebrey 1993: 40; Ko 2005: 128; Hu Yinglin 1964: 147; Tao Zongyi 1936: 158).

16 E. Ross 1914: 175; Turner 1997: 449; Doolittle 1865, vol. 2: 201; Ko 2005: 20–22, 131–32; Finnane 1998: 677–78.

17 Ko (2005: 20–22, 131–32) found claims of an urban-rural divide in Suzhou, but Fortune (1847: 246–57) observed small-footed women working in the nearby cotton fields (cf. Huang 1990: 56, 51–52).

18 Sources discussing footbinding in Guangdong include E. Ross (1914: 175), Yung (1995: 16, 22–24, 41), Zhang Qu ([1738] 1990: 52), and Faure (2007: 246).

19 See Turner (1997) and Ko (2005: 131, 139) on higher rates of binding in cities and among elites in the south.

20 Zhang Qu [1738] 1990: 52. The number of *jinshi* produced in Guangdong during the Song was less than a tenth of the number produced in Fujian (Chaffee 1985: 132–33), and Guangdong continued to lag in the Ming (P. Ho 1962: 229). The relatively shallow history of literati culture may help account for the footbinding fashion's failure to penetrate the working classes in Guangdong.

21 Several good treatments of the anti-footbinding movement, and the arguments it lodged against binding, can be found in Drucker (1981), C. Tao (1994), Lin Qiumin (1990), and F. Hong (1997).

22 Drucker 1981: 198–99.

23 In an interesting reversal from the days when women used special shoes to make cucumber feet look smaller, girls with bound feet feigned natural feet by wearing larger shoes in order to gain admission to schools open only to the natural-footed (Broadwin 1997: 434).

24 C. Tao 1994: 171.

25 Qian [ca. 1838] 1979: 630; Ko 2005: 141.

26 F. Hong 1997: 64.

27 E. Ross 1914: 181. In an analogous case, hockey players, fearing the ridicule of teammates and opponents directed at those who wore helmets, needed a rule-making authority to make them mandatory. Evidence that helmets would reduce serious injury was not enough to cause their voluntary adoption (Schelling 1978: 213–14).

28 *Guangxu chao shangyu dang* 1996, vol. 27: 272, No. 960; *Dezong shilu* 1985: 504–5 (*juan* 492, Guangxu 27.12 *yimao*).

29 C. Tao 1994: 170–71. Among these officials was Yuan Shikai, governor-general of Zhili (Hebei).

30 Zhang Ruohua 2014: 180, 187; Mallory 1926: 186.

31 These regulations were modeled on those devised by the reformist warlord Yan Xishan in his earlier campaigns against footbinding in Shanxi (see Lin Qiumin 1995; Ko 2005: 50ff; Gillin 1967).

32 Lin Qiumin 1990: 117–18; Yang Xingmei 1998: 114.

33 MacKinnon 2002: 166.

34 Strong 1935: 117.

35 F. Hong documents a 1939 prohibition in Shan-Gan-Ning that threatened parents with prison if they bound daughters' feet (1997: 197).

36 Johnson 1983: 70–71; Davin 1976: 205–6.

References

ABBREVIATIONS

Hebei 1928   *Hebei sheng shengzheng tongji gaiyao, Minguo shiqi niandu*
SPCF 1905   *The Special Population Census of Formosa, 1905*
TW   Taiwan Wenxian Congkan

TAIWAN CENSUS MATERIALS

Census of 1905, Kekka hyō. 1908. *Rinji Taiwan kokō chōsa, kekka hyō, Meiji 38-nen* (Results of the Taiwan provisional household census, 1905). Taiwan Sōtokufu Sōtoku Kambō, Rinji Taiwan Kokō Chōsabu.

Census of 1905, Shūkei gempyō, chihō no bu. 1907. *Rinji Taiwan kokō chōsa, shūkei gempyō, chihō no bu, Meiji 38-nen* (Detailed tables, by prefecture, Taiwan provisional household census, 1905). Taiwan Sōtokufu Sōtoku Kambō, Rinji Taiwan Kokō Chōsabu.

Census of 1905, Shūkei gempyō, zentō no bu. 1907. *Rinji Taiwan kokō chōsa, shūkei gempyō, zentō no bu, Meiji 38-nen* (Detailed tables, total island, Taiwan provisional household census, 1905). Taiwan Sōtokufu Sōtoku Kambō, Rinji Taiwan Kokō Chōsabu.

Census of 1915, Gairan hyō. 1917. *Dai-niji rinji Taiwan kokō chōsa gairan hyō, Taishō yo'nen* (Summary tables by locality, second provisional household census, 1915). Taiwan Sōtokufu Sōtoku Kambō, Rinji Taiwan Kokō Chōsabu.

Census of 1915, Kekka hyō. 1918. *Dai-niji rinji Taiwan kokō chōsa kekka hyō, Taishō yo'nen* (Results of second provisional household census, 1915). Taiwan Sōtokufu Sōtoku Kambō, Rinji Taiwan Kokō Chōsabu.

Census of 1915, Kijutsu hōbun. 1918. *Dai-niji rinji Taiwan kokō chōsa kijutsu hōbun, Taishō yo'nen* (Descriptive report, second provisional household census, 1915). Taiwan Sōtokufu Sōtoku Kambō, Rinji Taiwan Kokō Chōsabu.

Census of 1915, Shūkei gempyō, zentō no bu. 1917. *Dai-niji rinji Taiwan kokō chōsa shūkei gempyō, zentō no bu, Taishō yo'nen* (Detailed tables, total island, second provisional household census, 1915). Taiwan Sōtokufu Sōtoku Kambō, Rinji Taiwan Kokō Chōsabu.

Census of 1920, Shūkei gempyō, zentō no bu. 1923. *Dai-ikkai Taiwan kokusei chōsa, shūkei gempyō, zentō no bu, Taishō ku'nen* (First census of Taiwan, detailed tables, entire island, 1920). Taiwan Sōtokufu Sōtoku Kambō, Rinji Kokusei Chōsabu.

Census of 1920, Yōran hyō. 1922. *Dai-ikkai Taiwan kokusei chōsa, yōran hyō* (First census of Taiwan, summary tables by locality, 1920). Taiwan Sōtokufu Sōtoku Kambō, Rinji Kokusei Chōsabu.

Taiwan jinkō dōtai tōkei (Vital statistics of Taiwan, 1905–42). 1906–43. Sōtoku Kambō, Chōsaka.

OTHER SOURCES

Alexander, William, and George Henry Mason. 1988. *Views of 18th Century China: Costumes, History, Customs*. London: Studio Editions; New York: Portland House.

Ament, Rev. William S. 1899. "Strange People in the Mountains of Chihli." *Chinese Recorder* 30.7: 317–28.

Anonymous. 1835. "Small Feet of the Chinese Females: Remarks on the Origin of the Custom of Compressing the Feet; The Extent and Effects of the Practice; With an Anatomical Description of a Small Foot." *Chinese Repository* 3.12: 537–42.

Arthur M. Sackler Gallery. 2011. *Power/Play: China's Empress Dowager*. Special exhibit, Smithsonian Institution, Washington, DC, September 24, 2011–January 29, 2012. Accessed January 13, 2018. http://asia.si.edu/explore/china/powerplay/.

Atwell, Pamela. 1985. *British Mandarins and Chinese Reformers: The British Administration of Weihaiwei (1898–1930) and the Territory's Return to Chinese Rule*. Oxford: Oxford University Press.

Ball, J. Dyer. 1925. *Things Chinese*. 5th ed. Shanghai: Kelly and Walsh.

Banton, Michael. 1983. *Racial and Ethnic Competition*. Cambridge: Cambridge University Press.

Barclay, George W. 1954. *Colonial Development and Population in Taiwan*. Princeton, NJ: Princeton University Press.

Barclay, Thomas. 1890. "The Aborigine Tribes of Formosa." In *Records of the General Conference of the Protestant Missionaries of China, Held at Shanghai, May 7–20, 1890*, 668–75. Shanghai: American Presbyterian Mission Press.

Barnett, Suzanne W. 1985. "Justus Doolittle at Foochow: Christian Values in the Treaty Ports." In *Christianity in China: Early Protestant Writings*, ed. Suzanne W. Barnett and John King Fairbank, 107–19, 195–98. Cambridge, MA: Harvard University Press.

Barrow, John. 1805. *Travels in China: Containing Descriptions, Observations, and Comparisons*. Philadelphia: W. F. M'Laughlin.

Barth, Fredrik. 1969. Introduction to *Ethnic Groups and Boundaries*, ed. Fredrik Barth, 9–38. Boston: Little, Brown.

Bax, Capt. Bonham Ward. 1875. *The Eastern Seas*. London: John Murray.

Beijing nübao (Beijing women's news). 1905–9. Beijing.

Bertholet, Ferdinand M. 2011. *Concubines and Courtesans: Women in Chinese Erotic Art*. Photographs by Michiel Elsevier Stokmans. Munich: Prestel.

Biggerstaff, Knight. 1939. "Some Notes on the Tung-hua lu and the Shih-lu." *Harvard Journal of Asiatic Studies* 4.2: 101–15.

Blake, C. Fred. 1981. *Ethnic Groups and Social Change in a Chinese Market Town*. Honolulu: University Press of Hawaii.

———. 1994. "Foot-Binding in Neo-Confucian China and the Appropriation of Female Labor." *Signs: Journal of Women in Culture and Society* 19.3: 676–712.

Bossen, Laurel. 2002. *Chinese Women and Rural Development: Sixty Years of Change in Lu Village, Yunnan.* New York: Rowman and Littlefield.

Bossen, Laurel, and Hill Gates. 2017. *Bound Feet, Young Hands: Tracking the Demise of Footbinding in Village China.* Stanford, CA: Stanford University Press.

Boyd, Robert H. 1908. *Manchuria, and Our Mission There.* Belfast: Strain and Sons.

Broadwin, Julie. 1997. "Walking Contradictions: Chinese Women Unbound at the Turn of the Century." *Journal of Historical Sociology* 10.4: 418–43.

Brook, Timothy. 1998. *The Confusions of Pleasure: Commerce and Culture in Ming China.* Berkeley: University of California Press.

Brown, Melissa. 2004. *Is Taiwan Chinese? The Impact of Culture, Power, and Migration on Changing Identities.* Berkeley: University of California Press.

Brown, Melissa, Laurel Bossen, Hill Gates, and Damian Satterthwaite-Phillips. 2012. "Marriage Mobility and Footbinding in Pre-1949 Rural China: A Reconsideration of Gender, Economics, and Meaning in Social Causation." *Journal of Asian Studies* 71.4: 1035–67.

Bryan, William Jennings. 1907. *The Old World and Its Ways.* St. Louis: Thompson.

Buck, David D. 1978. *Urban Change in China: Politics and Development in Tsinan, Shantung, 1890–1949.* Madison: University of Wisconsin Press.

Buck, John Lossing. 1937. *Land Utilization in China.* Shanghai: North China Daily News.

Buxton, L. H. Dudley. 1923. "Present Conditions in Inner Mongolia." *Geographical Journal* 61.6: 393–409.

Cahill, James. 2010. *Pictures for Use and Pleasure: Vernacular Painting in High Qing China.* Berkeley: University of California Press.

———. 2013. *Beauty Revealed: Images of Women in Qing Dynasty Chinese Painting.* Berkeley: University of California, Berkeley Art Museum and Pacific Film Archive.

Campbell, George. 1888. "The Hakka Mission." *Baptist Missionary Magazine* 68.5: 140–41.

Campbell, William. [1913] 1972. *A Dictionary of the Amoy Vernacular.* Tainan: Taiwan Jiaohui Gongbaoshe.

———. 1915. *Sketches from Formosa.* London: Marshall Brothers.

Carl, Katharine A. 1906. *With the Empress Dowager of China.* London: E. Nash.

Chaffee, John W. 1985. *The Thorny Gates of Learning in Sung China: A Social History of Examinations.* Cambridge: Cambridge University Press.

———. 2001. "The Impact of the Song Imperial Clan on the Overseas Trade of Quanzhou." In *The Emporium of the World: Maritime Quanzhou, 1000–1400*, ed. Angela Schottenhammer, 13–46. Leiden: Brill.

Chang, Chun-shu, and Shelley Hsueh-lun Chang. 1998a. *Crisis and Transformation in Seventeenth-Century China: Society, Culture, and Modernity in Li Yu's World.* Ann Arbor: University of Michigan Press.

———. 1998b. *Redefining History: Ghosts, Spirits, and Human Society in P'u Sung-ling's World, 1640–1715.* Ann Arbor: University of Michigan Press.

Chang, Han-yu, and Ramon H. Myers. 1963. "Japanese Colonial Development Policy in Taiwan, 1895–1906: A Case of Bureaucratic Entrepreneurship." *Journal of Asian Studies* 22.2: 443–49.

Chang, Kang-i Sun. 1991. *The Late-Ming Poet Ch'en Tzu-lung: Crises of Love and Loyalism.* New Haven, CT: Yale University Press.

———. 2006. "Qian Qianyi and His Place in History." In *Trauma and Transcendence in Early Qing Literature*, ed. Wilt L. Idema, Wai-yee Li, and Ellen Widmer, 199–218. Cambridge, MA: Harvard University Asia Center.

Chang, Kun. 1956. *A Regional Handbook on the Inner Mongolia Autonomous Region.* New Haven, CT: Human Relations Area Files.

Chang Lung-chih. 2003. "From Island Frontier to Imperial Colony: Qing and Japanese Sovereignty Debate and Territorial Projects in Taiwan, 1874–1906." Ph.D. dissertation, Harvard University.

Chang Mo-chun [Zhang Mojun]. 1992. "Opposition to Footbinding." In *Chinese Women through Chinese Eyes*, ed. Li Yu-ning, 125–28. Armonk, NY: M. E. Sharpe.

Chanzu zhi bihai ji jiuji (Footbinding, its harms and how to relieve them). 1915. Preface by Uchida Kakichi. Taipei: Nichinichi Shinpōsha.

Chao Kang. 1977. *The Development of Cotton Textile Production in China.* Cambridge, MA: East Asian Research Center, Harvard University.

Chapin, William W. 1910. "Glimpses of Korea and China." *National Geographic Magazine* 21.11: 895–934.

Ch'en Ch'ing-ch'ih. 1975. "The Japanese Adaptation of the *Pao-Chia* System in Taiwan, 1895–1945." *Journal of Asian Studies* 34.2: 391–416.

Chen Dongsheng. 2015. *Haixia liang'an de Kejia fushi wenhua yu yishu* (The art and culture of Hakka dress on both sides of the Taiwan straits). Beijing: Zhongguo Shehuixue Chubanshe.

Chen Dongyuan. [1937] 1984. *Zhongguo funü shenghuo shi* (History of Chinese women). Shanghai: Shanghai Shudian.

Chen Han-seng. 1936. *Landlord and Peasant in China.* New York: International Publishers.

Chen Shengxi. 1985. "Qingchu tifa ling de shishi yu hanzu dizhu jieji de paixi douzheng" (The implementation of the tonsure command in the early Qing and factional conflict within the Han landlord class). *Lishi yanjiu* 4:67–77.

Chen Shu-juo. 2008. "How Han Are Taiwanese Han? Genetic Inference of Plains Indigenous Ancestry among Taiwanese Han and Its Implications for Taiwan Identity." Ph.D. dissertation. Stanford University.

Chou, Shengfang. 2009. "Manchu Horse-Hoof Shoes: Footwear and Cultural Identity." *V&A Online Journal* (Victoria and Albert Museum) 2 (Autumn). Accessed May 2, 2012. www.vam.ac.uk/content/journals/research-journal/issue-02/manchu-horse -hoof-shoes-footwear-and-cultural-identity/.

Chow, a Chu-jen. 1896. "Appeal to the People, Posted on the Walls of Sui-fu and Signed by a Chu-jen and Five Literati." ["Suifu Appeal"]. *Chinese Recorder* 27 (November): 584–87.

Christie, Dugald. 1914. *Thirty Years in Moukden, 1883–1913, Being the Experiences and Recollections of Dugald Christie, C.M.G.* London: Constable.

Chu, T. S., and T. Chin. 1929. *Marketing of Cotton in Hebei Province.* Beijing: Institute of Social Research.

Chuang Ying-chang. 1994. *Jiazu yu hunyin: Taiwan beibu liangge Min Ke cunluo zhi yanjiu* (Family and marriage: Hokkien and Hakka villages in North Taiwan). Taipei: Institute of Ethnology, Academia Sinica.

Chuang Ying-chang and Arthur P. Wolf. 1995. "Marriage in Taiwan, 1881–1905: An Example of Regional Diversity." *Journal of Asian Studies* 54.3: 781–95.

Clark, Hugh R. 1991. *Community, Trade, and Networks: Southern Fujian Province from the Third to the Thirteenth Century*. Cambridge: Cambridge University Press.

———. 2001. "Overseas Trade and Social Change in Quanzhou through the Song." In *The Emporium of the World: Maritime Quanzhou, 1000–1400*, ed. Angela Schottenhammer, 47–94. Leiden: Brill.

Clunas, Craig. 1991. *Superfluous Things: Material Culture and Social Status in Early Modern China*. Urbana: University of Illinois Press.

Cody, Jeffrey W., and Frances Terpak. 2011. *Brush and Shutter: Early Photography in China*. Los Angeles: Getty Research Institute.

Cohen, Myron L. 1976. *House United, House Divided: The Chinese Family in Taiwan*. New York: Columbia University Press.

———. 2005. *Kinship, Contract, Community, and State: Anthropological Perspectives on China*. Stanford, CA: Stanford University Press.

Cohen, Paul A. 1997. *History in Three Keys: The Boxers as Event, Experience, and Myth*. New York: Columbia University Press.

Collingwood, Dr. Cuthbert. 1868. "Visit to the Kibalan Village of Sano Bay, North-East Coast of Formosa." *Transactions of the Ethnological Society of London*, n.s., 6:135–43.

Conger, Sarah Pike. 1909. *Letters from China, with Particular Reference to the Empress Dowager and the Women of China*. Chicago: A. C. McClurg.

Constable, Nicole. 2000. "Ethnicity and Gender in Hakka Studies." In *Juluo, zongzu yu zuqun guanxi, disijie guoji kejiaxue yantaohui lunwenji* (Community, lineage, and ethnic relations: Proceedings of the International Conference on Hakkology), ed. Hsu Cheng-kuang, 365–96. Nankang, Taipei: Institute of Ethnology, Academia Sinica.

Cressey, George B. 1932. "Chinese Colonization in Mongolia: A General Survey." In *Pioneer Settlement: Cooperative Studies*, ed. W. L. G. Joerg, 273–87. Special Publication no. 14. New York: American Geographical Society.

Crossley, Pamela Kyle. 1999. *A Translucent Mirror: History and Identity in Qing Imperial Ideology*. Berkeley: University of California Press.

Customs Trade Reports. 1866–1920. [Annual, title varies: *Returns of Trade and Trade Reports* (Hai kuan tsung shui wu ssu shu)]. Shanghai: Statistical Department of the Inspectorate-General of Customs.

Dajia zhenzhi (Dajia Township gazetteer). 2009. Ed. Liao Ruiming. Taizhong County: Dajia zhen gongsuo.

Danshui tingzhi (Gazetteer of Danshui Subprefecture). 1870. Ed. Chen Peigui. TW 172.

Davidson, James W. 1903. *The Island of Formosa: Historical View from 1430 to 1900*. New York: Macmillan.

Davin, Delia. 1976. *Woman-Work: Women and the Party in Revolutionary China*. Oxford, UK: Clarendon Press.

Davis, John Francis. 1836. *The Chinese: A General Description of the Empire of China and Its Inhabitants*. 2 vols. New York: Harper and Brothers.

DeGlopper, Donald R. 1995. *Lukang: Commerce and Community in a Chinese City*. Albany: State University of New York Press.

Der Ling, Princess. 1914. *Two Years in the Forbidden City*. New York: Moffat, Yard.

———. 1933. *Imperial Incense*. New York: Dodd, Mead.

Dezong shilu (Veritable Records of Emperor Dezong). 1985. In *Qing shilu* (Veritable Records of the Qing), vol. 58, *Dezong Jing huangdi shilu* (Veritable Records of Emperor Dezong Jing [Guangxu reign]). Beijing: Zhonghua Shuju.

Ding Yizhuang. 1999. *Zuihou de jiyi: Shiliuwei qiren funü di koushu lishi* (Last memories: Oral histories of sixteen bannerwomen). Beijing: Zhongguo Guangbo Chubanshe.

———. 2002. *Qingdai baqi zhufang yanjiu* (Researches on the Qing Eight Banner garrisons). Shenyang: Liaoning Minzu Chubanshe.

———. 2004. *Liaodong yiminzhong de qiren shehui: Lishi wenxian, renkou tongji yu tianye diaocha* (Immigration and Eight Banner society in Liaodong: Historical documents, population data, and field surveys). Shanghai: Shanghai Shehui Kexueyuan Chubanshe.

Donghua lu (Records from within the Eastern Gate). 1968. Comp. Jiang Liangqi and Wang Xianqian. *Shierchao donghua lu* (Records of twelve reigns from within the Eastern Gate). 30 vols. Tainan: Dadong Shuju.

Doolittle, Rev. Justus. 1865. *Social Life of the Chinese*. 2 vols. New York: Harper and Brothers.

Douglas, Carstairs. [1873] 1970. *Chinese-English Dictionary of the Vernacular or Spoken Language of Amoy*. London: Trubner. Reprint, Taipei: Guting Bookstore.

Drucker, Alison. 1981. "The Influence of Western Women on the Anti-Footbinding Movement, 1840–1911." *Historical Reflections* 8.3: 179–99.

Du Shuying. 2010. *Ping dian Li Yu: "Xian qing ou ji" "Kui ci guan jian" yanjiu* (Critical edition of Li Yu: Researches on "Xian qing ou ji" and "Kui ci guan jian"). Shanghai: Dongfang Chuban Zhongxin.

Duara, Prasenjit. 1988. *Culture, Power, and the State: Rural North China, 1900–1942*. Stanford, CA: Stanford University Press.

Dudgeon, John, M.D. 1869. "The Small Feet of Chinese Women." *Chinese Recorder and Missionary Journal* 2 (September): 93–96; (October): 130–33.

Dukes, Edwin Joshua. 1885. *Everyday Life in China, or Scenes along River and Road in Fuhkien*. London: Religious Tract Society.

Duncan, Robert Moore. 1933. *Peiping Municipality and the Diplomatic Quarter*. Peiping: Yenching University.

Duus, Peter. 1995. *The Abacus and the Sword: The Japanese Penetration of Korea, 1895–1910*. Berkeley: University of California Press.

Duyiwotuishi. [1930] 1973. *Xiaoxiao lu* (Collected humor). In *Biji xiaoshuo daguan zhengbian* (First collectanea of essays and fiction), vol. 5: 3067–150. Taipei: Xinxing Shuju.

Eberhard, Wolfram. 1971. "What Is Beautiful in a Chinese Woman?" In *Moral and Social Values of the Chinese: Collected Essays*, 271–304. Taipei: Ch'eng-wen. Distributed by Chinese Materials and Research Aids Service Center.

Ebrey, Patricia. 1990. "Women, Marriage, and the Family in Chinese History." In *Heritage of China: Contemporary Perspectives on Chinese Civilization*, ed. Paul S. Ropp and T. H. Barrett, 197–223. Berkeley: University of California Press.

———. 1993. *The Inner Quarters: Marriage and the Lives of Chinese Women in the Sung Period*. Berkeley: University of California Press.

———. 1996. "Surnames and Han Chinese Identity." In *Negotiating Ethnicities in China and Taiwan*, ed. Melissa Brown, 19–36. Berkeley: Institute of East Asian Studies, University of California.

———. 1999. "Gender and Sinology: Shifting Western Interpretations of Footbinding, 1300–1890." *Late Imperial China* 20.2: 1–34.

Edwards, E. H. 1903. *Fire and Sword in Shansi*. Edinburgh: Oliphant Anderson and Ferrier.

Elliott, Mark C. 2001. *The Manchu Way*. Stanford, CA: Stanford University Press.

Elman, Benjamin A. 1994. "Changes in Confucian Civil Service Examinations from the Ming to the Ch'ing Dynasty." In *Education and Society in Late Imperial China, 1600–1900*, ed. Benjamin A. Elman and Alexander Woodside, 110–49. Berkeley: University of California Press.

Elvin, Mark. 1999. "Blood and Statistics: Reconstructing the Population Dynamics of Late Imperial China from the Biographies of Virtuous Women in Local Gazetteers." In *Chinese Women in the Imperial Past*, ed. Harriet T. Zurndorfer, 135–222. Leiden: Brill.

Enatsu, Yoshiki. 2004. *Banner Legacy: The Rise of the Fengtian Local Elite at the End of the Qing*. Ann Arbor: Center for Chinese Studies, University of Michigan.

Fairbank, John King, and Merle Goldman. 1998. *China: A New History*. Cambridge, MA: Harvard University Press.

Faure, David. 2007. *Emperor and Ancestor: State and Lineage in South China*. Stanford, CA: Stanford University Press.

Feng Erkang. 1986. "Qingdai de hunyin zhidu yu funü de shehui diwei shulun" (The marriage system and women's social status in the Qing dynasty). *Qingshi yanjiu ji* 5:305–43.

Feng Erkang and Chang Jianhua. 2002. *Qing ren shehui shenghuo* (Social life in the Qing dynasty). Shenyang: Shenyang Chubanshe.

Feng Jicai. 1994. *The Three-Inch Golden Lotus*. Trans. David Wakefield. Honolulu: University of Hawaii Press.

———. 2004. *Sancun jinlian tuwenben* (Three-inch golden lotus; illustrated edition). Beijing: Zuojia Chubanshe.

Fengtian tongzhi (Gazetteer of Fengtian). 1983. Ed. Wang Shunan et al. 5 vols. Shenyang: Gujiu Shudian.

Feuerwerker, Albert. 1969. *The Chinese Economy, ca. 1870–1911*. Michigan Papers in Chinese Studies, no. 5. Ann Arbor: Center for Chinese Studies, University of Michigan.

Fielde, Adele M. 1878. *First Lessons in the Swatow Dialect*. Swatow: Swatow Printing Office.

———. 1883. *A Pronouncing and Defining Dictionary of the Swatow Dialect, Arranged according to Syllables and Tones*. Shanghai: American Presbyterian Mission Press.

———. 1887. *Pagoda Shadows: Studies from Life in China*. London: T. Ogilvie Smith.

———. 1894. *A Corner of Cathay: Studies from Life among Chinese*. New York: Macmillan.

Finnane, Antonia. 1998. "Water, Love, and Labor, Aspects of a Gendered Environment." In *Sediments of Time: Environment and Society in Chinese History,* ed. Mark Elvin and Liu Ts'ui-jung, 657–89. Cambridge: Cambridge University Press.

———. 2004. *Speaking of Yangzhou: A Chinese City, 1550–1850.* Cambridge, MA: Harvard University Asia Center.

Fisher, T. S. 1977. "Accommodation and Loyalism: The Life of Lu Liu-liang (1629–1683)." *Papers on Far Eastern History* 15 (March): 97–104.

Fong, Grace S. 2008. *Herself an Author: Gender, Agency, and Writing in Late Imperial China.* Honolulu: University of Hawaii Press.

———. 2010. "Writing and Illness: A Feminine Condition in Women's Poetry of the Ming and Qing." In *The Inner Quarters and Beyond: Women Writers from Ming through Qing,* ed. Grace S. Fong and Ellen Widmer, 19–48. Leiden: Brill.

Fong, Grace S., and Ellen Widmer, eds. 2010. *The Inner Quarters and Beyond: Women Writers from Ming through Qing.* Leiden: Brill.

Fong, H. D. [Fang Xianting]. [1932] 2014. *Cotton Industry and Trade in China.* Beijing: Commercial Press.

———. 1933. *Rural Industries in China.* With Wu Chih. China Institute of Pacific Relations. Tientsin: Chihli Press.

———. 1934. "Terminal Marketing of Tientsin Cotton." *Monthly Bulletin on Economic China* 7.7: 275–321.

———. 1935. "Rural Weaving and the Merchant Employers in a North China District." *Nankai Social and Economic Quarterly,* pt. 1, 8.1: 75–120; pt. 2, 8.2: 274–308.

———. 1936. "The Growth and Decline of Rural Industrial Enterprise in North China: A Case Study of the Cotton Handloom Weaving Industry in Paoti." With H. H. Pi (Bi Xianghui). *Nankai Social and Economic Quarterly* 8.4: 691–772.

Fortune, Robert. 1847. *Three Years' Wanderings in the Northern Provinces of China.* London: J. Murray.

Franck, Harry A. 1923. *Wandering in Northern China.* New York: Century.

Fu Yuguang. 2008. *Tuxiang zhongguo Manzu fengsu xulu* (Manchu customs illustrated). Jinan: Shandong Huabao Chubanshe.

Fu-ge. [1860] 1984. *Tingyu congtan* (Talks collected while listening to the rain). 2nd ed. Beijing: Zhonghua Shuju.

Gamble, Sidney D. 1921. *Peking: A Social Survey.* New York: George H. Doran.

———. 1943. "The Disappearance of Foot-Binding in Tinghsien." *American Journal of Sociology* 49.2: 181–83.

———. [1954] 1968. *Ting Hsien: A North China Rural Community.* Stanford, CA: Stanford University Press.

———. 1963. *North China Villages: Social, Political, and Economic Activities before 1933.* Berkeley: University of California Press.

Gao Hongxing. 2007. *Chanzu shi* (A history of footbinding). Shanghai: Shanghai Wenyi Chubanshe.

Garrett, Valery M. 1994. *Chinese Clothing: An Illustrated Guide.* Hong Kong: Oxford University Press.

Gates, Hill. 1997a. "Footbinding and Handspinning in Sichuan." In *Constructing China: The Interaction of Culture and Economics*, ed. Kenneth Lieberthal, Shuen-fu Lin, and Ernest Young, 177–94. Ann Arbor: Center for Chinese Studies, University of Michigan.

———. 1997b. "On a New Footing: Footbinding and the Coming of Modernity." *Jindai zhongguo funü shi yanjiu* (Research on women in modern Chinese history) 5:115–35.

———. 1999. "Chinese Modernity in Taiwan: The View from the Bound Foot." In *Renlei xue zai Taiwan di fazhan, jingyan yanjiu pian* (Anthropological studies in Taiwan, empirical research), ed. Xu Zhengguang and Lin Meirong, 291–318. Taipei: Institute of Ethnology, Academia Sinica.

———. 2001. "Footloose in Fujian: Economic Correlates of Footbinding." *Comparative Studies in Society and History* 43:130–48.

———. 2008. "Bound Feet: How Sexy Were They?" *History of the Family* 13:58–70.

———. 2015. *Footbinding and Women's Labor in Sichuan*. New York: Routledge.

Gibson, J. Campbell. 1901. *Mission Problems and Mission Methods in South China*. 2nd ed. New York: Young People's Missionary Movement.

Giersch, C. Patterson. 2006. *Asian Borderlands: The Transformation of Qing China's Yunnan Frontier*. Cambridge, MA: Harvard University Press.

Gillin, Donald G. 1967. *Warlord: Yen Hsi-shan in Shansi Province, 1911–1949*. Princeton, NJ: Princeton University Press.

Godley, Michael R. 1994. "The End of the Queue: Hair as a Symbol in Chinese History." *East Asian History* 8:53–72.

Goldstein, Joshua R., and Sebastian Klüsener. 2014. "Spatial Analysis of the Causes of Fertility Decline in Prussia." *Population and Development Review* 40.3: 497–525.

Gotō Shimpei. 1909. "The Administration of Formosa (Taiwan)." In *Fifty Years of New Japan*, comp. Count Shigenobu Okuma, 530–53. English version, ed. Marcus B. Huish. London: Smith, Elder.

Gottschang, Thomas R., and Diana Lary. 2000. *Swallows and Settlers: The Great Migration from North China to Manchuria*. Ann Arbor: Center for Chinese Studies, University of Michigan.

Gray, John Henry. 1878. *China: A History of the Laws, Manners, and Customs of the People*. 2 vols. London: Macmillan.

Grove, Linda. 1993. "Mechanization and Women's Work in Early Twentieth Century China." In *Yanagida Setsuko Sensei koki kinen Chūgoku no dentō shakai to kazoku* (Essays in honor of the seventieth birthday of Professor Yanagida Setsuko on the family and traditional society in China), 95–120. Tokyo: Kyūko Shoin.

Gu Cheng. 1997. *Nan Ming shi* (History of the Southern Ming). Beijing: Zhongguo Qingnian Chubanshe.

Gu Yanwu. 1983. *Gu Tinglin shiji huizhu* (Collected poems of Gu Tinglin). Shanghai: Shanghai Guji Chubanshe.

Guangxu chao shangyu dang (Imperial edicts of the Guangxu reign). 1996. Ed. Zhongguo Diyi Lishi Dang'an. 34 vols. Guilin: Guangxi Shifan Daxue Chubanshe.

Gully, Robert, and Capt. Frank Denham. 1844. *Journals Kept by Mr. Gully and Capt. Denham, during a Captivity in China, in the Year 1842. Edited by a Barrister.* London: Chapman and Hall.

Hakka Affairs Council. 2011. *Xingzhengyuan Kejia weiyuanhui 99 nian zhi 100 nian quanguo kejia renkou jichu ziliao diaocha yanjiu* (Report of the 2010–11 National Hakka Population Survey of the Hakka Affairs Council, Executive Yuan). Taipei: Xingzhengyuan, Kejia Weiyuanhui.

Han Guanghui. 1996. *Beijing lishi renkou dili* (Historical geography of population in Beijing). Beijing: Beijing Daxue Chubanshe

Han Yanlong, ed. 1993. *Zhongguo jindai jingcha zhidu* (The police system of modern China). Beijing: Zhongguo Renmin Gong'an Daxue Chubanshe.

Han Yaoqi and Lin Qian. 1990. *Qingdai Manzu fengqing* (Manchu styles in the Qing). Changchun: Jilin Wenshi Chubanshe.

Hanan, Patrick. 1988. *The Invention of Li Yu.* Cambridge, MA: Harvard University Press.

Harrison, Henrietta. 2000. *The Making of the Republican Citizen.* New York: Oxford University Press.

Hashimoto, Mantaro J. 1973. *The Hakka Dialect.* Cambridge: Cambridge University Press.

Hastings, Sally A. 1993. "The Empress' New Clothes and Japanese Women, 1868–1912." *Historian* 55.4: 677–92.

Hayami, Akira. 2001. *The Historical Demography of Pre-modern Japan.* Tokyo: University of Tokyo Press.

Hebei sheng gexian gaikuang yilan (An outline of conditions in individual counties in Hebei Province). 1933. Baoding: Hebei Sheng Minzhengting.

Hebei sheng shengzheng tongji gaiyao, Minguo shiqi niandu (Administrative statistics of the province of Hebei for the year 1928). 1930. Qingyuan: Hebei Sheng Zhengfu Mishuchu.

Hebei tongzhi gao [Minguo] (Gazetteer of Hebei in the Republican period). [1935] 1993. Ed. Hebeisheng Difangzhi Bangongshi. 3 vols. Shijiazhuang: Beijing Yanshan Chubanshe.

Hedley, John. 1910. *Tramps in Dark Mongolia.* London: T. Fisher Unwin.

Hindman, Hugh D. 2009. *The World of Child Labor: An Historical and Regional Survey.* Armonk, NY: M. E. Sharpe.

Hinton, Carma, and Richard Gordon, dirs. 1987. *Small Happiness: Xiao Xi.* New York: Long Bow Group. Video recording.

Hirano Ken'ichiro. 1993. "The Westernization of Clothes and the State in Meiji Japan." In *The State and Cultural Transformation: Perspectives from East Asia*, ed. Hirano Ken'ichiro, 121–31. Tokyo: United Nations University Press.

Ho, Samuel. 1978. *Economic Development of Taiwan, 1860–1970.* New Haven, CT: Yale University Press.

Ho Ping-ti. 1959. *Studies on the Population of China, 1368–1953.* Cambridge, MA: Harvard University Press.

———. 1962. *The Ladder of Success in Imperial China: Aspects of Social Mobility, 1368–1911.* New York: Columbia University Press.

Holmes, Burton. 1914. *Burton Holmes Travelogues.* Vol. 9, *Down the Amur; Peking, the Forbidden City.* Chicago: Travelogue Bureau.

Hong, Fan. 1997. *Footbinding, Feminism, and Freedom: The Liberation of Women's Bodies in Modern China*. London: Frank Cass.

Hong Minlin. 1976. "Chanjiao yu Taiwan di tianran zu yundong" (Footbinding and the campaign for natural feet in Taiwan). *Taiwan wenxian* 27.3: 143–52.

Hong Rumao. 2005. *Rizhi shiqi huji dengji falü ji yongyu bianyi* (Household registration law and terminology in the Japanese period). Taichung, Taiwan: Taizhong Xian Zhengfu.

Hosie, Alexander. 1910. *Manchuria: Its People, Resources and Recent History*. Boston: J. B. Millet.

Hsieh, T'ing-yu. 1929. "Origin and Migrations of the Hakkas." *Chinese Social and Political Science Review* 13:202–27.

Hsu Wen-hsiung. 1980. "Frontier Social Organization and Social Disorder in Ch'ing Taiwan." In *China's Island Frontier*, ed. Ronald G. Knapp, 87–105. Honolulu: University Press of Hawaii.

Hu Piyun. 1995. *Jiu jing shi zhao* (Historical photos of old Beijing). Beijing: Beijing Chubanshe.

Hu Siao-chen. 2010. "War, Violence, and the Metaphor of Blood in Tanci Narratives by Women Authors." In *The Inner Quarters and Beyond: Women Writers from Ming through Qing*, ed. Grace S. Fong and Ellen Widmer, 249–80. Leiden: Brill.

Hu Yinglin. 1964. *Shaoshi shanfang bicong* (Notes from the Shaoshishan studio). Shanghai: Zhonghua Shuju.

Huang, Philip C. C. 1985. *The Peasant Economy and Social Change in North China*. Stanford, CA: Stanford University Press.

——. 1990. *The Peasant Family and Rural Development in the Yangzi Delta, 1350–1988*. Stanford, CA: Stanford University Press.

Hummel, Arthur W. 1943–44. *Eminent Chinese of the Ch'ing Period*. 2 vols. Washington, DC: Government Printing Office.

Idema, Wilt L., Wai-yee Li, and Ellen Widmer, eds. 2006. *Trauma and Transcendence in Early Qing Literature*. Cambridge, MA: Harvard University Asia Center.

Illustrated Catalogue of the Chinese Collection of Exhibits for the International Health Exhibition, London, 1884. 1884. China, Imperial Maritime Customs, II — Miscellaneous Series, no. 12. Published by order of the Inspector General of Customs. London: William Clowes and Sons.

Imanishi Shunjū, trans. 1969. *Kyū Shingo yakkai, Chiu-ch'ing-yü, Translated and Explained* [Old Manchu documents]. Tōhōgaku kiyō, 3. Tenri: Tenri Daigaku Oyasato Kenkyūjo.

Ino Yoshinori. 1905. "Shina kanzoku no joshi ni okonaruru tensoku no fū" (The footbinding custom practiced among Han women in China). *Tōkyō jinrui gakkai zasshi* (Journal of the Anthropological Society of Tokyo) 20.229: 301–11.

Isett, Christopher. 2007. *State, Peasant, and Merchant in Qing Manchuria, 1644–1862*. Stanford, CA: Stanford University Press.

Jackson, Beverly. 1997. *Splendid Slippers: A Thousand Years of an Erotic Tradition*. Berkeley: Ten Speed Press.

James, H. E. M. [Henry Evan Murchison]. [1888] 1968. *The Long White Mountain, or A Journey in Manchuria*. New York: Greenwood Press.

Jen Yu-wen. 1973. *The Taiping Revolutionary Movement*. New Haven, CT: Yale University Press.

Jennings, John M. 1997. *The Opium Empire: Japanese Imperialism and Drug Trafficking in Asia, 1895–1945*. Westport, CT: Praeger.

Jia Shen [Jia Yijun]. 1929. *Zhonghua funü chanzu kao* (Investigations of footbinding among Chinese women). Beijing: Wenhua Xueshe.

Jiang Longzhao. 1992. *Xiang fei kaozheng yanjiu xuji* (Further researches on the Fragrant Concubine). Taipei: Wenshizhe Chubanshe

Jin Qizong. 1989. *Beijing jiaoqu de Manzu* (Manchus in the outskirts of Beijing). Hohhot: Neimenggu Daxue Chubanshe.

Johnson, Kay Ann. 1983. *Women, the Family and Peasant Revolution in China*. Chicago: University of Chicago Press.

Johnston, Meta, and Lena Johnston. 1907. *Jin Ko-niu: A Brief Sketch of the Life of Jessie M. Johnston, for Eighteen Years W.M.A. Missionary in Amoy, China*. London: T. French Downie.

Johnston, Reginald. F. [1910] 1977. *Lion and Dragon in Northern China*. Reprint, Taipei: Southern Materials Center.

Kang Youwei. 2007. *Kang Youwei quan ji* (Complete works of Kang Youwei). 12 vols. Beijing: Zhongguo Renmin Daxue Chubanshe.

Kawachi Yoshihiro. 2010. *Naikokushiin manbun tōan yakuchū: Chūgoku daiichi rekishi tōankan zō; Sūtoku ni sannenbun* (Translated and annotated Manchu-language archives from the Inner Historical Office, held in the First Historical Archives, second and third years of the Chongde reign). Kyoto: Shōkadō Shoten.

Ke Jisheng. 1995. *Sancun jinlian: Aomi, meili, jinji* (Three-inch golden lotus: Mystery, glamour, taboo). Taipei: Chanye Qingbao Zazhishe.

———. 1998. *Shengui hongyan lei: Sancun jinlian wenwuzhan* (Tears from the boudoir: A three-inch golden lotus exhibition). Banqiao, Taiwan: Taipei Xianli Wenhua Zhongxin.

———. 2003. *Qian zai jinlian fenghua: Chanzu wenwuzhan* (A thousand years of bound feet: A footbinding exhibition). Taipei: Guoli Lishi Bowuguan.

Ko, Dorothy. 1994. *Teachers of the Inner Chambers: Women and Culture in Seventeenth-Century China*. Stanford, CA: Stanford University Press.

———. 1997. "The Body as Attire: The Shifting Meanings of Footbinding in Seventeenth-Century China." *Journal of Women's History* 8.4: 8–28.

———. 1998. "The Emperor and His Women: Three Views of Footbinding, Ethnicity, and Empire." In "Life in the Imperial Court of Qing Dynasty China," ed. Chuimei Ho and Cheri A. Jones. *Proceedings of the Denver Museum of Natural History*, ser. 3, no. 15: 37–48.

———. 2001. *Every Step a Lotus: Shoes for Bound Feet*. Berkeley: University of California Press.

———. 2002. "Footbinding as Female Inscription." In *Rethinking Confucianism: Past and Present in China, Japan, Korea, and Vietnam*, ed. Benjamin A. Elman, John B. Duncan, and Herman Ooms, 147–77. Los Angeles: Asia Institute, University of California, Los Angeles.

———. 2004. "High Heels and Platform Shoes." In *Splendors of China's Forbidden City: The Glorious Reign of Emperor Qianlong*, ed. Chuimei Ho and Bennet Bronson, 70–71. London: Merrell.

———. 2005. *Cinderella's Sisters: A Revisionist History of Footbinding*. Berkeley: University of California Press.

Kraus, Richard A. 1980. *Cotton and Cotton Goods in China, 1918–1936*. New York: Garland.

Kuhn, Philip A. 1990. *Soulstealers: The Chinese Sorcery Scare of 1768*. Cambridge, MA: Harvard University Press.

Lamley, Harry. 1964. "The Taiwan Literati and Early Japanese Rule, 1895–1915." Ph.D. dissertation, University of Washington, Seattle.

———. 1970. "The 1895 Taiwan War of Resistance: Local Chinese Efforts against a Foreign Power." In *Taiwan: Studies in Chinese Local History*, ed. Leonard H. D. Gordon, 23–77. New York: Columbia University Press.

———. 1977. "The Formation of Cities: Initiative and Motivation in Building Three Walled Cities in Taiwan." In *The City in Late Imperial China*, ed. G. William Skinner, 155–209. Stanford, CA: Stanford University Press.

———. 1981. "Subethnic Rivalry in the Ch'ing Period." In *The Anthropology of Taiwanese Society*, ed. Emily Ahern and Hill Gates, 282–318. Stanford, CA: Stanford University Press.

———. 2007. "Taiwan under Japanese Rule, 1895–1945: The Vicissitudes of Colonialism." In *Taiwan: A New History*, ed. Murray A. Rubinstein, 201–60. Expanded ed. Armonk, NY: M. E. Sharpe.

Lattimore, Owen. 1932a. "Chinese Colonization in Inner Mongolia: Its History and Present Development." In *Pioneer Settlement: Cooperative Studies*, ed. W. L. G. Joerg, 288–312. Special Publication no. 14. New York: American Geographical Society.

———. 1932b. *Manchuria, Cradle of Conflict*. New York: Macmillan.

———. 1934. *The Mongols of Manchuria*. New York: John Day.

Lechler, Rev. Rudolf. 1878. "The Hakka Chinese." *Chinese Recorder and Missionary Journal* 9.5: 352–59.

Lee, James, and Cameron Campbell. 1997. *Fate and Fortune in Rural China*. Cambridge: Cambridge University Press.

Lee Kyung Ja, Hong Na Young, and Chang Sook Hwan. 2005. *Traditional Korean Costume*. Folkestone, UK: Global Oriental.

Leong, Sow-Theng. 1997. *Migration and Ethnicity in Chinese History: Hakkas, Pengmin, and Their Neighbors*, ed. Tim Wright. Stanford, CA: Stanford University Press.

Levy, Howard S. 1966. *A Feast of Mist and Flowers: The Gay Quarters of Nanking at the End of the Ming*. Translation of *Ban qiao zaji* (Diverse records of wooden bridge), by Yu Huai. Yokohama, Japan: privately printed.

———. 1967. *Chinese Footbinding: The History of a Curious Erotic Custom*. New York: Bell.

Li, Huaiyin. 2005. *Village Governance in North China, 1875–1936*. Stanford, CA: Stanford University Press.

Li, Wai-yee. 1999. "Heroic Transformations: Women and National Trauma in Early Qing Literature." *Harvard Journal of Asiatic Studies* 59.2: 363–443.

———. 2005. "Women as Emblems of Dynastic Fall in Qing Literature." In *Dynastic Crisis and Cultural Innovation: From the Late Ming to the Late Qing and Beyond*, ed. David Der-wei Wang and Shang Wei, 93–150. Cambridge, MA: Harvard University Asia Center.

———. 2006. Introduction to *Trauma and Transcendence in Early Qing Literature*, ed. Wilt L. Idema, Wai-yee Li, and Ellen Widmer, 1–70. Cambridge, MA: Harvard University Asia Center.

———. 2010. "Women Writers and Gender Boundaries during the Ming-Qing Transition." In *The Inner Quarters and Beyond: Women Writers from Ming through Qing*, ed. Grace S. Fong and Ellen Widmer, 179–213. Leiden: Brill.

———. 2012. "Romantic Recollections of Women as Sources of Women's History." In *Overt and Covert Treasures: Essays on the Sources for Chinese Women's History*, ed. Clara Wing-chung Ho, 337–67. Hong Kong: Chinese University Press.

———. 2014. *Women and National Trauma in Late Imperial Chinese Literature*. Harvard-Yenching Institute Monograph Series. Cambridge, MA: Harvard University Press.

Li, Wen Lang. 1967. "Inter-prefectural Migration of the Native Population in Taiwan, 1905–1940." Ph.D. dissertation, University of Pennsylvania.

Li Chun-hao, Yang Wen-shan, and Chuang Ying-chang. 2011. "How Reliable Is Taiwan's Colonial Period Demographic Data?" In *Death at the Opposite Ends of the Eurasian Continent*, ed. Theo Engelen, John R. Shepherd, and Yang Wen-shan, 349–74. Amsterdam: Aksant Academic Publishers.

Li Feng. 1934. "Wushinian lai shangye ziben zai Hebei xiangcun mianzhi shougongye-zhong zhi fazhan jincheng" (The development of commercial capital in the handicraft cotton textile industry in the rural areas in Hebei in the past fifty years). *Zhongguo nongcun* 1.3: 61–76.

Li Jinghan. 1933. *Dingxian shehui gaikuang diaocha* (Investigations of Ding County society). Beijing: Zhonghua Pingmin Jiaoyu Cujinhui.

Li Nan, Feng Jicai, and Ke Jisheng. 2005. *Jueshi jinlian* (The last generation of the golden lotus). Shijiazhuang: Huashan Wenyi Chubanshe.

Li Rongmei. [1936] 1998. "Zhonghua funü chanzu shi tan" (History of footbinding among Chinese women). In *Caifeilu* (Gathered fragrances), ed. Yao Lingxi, 1–23. Shanghai: Shanghai Shudian Chubanshe.

Lian Heng. 1979. *Taiwan tongshi* (Comprehensive history of Taiwan). Taipei: Guting Shuwu.

Liang Qichao. 1999. *Liang Qichao quanji* (Complete works of Liang Qichao). Ed. Yang Gang and Wang Xiangyi. 10 vols. Beijing: Beijing Chubanshe.

Lin Hsin-yi. 2011. "The Formation of Taiwan Society: The Case of the Zhuqian Area (1723–1895)." Ph.D. dissertation, University of Oxford.

Lin Qiumin. 1990. "Jindai Zhongguo de buchanzu yundong (1895–1937)" (The anti-footbinding movement in modern China, 1895–1937). Master's thesis, Guoli Zhengzhi Daxue Shixue Yanjiusuo.

———. 1995. "Yan Xishan yu Shanxi de tianzu yundong" (Yan Xishan and the natural foot movement in Shanxi). *Guoshiguan guankan, fukan* (Journal of the National History Museum, n.s.) 18:129–44.

Lin Yutang. [1935] 1992. "Feminist Thought in Ancient China." In *Chinese Women through Chinese Eyes*, ed. Li Yu-ning, 34–58. Armonk, NY: M. E. Sharpe.

———. 1960. *The Importance of Understanding: Translations from the Chinese*. Cleveland: World Publishing.

Little, Mrs. Archibald [Alicia]. 1901. *Intimate China*. London: Hutchinson.

———. 1908. *In the Land of the Blue Gown*. 2nd ed. London: T. Fisher Unwin.

Liu, Cheng-yuan. 2005. "Negotiating Colonialism in a Taiwanese Sugar Town." Ph.D. dissertation, Australian National University.

Liu, Kwang-ching, and Richard J. Smith. 1976. "The Military Challenge: The North-West and the Coast." In *Cambridge History of China*, vol. 11, *Late Ch'ing, 1800–1911*, pt. 2, ed. John King Fairbank and Kwang-ching Liu, 202–73. Cambridge: Cambridge University Press.

Liu, Nanming I. 1935. *Contribution à l'étude de la population chinoise*. Geneva: Imprimerie et Editions Union.

Lockhart, William. 1864. "Medical Missionary Practice in Peking in 1861-2." *Chinese and Japanese Repository*, May 3, 472–80; June 3, 483–94.

Lu, Hanchao. 2010. *The Birth of a Republic: Francis Stafford's Photographs of China's 1911 Revolution and Beyond*. Seattle: University of Washington Press.

Lucas, Christopher J., ed. 1990. *James Ricalton's Photographs of China during the Boxer Rebellion: His Illustrated Travelogue of 1900*. Lewiston, NY: Edwin Mellen Press.

Ma, Shirley See Yan. 2010. *Footbinding: A Jungian Engagement with Chinese Culture and Psychology*. New York: Routledge.

Ma Junya and Tim Wright. 2010. "Industrialization and Handicraft Cloth: The Jiangsu Peasant Economy in the Late Nineteenth and Early Twentieth Centuries." *Modern Asian Studies* 44.6: 1337–72.

Macgowan, John. 1913. *How England Saved China*. London: T. Fisher Unwin.

Mackay, George Leslie. 1895. *From Far Formosa*. New York: Fleming H. Revell.

Mackie, Gerry. 1996. "Ending Footbinding and Infibulation: A Convention Account." *American Sociological Review* 61.6: 999–1017.

MacKinnon, Stephen R. 1980. *Power and Politics in Late Imperial China: Yuan Shi-kai in Beijing and Tianjin, 1901–1908*. Berkeley: University of California Press.

———. 2002. "Wuhan's Search for Identity in the Republican Period." In *Remaking the Chinese City: Modernity and National Identity, 1900–1950*, ed. Joseph Esherick, 161–73. Honolulu: University of Hawaii Press

Mallory, Walter H. 1926. *China: Land of Famine*. New York: American Geographical Society.

Manbun rōtō (Old Manchu archives). 1955–63. Trans. Nobuo Kanda and the Manbun Rōtō Kenkyūkai. 7 vols. Tokyo: Tōyō Bunko.

Mann, Susan. 1997. *Precious Records: Women in China's Long Eighteenth Century*. Stanford, CA: Stanford University Press.

———. 2002. "Women, Families, and Gender Relations." In *The Cambridge History of China*, vol. 9, *The Ch'ing Empire to 1800*, pt. 1, ed. Willard J. Peterson, 428–72. Cambridge: Cambridge University Press.

Manshū chihōshi: Sōkō (Draft local history of Manchuria). 1912. 8 vols. Kantō Totokufu.

Manshū shi sōkō (Draft gazetteer of Manchuria). [1911] 2000. Ed. Kantō Totokufu Rikugun Keiribu. 15 vols. Tokyo: Kuresu Shuppan.

Manzhou shilu (Veritable Records of the Manchus). 1985. In *Qing shilu* (Veritable Records of the Qing), vol. 1, *Taizu Gao huangdi shilu* (Veritable Records of Emperor Taizu Gao [Tianming reign]). Beijing: Zhonghua Shuju.

Manzu minjian gushi xuan (Selected Manchu folktales). 1981–83. Ed. Zhongguo Minjian Wenyi Yanjiu Hui and Liaoning, Jilin, Heilongjiang Sansheng Fenhui. 2 vols. Shenyang: Chunfeng Wenyi Chubanshe.

Manzu minjian gushi xuan (Selected Manchu folktales). 1983. Ed. Wu Bingan and Li Wengang. Zhongguo xiaoshu minzu minjian wenxue congshu (Folk literature of China's minority nationalities). Shanghai: Shanghai Wenyi Chubanshe.

Manzu shehui lishi diaocha (Investigations into the social history of the Manchus). 1985. Ed. Minzu Wenti Wuzhong Congshu, Liaoning Sheng Bianji Weiyuanhui. Shenyang: Liaoning Renmin Chubanshe.

Mao Zhibin. 1973. "Jin chan zu biao" (Manifesto to prohibit footbinding). In "Jian hu ji" (Hard gourd collection), by Chu Jiaxuan [1630–ca.1705], 8 *ji*, *juan* 4, 10a–b, p. 3591. In *Biji xiaoshuo daguan xubian* (Collectanea of essays and fiction continued), vol. 16: 3337–66. Taipei: Xinxing Shuju.

McLaren, Anne E. 2008. *Performing Grief: Bridal Laments in Rural China*. Honolulu: University of Hawaii Press.

McNabb, Robert Leroy. 1903. *The Women of the Middle Kingdom*. New York: Eaton and Mains.

Miao Yanwei. 2013. "Cong 'tianran zu hui' dao 'jiechan hui': Rizhi chuqi Taiwan de nüti zhengzhi (1900–1915)" (From "Natural feet societies" to "Footbinding liberation societies": The politics of the female body in early colonial Taiwan [1900–1915]). *Taiwan shehui yanjiu jikan* 91:125–74.

Miaoli xianzhi (Gazetteer of Miaoli County). 1893. Ed. Shen Maoyin. TW 159.

Michie, Alexander. 1863. "Narrative of a Journey from Tientsin to Moukden in Manchuria in July, 1861." *Journal of the Royal Geographical Society of London* 33:153–66.

Ming Qing shiliao, ding bian (Historical materials of the Ming and Qing, fourth compilation). [1951] 1972. Taipei: Institute of History and Philology, Academia Sinica.

Minguo shiqinian ge sheng shi hukou diaocha tongji baogao (Statistical report of the census taken in various provinces and municipalities in 1928). 1931. Nanjing: Neizhengbu Tongjisi.

Montgomery, Mark R., and John B. Casterline. 1993. "The Diffusion of Fertility Control in Taiwan: Evidence from Pooled Cross-Section Time-Series Models." *Population Studies* 47.3: 457–79.

———. 1996. "Social Learning, Social Influence, and New Models of Fertility." *Population and Development Review* 22 (Supp.): S151–S175.

Myers, Ramon H. 1972. "Taiwan under Ch'ing Imperial Rule, 1684–1895: The Traditional Economy." *Journal of the Institute of Chinese Studies of the Chinese University of Hong Kong* 2:373–411.

Nagao Ryūzō. 1942. *Shina minzoku shi* (Chinese customs). Vol. 6. Tokyo: Shina Minzokushi Kankōkai.

Nankai Weekly Statistical Service. 1933. "Home Industries in Hopei, 1928." 6.22 (May 29): 105, 107–11.

Naquin, Susan. 2000. *Peking: Temples and City Life, 1400–1900.* Berkeley: University of California Press.

Neizheng gongbao (Bulletin of the Ministry of the Interior). 1928–40. Nanjing: Neizhengbu Zongwusi.

Neizheng nianjian (Yearbook of the Ministry of the Interior). 1936. Neizhengbu. Shanghai: Shangwu Yinshuguan.

Ng, Chin-keong. 1983. *Trade and Society: The Amoy Network on the China Coast, 1683–1785.* Singapore: Singapore University Press.

Nōgyō kihon chōsasho (Basic researches in agriculture). 1923a. Vol. 2, *Kōchi bun-pai oyobi keiei chōsa, 1921* (Distribution and management of cultivated land, 1921). Taipei: Taiwan Sōtokufu Shokusankyoku.

———. 1923b. Vol. 4, *Shuyō nōsakubutsu seisan chōsa, saibai kosū, sakutsuke menseki, 1921* (Researches on the production of important crops, number of cultivator households, and cultivated area, 1921). Taipei: Taiwan Sōtokufu Shokusankyoku.

Norman, Jerry. 1978. *A Concise Manchu-English Lexicon.* Seattle: University of Washington Press.

Okada, Hidehiro. 1993. "Mandarin, a Language of the Manchus: How Altaic?" *Aetas Manjurica* 3:165–87.

Okinawa Soba [pseud.]. 2013. Lantern slide of two Manchu women walking. Accessed August 15, 2013. www.flickr.com/photos/24443965@N08/3463650657/in/set -72157616817817339.

Ono, Kazuko. 1989. *Chinese Women in a Century of Revolution, 1850–1950.* Stanford, CA: Stanford University Press.

The Origins of Manchu Chopine. 2013. Accessed July 20, 2013. http://traditions.cultural -china.com/en/15Traditions7950.html.

Oxnam, Robert B. 1973. "Policies and Institutions of the Oboi Regency, 1661–1669." *Journal of Asian Studies* 32.2: 265–86.

———. 1975. *Ruling from Horseback: Manchu Politics in the Oboi Regency, 1661–1669.* Chicago: University of Chicago Press.

Pasternak, Burton. 1972. *Kinship and Community in Two Chinese Villages.* Stanford, CA: Stanford University Press.

———. 1983. *Guests in the Dragon.* New York: Columbia University Press.

Patterson, Orlando. 1975. "Context and Choice in Ethnic Allegiance: A Theoretical Framework and Caribbean Case Study." In *Ethnicity: Theory and Experience*, ed. Nathan Glazer and Daniel P. Moynihan, 305–49. Cambridge, MA: Harvard University Press.

Peattie, Mark R. 1984. "Japanese Attitudes toward Colonialism, 1895–1945." In *The Japanese Colonial Empire, 1895–1945*, ed. Ramon H. Myers and Mark R. Peattie, 80–127. Princeton, NJ: Princeton University Press.

Perckhammer, Heinz von. 1928. *Peking.* Berlin: Albertus.

Pickering, William A. 1898. *Pioneering in Formosa.* London: Hurst and Blackett.

Pruitt, Ida. [1945] 1967. *A Daughter of Han: The Autobiography of a Chinese Working Woman; From the Story Told Her by Ning Lao T'ai-t'ai*. Stanford, CA: Stanford University Press.

Putnam Weale, B. L. [Bertram Lenox Simpson]. 1904. *Manchu and Muscovite*. London: Macmillan.

Pyle, Kenneth B. 1969. *The New Generation in Meiji Japan: Problems of Cultural Identity, 1885-1895*. Stanford, CA: Stanford University Press.

Qian Yong. [Ca. 1838] 1979. *Lüyuan conghua* (Collected works from Lüyuan). Vol. 2. Beijing: Zhonghua Shuju.

Qicai shen huo, Manzu minjian chuanshuo gushi (Seven-colored torch, Manchu folk legends). 1984. Ed. Yu Guang [Fu Yuguang]. Jilin: Jilin Renmin Chubanshe.

Qing huidian shili (Collected regulations and precedents of the Qing dynasty). [1899] 1991. Beijing: Zhonghua Shuju.

Qing shi gao (Draft history of the Qing). [1927] 1977. Ed. Zhao Erxun. Beijing: Zhonghua Shuju.

Qing Taizong shilu gaoben (Draft Veritable Records of the Taizong emperor [Chongde reign]). 1978. Qingchu shiliao congkan di san Zhong (Third collection of historical materials of the early Qing). Shenyang: Liaoning Daxue Lishixi.

Qingchao yeshi daguan (Unofficial history of the Qing dynasty). 1921. Anonymous [Xiao-heng-xiang-shi-zhu-ren, pseud.]. 12 vols. Shanghai: Zhonghua Shuju.

Qingchu neiguo shiyuan manwen dang'an yibian (Translated compilation of the Manchu archive of the early Qing Inner Historical Office). 1986. Comp. Zhongguo Diyi Lishi Dang'an Guan. 3 vols. Beijing: Guangming Ribao Chubanshe.

Qingshi liezhuan (Qing history biographies). 1962. 10 vols. Taipei: Zhonghua Shuju.

Qiu Weixuan. [1914] 1991. "Shuyuan zhuitan jielu" (Extracts of superfluous talks from Shu garden). In *Xiangyan congshu* (Collectanea of romances), *ji* 8, *juan* 3, vol. 4: 455–92. Shanghai: Shanghai Shudian.

Qu Tongzu [Ch'u T'ung-tsu]. 1965. *Law and Society in Traditional China*. Paris: Mouton.

Qu Xuanying. [1937] 2009. *Zhongguo shehui shiliao congchao: Jia ji* (First collection of copies of historical materials on Chinese society). Changsha: Hunan Jiaoyu Chubanshe.

Rawski, Evelyn Sakakida. 1972. *Agricultural Change and the Peasant Economy of South China*. Cambridge, MA: Harvard University Press.

———. 1985. "Economic and Social Foundations of Late Imperial Culture." In *Popular Culture in Late Imperial China*, ed. David Johnson, Andrew J. Nathan, and Evelyn Sakakida Rawski, 3–33. Berkeley: University of California Press.

———. 1998. *The Last Emperors*. Berkeley: University of California Press.

Reardon-Anderson, James. 2005. *Reluctant Pioneers: China's Expansion Northward, 1644-1937*. Stanford, CA: Stanford University Press.

Reynolds, Douglas R. 1993. *China, 1898-1912: The Xinzheng Revolution and Japan*. Cambridge, MA: Harvard University Press.

Rhoads, Edward J. M. 2000. *Manchus and Han: Ethnic Relations and Political Power in Late Qing and Early Republican China, 1861-1928*. Seattle: University of Washington Press.

Riddell, Rev. W. 1901. "Map of Swatow Mission Field." In *Mission Problems and Mission Methods in South China*, by J. Campbell Gibson. 2nd ed. New York: Young People's Missionary Movement.

Roberts, Glenn, and Valerie Steele. 1997. "The Three-Inch Golden Lotus: A Collection of Chinese Bound Foot Shoes." *Arts of Asia* 27.2: 69–85.

Ropp, Paul S. 1981. *Dissent in Early Modern China: Ju-lin Wai-shih and Ch'ing Social Criticism*. Ann Arbor: University of Michigan Press.

Ross, Edward Alsworth. 1914. *The Changing Chinese: The Conflict of Oriental and Western Cultures in China*. New York: Century.

Ross, John. 1908. *Mission Methods in Manchuria*. Edinburgh: Oliphant Anderson and Ferrier.

Roth, Gertraude. 1979. "The Manchu-Chinese Relationship, 1618–1636." In *From Ming to Ch'ing*, ed. Jonathan D. Spence and John E. Wills Jr., 3–38. New Haven, CT: Yale University Press.

Roth Li, Gertraude. 2010. *Manchu: A Textbook for Reading Documents*. 2nd ed. Honolulu: University of Hawaii Press.

Rowe, William T. 2009. *China's Last Empire: The Great Qing*. Cambridge, MA: Harvard University Press.

Sando, Ruth Ann. 1981. "The Meaning of Development for Rural Areas: Depopulation in a Taiwanese Farming Community." Ph.D. dissertation, University of Hawaii.

Santangelo, Paolo. 1988. "'Chinese and Barbarians' in Gu Yanwu's Thought." In *Collected Papers of the XXIXth Congress of Chinese Studies*, ed. Tilemann Grimm, 183–99. Tübingen: Tübingen University Press.

Schafer, Edward H. 1954. *The Empire of Min*. Rutland, VT: Charles E. Tuttle.

Schelling, Thomas C. 1978. *Micromotives and Macrobehavior*. New York: W. W. Norton.

Schmidt, J. D. 2008. "Yuan Mei (1716–98) on Women." In *Late Imperial China* 29.2: 129–85.

Scott, A. C. 1958. *Chinese Costume in Transition*. Singapore: Donald Moore.

———. 1959. *An Introduction to the Chinese Theatre*. New York: Theatre Arts Books.

Shan Guoqiang. 1995. "Gentlewomen Paintings of the Qing Palace Ateliers." *Orientations* 26.7: 56–59.

Shao Dan. 2011. *Remote Homeland, Recovered Borderland: Manchus, Manchoukuo, and Manchuria, 1907–1985*. Honolulu: University of Hawaii Press.

Shen Defu. 1997. "Furen gongzu" (Bowed feet among women). In *Wanli yehuo bian* (Private gleanings in the reign of Wanli [1573–1620]), *juan* 23, vol. 2: 598–99. Beijing: Zhonghua Shuju.

Shengzu shilu (Veritable Records of Emperor Shengzu). 1985. In *Qing shilu* (Veritable Records of the Qing), vol. 4, *Shengzu Ren huangdi shilu* (Veritable Records of Emperor Shengzu Ren [Kangxi reign, years 1–20]). Beijing: Zhonghua Shuju.

Shepherd, John R. 1991. "Marriage Mode and Marriage Market: Spatial, Temporal, and Class Variation in Taiwan." Unpublished manuscript.

———. 1993. *Statecraft and Political Economy on the Taiwan Frontier, 1600–1800*. Stanford, CA: Stanford University Press.

————. 1996. "From Barbarians to Sinners: Collective Conversion among Plains Aborigines in Qing Taiwan, 1859–1895." In *Christianity in China: From the Eighteenth Century to the Present*, ed. Daniel H. Bays, 120–37. Stanford, CA: Stanford University Press.

————. 2003. "Siraya Marriage Practices in Late Nineteenth and Early Twentieth Century Taiwan: Preliminary Explorations in the Household Registers." In *Zuqun yishi yu wenhua rentong* (Ethnicity and cultural identity), ed. Yeh Chuen-jong, 241–86. Taipei: Institute of Ethnology, Academia Sinica.

————. 2004. "Some Demographic Characteristics of Chinese Immigrant Populations: Lessons for the Study of Taiwan's Population History." In *Maritime China in Transition, 1750–1850*, ed. Wang Gungwu and Ng Chin-keong, 115–37. Wiesbaden: Harrassowitz.

————. 2011. "Regional and Ethnic Variation in Mortality in Japanese Colonial Period Taiwan." In *Death at the Opposite Ends of the Eurasian Continent: Mortality Trends in Taiwan and the Netherlands, 1850–1945*, ed. Theo Engelen, John R. Shepherd, and Yang Wen-shan, 99–151. Amsterdam: Aksant Academic Publishers.

————. 2015. "Hakka-Hoklo Interaction: Exploring the Evidence." In *Zuqun, shehui yu lishi: Zhuang Yingzhang Jiaoshou rongtui xueshu yantaohui lunwenji* (Ethnicity, society and history: A festschrift in honor of the retirement of Professor Zhuang Yingzhang), ed. Zhang Weian and Lian Ruizhi, 61–96. Xinzhu: Jiao Tong University Press.

————. 2016. "The Qing, the Manchus, and Footbinding: Sources and Assumptions under Scrutiny." *Frontiers of History in China* 11.2: 279–322.

Shepherd, John R., Pan Inghai, Jan Kok, Claudia Engel, Theo Engelen, and Melissa Brown. 2006. "Group Identity and Fertility: An Evaluation of the Role of Religion and Ethnicity in the Netherlands and Taiwan." In *Positive or Preventive? Reproduction in Taiwan and the Netherlands, 1850–1940*, ed. Chuang Ying-chang, Theo Engelen, and Arthur P. Wolf, 121–61. Amsterdam: Aksant Academic Publishers.

Sheridan, James E. 1975. *China in Disintegration*. New York: Free Press.

Shi Dun. 1959. *Tongyu zaji* (Miscellaneous sorrows). Reprinted with Zhao Shijin, *Jiashen ji shi* (Record of events of the year 1644), 61–93. Beijing: Zhonghua Shuju.

Shibusawa, Keizō, ed. 1958. *Japanese Life and Culture in the Meiji Era*. Trans. and adapted Charles S. Terry. Tokyo: Ōbunsha.

Shih, Vincent Y. C. 1967. *The Taiping Ideology*. Seattle: University of Washington Press.

Shizu shilu (Veritable Records of Emperor Shizu). 1985. In *Qing shilu* (Veritable Records of the Qing), vol. 3, *Shizu Zhang huangdi shilu* (Veritable Records of Emperor Shizu Zhang [Shunzhi reign]). Beijing: Zhonghua Shuju.

Shoberl, Frederic, ed. 1823. *China, Containing the Illustrations of the Manners, Customs, Character and Costumes of the People of That Empire*. Vols. 38–39 of *The World in Miniature*. London: R. Ackermann.

Sidney D. Gamble Photographs. Archive of Documentary Arts, David M. Rubenstein Rare Book and Manuscript Library, Duke University. http://library.duke.edu/digitalcollections/gamble/.

Skinner, G. William. 1987. "Sichuan's Population in the Nineteenth Century: Lessons from Disaggregated Data." *Late Imperial China* 8.1: 1–79.

Smith, Arthur H. [1899] 1970. *Village Life in China*. Boston: Little, Brown.

Souwen xubi (Further essays on rumors). 1974. Attributed to Ming remnant subjects (*Ming yimin*). In *Biji xiaoshuo daguan zheng bian* (First collectanea of essays and fiction), vol. 3: 1550–98. Taipei: Xinxing Shuju. [Also referred to as *Souwen xubi* (Further essays in search of hearsay), attributed to Zhang Yi, 1608–1695.]

The Special Population Census of Formosa, 1905. 1909. Report of the Committee of the Formosan Special Census Investigation. Tokyo: Imperial Printing Bureau.

Spence, Jonathan D. 1999. *The Search for Modern China*. 2nd ed. New York: W. W. Norton.

———. 2002. "The K'ang-hsi Reign." In *The Cambridge History of China*, vol. 9, *The Ch'ing Empire to 1800*, pt. 1, ed. Willard J. Peterson, 120–82. Cambridge: Cambridge University Press.

Statistical Summary of Taiwan. 1912. Government-General of Taiwan. Tokyo.

Staunton, Sir George. 1798. *An Authentic Account of an Embassy from the King of Great Britain to the Emperor of China*. 3 vols. 2nd ed. London: G. Nicol.

Steere, Joseph B. 1874. "Formosa." *Journal of the American Geographical Society of New York* 6:302–34.

———. 2002. *Formosa and Its Inhabitants*. Ed. Paul Jen-kuei Li. Taipei: Institute of Taiwan History, Academia Sinica.

Stevens, Helen Norton. 1918. *Memorial Biography of Adele M. Fielde, Humanitarian*. Seattle: Pigott Printing.

Strand, David. 1989. *Rickshaw Beijing: City People and Politics in the 1920s*. Berkeley: University of California Press.

Strong, Anna Louise. 1935. *China's Millions: The Revolutionary Struggles from 1927 to 1935*. New York: Knight.

Struve, Lynn A. 1984. *The Southern Ming, 1644–1662*. New Haven, CT: Yale University Press.

———, ed. and trans. 1993. *Voices from the Ming-Qing Cataclysm: China in Tigers' Jaws*. New Haven, CT: Yale University Press.

———. 2004. "Ruling from Sedan Chair: Wei Yijie (1616–1686) and the Examination Reform of the 'Oboi' Regency." *Late Imperial China* 25.2: 1–32.

Suleski, Ronald. 2002. *Civil Government in Warlord China: Tradition, Modernization and Manchuria*. New York: Peter Lang.

Sun, E-tu Zen. 1952. "Results of Culture Contact in Two Mongol-Chinese Communities." *Southwestern Journal of Anthropology* 8.2: 182–210.

Sun Wenliang, ed. 1990. *Manzu da cidian* (Dictionary of the Manchu nationality). Shenyang: Liaoning Daxue Chubanshe.

Taiwan aikoku fujin (Patriotic women of Taiwan). 1914–15. [Kanbun / Han wen edition]. Aikoku Fujinkai Taiwan Shibu. Taipei: Nichinichi Shinpōsha.

Taiwan guanxi jishi (Taiwan folk customs). 1984. Taichung: Taiwan Sheng Wenxian Weiyuanhui. Translated into Chinese from the Japanese original, *Taiwan kanshu kiji*.

Taiwan Household Register Database. Maintained by the Program for Historical Demography, Research Center for Humanities and Social Sciences, Academia Sinica, Nankang, Taiwan.

Taiwan Sōtokufu tōkeisho (Statistical yearbook of the Government-General of Taiwan). 1899–1944. Taipei: Sōtoku Kambō.

Taiwan tōkei zuhyō (Statistics of Taiwan graphically presented). 1912. Taiwan Sōtokufu.

Taiwan Wenxian Congkan (Literary collectanea on Taiwan). 1957–72. Ed. Taiwan Yinhang Jingji Yanjiu Shi. 309 titles. Taipei: Taiwan Yinhang.

Taiwan zaiseki kan'minzoku kyōkanbetsu chōsa (An investigation of the native places of Taiwan's Han population). 1928. Taipei: Taiwan Sōtoku Kambō Chōsaka.

Taizong shilu (Veritable Records of Emperor Taizong). 1985. In *Qing shilu* (Veritable Records of the Qing), vol. 2, *Taizong Wen huangdi shilu* (Veritable Records of Emperor Taizong Wen [Tiancong and Chongde reigns]). Beijing: Zhonghua Shuju.

Takekoshi Yosaburō. 1907. *Japanese Rule in Formosa*. Trans. George Braithwaite. London: Longmans, Green.

Tan Qian. 1960. *Beiyou lu* (Records of travel in the north). Beijing: Zhonghua Shuju.

Tao, Chia-lin Pao. 1994. "The Anti-Footbinding Movement in Late Ch'ing China: Indigenous Development and Western Influence." *Jindai zhongguo funüshi yanjiu* (Research on women in modern Chinese history) 2:141–78.

Tao Zongyi. 1936. *Chuo geng lu* (Sketches after farmwork). Congshu Jicheng Chubian. Shanghai: Shangwu Yinshuguan.

Theiss, Janet M. 2004. *Disgraceful Matters: The Politics of Chastity in Eighteenth-Century China*. Berkeley: University of California Press.

Tianjin renkou shi (Population history of Tianjin). 1990. Ed. Li Jingneng. Tianjin: Nankai Daxue Chubanshe.

T'ien Ju-k'ang. 1988. *Male Anxiety and Female Chastity: A Comparative Study of Chinese Ethical Values in Ming-Ch'ing Times*. Leiden: Brill.

Tong Te-kong and Li Tsung-jen. 1979. *The Memoirs of Li Tsung-jen*. Boulder, CO: Westview Press.

Torbert, Preston. 1977. *The Ch'ing Imperial Household Department*. Cambridge, MA: Harvard University Press.

Trudgill, Peter. 2010. *Investigations in Sociohistorical Linguistics*. Cambridge: Cambridge University Press.

Ts'ai, Hui-yu Caroline. 1990. "One Kind of Control: The 'Hoko' System in Taiwan under Japanese Rule, 1894–1945." Ph.D. dissertation, Columbia University.

———. 2009. *Taiwan in Japan's Empire Building: An Institutional Approach to Colonial Engineering*. London: Routledge.

Tsurumi, E. Patricia. 1977. *Japanese Colonial Education in Taiwan, 1895–1945*. Cambridge, MA: Harvard University Press.

Turner, Christena L. 1997. "Locating Footbinding: Variations across Class and Space in Nineteenth and Early Twentieth Century China." *Journal of Historical Sociology* 10.4: 444–79.

Tuttle, Carolyn. 1999. *Hard at Work in Factories and Mines: The Economics of Child Labor during the British Industrial Revolution*. Boulder, CO: Westview Press.

Vollmer, John. 1977. *In the Presence of the Dragon Throne: Ch'ing Dynasty Costume (1644–1911) in the Royal Ontario Museum*. Toronto: Royal Ontario Museum.

Wachter, Kenneth W. 2006. *Essential Demographic Methods*. Berkeley: Department of Demography, University of California.

Wadley, Stephen A. 1991. *The Mixed-Language Verses from the Manchu Dynasty in China.* Papers on Inner Asia, no. 16. Bloomington: Research Institute for Inner Asian Studies, Indiana University.

Wakeman, Frederic, Jr. 1985. *The Great Enterprise.* 2 vols. (continuously paginated). Berkeley: University of California Press.

Wang, David Der-wei, and Shang Wei, eds. 2005. *Dynastic Crisis and Cultural Innovation: From the Late Ming to the Late Qing and Beyond.* Cambridge, MA: Harvard University Asia Center.

Wang, Siping, Jan Kok, and Chuang Ying-chang. 2008. "Who Married How? Modeling Marital Decisions in Early Twentieth Century Taiwan." *Journal of Family History* 33.4: 430–45.

Wang, Sung-hsing, and Raymond Apthorpe. 1974. *Rice Farming in Taiwan: Three Village Studies.* Nankang, Taipei: Institute of Ethnology, Academia Sinica.

Wang Bu. 1974. *Yin'an suoyu* (Trivial thoughts in Yin An). In *Biji xiaoshuo daguan san bian* (Third collectanea of essays and fiction), vol. 10: 6476–92. Taipei: Xinxing Shuju.

———. 1995. "Yin'an suoyu" (Trivial thoughts in Yin An). In *Sikuquanshu cunmu congshu, zibu* (Collectanea of works mentioned in the *cunmu* catalog of the Sikuquanshu, Masters section), ed. Sikuquanshu Cunmu Congshu Bianzuan Weiyuan Hui, vol. 249: 572–83. Jinan: Qi Lu Shushe.

Wang Fuchang. 1993. "Guangfuhou Taiwan hanren zuqun tunghun de yuanyin yu xingshi chutan" (Causes and patterns of ethnic intermarriage in postwar Taiwan). *Bulletin of the Institute of Ethnology, Academia Sinica* 76:43–96.

Wang Honggang and Fu Yuguang. 1991. *Manzu fengsu zhi* (Manchu customs). Beijing: Zhongyang Minzu Xueyuan.

Wang Jiajian. 1984. *Qingmo minchu woguo jingcha zhidu xiandaihua de licheng, 1901–1928.* (The modernization of the police system in the late Qing and early Republic). Taipei: Taiwan Shangwu Yinshuguan.

Wang Ping. 2002. *Aching for Beauty: Footbinding in China.* New York: Anchor Books.

Wang Shida. 1932–33. "Minzhengbu hukou diaocha ji gejia guji" (The Ministry of Civil Affairs census and population estimates by various experts). *Shehui kexue zazhi* 3.3 (September 1932): 264–322; 4.1 (March 1933): 68–135.

Wang Shizhen. [1691] 1982. *Chibei outan* (Casual talks by the north side of the pond). 2 vols. Beijing: Zhonghua Shuju.

———. 1992. *Yuyang shanren zizhuan nianpu* (The self-compiled biography of Yuyang Shanren). In *Wang Shizhen nianpu* (Biography of Wang Shizhen), 1–61. Beijing: Zhonghua Shuju. *Wang Shizhen nianpu* first published in the Yongzheng reign, 1723–35.

Wang Shuo. 2006. "Manchu Women in Transition: Gender Relations and Sexuality." In *Proceedings of the First North American Conference on Manchu Studies (Portland, OR, May 9–10, 2003)*, ed. Stephen A. Wadley and Carsten Naeher, vol. 1: 105–30. Wiesbaden: Harrassowitz.

Wang Xi. [1707] 2009. *Wang Wenjing gong ji: Ershisi juan, nianpu yi juan, fulu yi juan* (Collected works of Wang Wenjing: In twenty-four chapters, biography in one chapter, supplementary materials in one chapter). In *Qingdai shiwenji huibian*

(Compilation of works of the Qing dynasty), vol. 109: 92–513. Guojia Qingshi bianzuan weiyuan hui wenxian congkan (Literary collectanea of the National Committee for Compiling Qing History). Shanghai: Shanghai Guji Chubanshe.

Wang Yigang. 1960. "Riju chuqi di xisu gailiang yondong" (The campaign to reform customs in the early period of the Japanese occupation). *Taipei wenwu* 9.2–3: 13–22.

Washizu Atsuya. 1940. "Taiwan tōchi kaiko dan (10): Fuzōku shūkan no hensen oyobi kōminka undo" (Reflections on governing Taiwan (10): Changing customs and the imperialization movement). *Taiwan chihō gyōsei* 6.3: 115–28.

Wei Manzhouguo zhengfu gongbao (Manzhouguo government gazette; J: Manshūkoku seifu kōhō). 1990. 120 volumes. Reprint, Shenyang: Liaoshen Shushe.

Widmer, Ellen, and Kang-i Sun Chang, eds. 1997. *Writing Women in Late Imperial China.* Stanford, CA: Stanford University Press.

Wiens, Mi-chu. 1969. "Anti-Manchu Thought during the Early Ch'ing." *Papers on China* (East Asian Research Center, Harvard University) 22A: 1–24.

Williamson, Alexander. 1870. *Journeys in North China, Manchuria, and Eastern Mongolia; With Some Account of Corea.* 2 vols. London: Smith, Elder.

Wolf, Arthur P. 1995. *Sexual Attraction and Childhood Association: A Chinese Brief for Edward Westermarck.* Stanford, CA: Stanford University Press.

Wolf, Arthur P., and Chuang Ying-chang. 1994. "Fertility and Women's Labor: Two Negative (but Instructive) Findings." *Population Studies* 48:427–33.

Wolf, Arthur P., and Huang Chieh-shan. 1980. *Marriage and Adoption in China, 1845–1945.* Stanford, CA: Stanford University Press.

Wolf, Margery. 1968. *The House of Lim: A Study of a Chinese Farm Family.* New York: Appleton-Century-Crofts.

———. 1972. *Women and the Family in Rural Taiwan.* Stanford, CA: Stanford University Press.

———. 1985. *Revolution Postponed: Women in Contemporary China.* Stanford, CA: Stanford University Press.

Wu, David Y. H. 1981. "Child Abuse in Taiwan." In *Child Abuse and Neglect: Cross-Cultural Perspectives,* ed. Jill E. Korbin, 139–65. Berkeley: University of California Press.

Wu, Silas H. L. 1970. *Communication and Imperial Control in China.* Cambridge, MA: Harvard University Press.

Wu Hong. 1997. "Beyond Stereotypes: The Twelve Beauties in Qing Court Art and the *Dream of the Red Chamber.*" In *Writing Women in Late Imperial China,* ed. Ellen Widmer and Kang-i Sun Chang, 306–65. Stanford, CA: Stanford University Press.

Wu Wenxing. 1986. "Riju shiqi Taiwan di fangzu duanfa yundong" (The anti-footbinding and queue-cutting campaigns in Japanese-occupied Taiwan). In *Taiwan shehui yu wenhua bianqian* (Social and cultural change in Taiwan), ed. Qu Haiyuan and Zhang Yinghua, 1:69–108. Monograph Series B, no. 16. Nankang, Taipei: Institute of Ethnography, Academia Sinica.

Wu Zhenfang. 1936. *Lingnan zaji* (Random notes on Guangdong). Shanghai: Shangwu Yinshuguan.

Wu Zhenyu. 2005. *Yangji zhai conglu* (Collected records of the Yangji studio). Beijing: Zhonghua Shuju.

Wynne, Waller. 1958. "The Population of Manchuria." *International Population Statistics Reports*. Washington, DC: U.S. Department of Commerce, Bureau of the Census.

Xia Xiaohong. 2004. "Lishi jiyi de chonggou: Wan Qing 'Nan xiang, nü bu xiang' shiyi" (The invention of historical memory: Explaining the late Qing phrase "Men surrendered, women did not"). In *Wan Qing nüxing yu jindai Zhongguo* (Late Qing womanhood and modern China), by Xia Xiaohong, 114–41. Beijing: Beijing University Press.

Xie Aijie. 2002. "Dui kejia bu chanzu zhi kanfa" (Views on the rejection of footbinding among Hakka). In *Kejia wenhua xueshu yantao hui lunwen ji* (Collected essays on Hakka culture), ed. Lai Zehan, 553–85. Taipei: Xingzhengyuan Kejia Weiyuanhui.

Xie Guozhen. 1982. " 'Liaozhai zhiyi' suo sheji de Qingchu nongmin chiyi shiji buzheng" (Additional notes on the deeds of early Qing peasant uprisings referred to in the "Strange tales from Liaozhai studio"). In *Mingmo Qingchu de xuefeng* (The intellectual atmosphere of the late Ming and early Qing), by Xie Guozhen, 262–74. Beijing: Renmin Chubanshe.

Xu Jiaming. 1973. "Zhanghua pingyuan fulaoke di diyu zuzhi" (Territorial organization of Hoklorized Hakka in the Zhanghua plain). *Bulletin of the Institute of Ethnology, Academia Sinica* 36:165–90.

Xu Ke. [1914] 1989. *Tianzu kaolüe* (A study of natural feet). In *Cong shu jicheng xubian* (Additional compilation of series of collected works), vol. 212: 365–74. Taipei: Xinwenfeng Chuban Gongsi.

———. [1928] 1966. *Qingbai leichao* (Classified anthology of Qing anecdotes). 48 vols. Taipei: Taiwan Shangwu Yinshuguan.

Xu Xuzeng. [1815] 1965. "Fenghu zaji" (Miscellaneous notes from Fenghu). In *Kejia shiliao huipian* (Historical sources for the study of the Hakkas), comp. Luo Xianglin, 297–99. Hong Kong: Zhongguo Xueshe.

Yan Gui. 1941. "Baqi funü zhi chanzu" (Footbinding among Eight Banner women). In *Caifei jinghua lu* (The best of gathered fragrances), comp. Yao Lingxi, 266–67. Tianjin: Tianjin Shuju.

Yang, Martin C. 1945. *A Chinese Village: Taitou, Shantung Province*. New York: Columbia University Press.

Yang Xichun. 1988. *Manzu fengsu kao* (A study of Manchu customs). Harbin: Heilongjiang Renmin Chubanshe.

Yang Xingmei. 1998. "Nanjing guomin zhengfu jinzhi funü chanzu de nuli ji qi chengxiao" (The Nanjing government's prohibition of footbinding: Efforts and results). *Lishi yanjiu* 3:113–29.

Yantang jianwen zaji (Miscellaneous notes of things seen and heard from the hall of studies). 1968. Attributed to Wang Jiazhen. TW 254.

Yao Lingxi, comp. 1938. *Caifeilu siji* (Fourth collection of gathered fragrances). Tianjin: Tianjin Shuju.

Ye Gaohua. 2017. "Dang chanzu yushang tianranzu: Duqun ronghe yu shehui yali" (When bound feet meet natural feet: Ethnic mixing and social pressure). *Minsu quyi* 197.9: 107–33.

Ye Mengzhu. 2007. *Yue shi bian* (Collected writings examining the world). Beijing: Zhonghua Shuju.

Young, C. Walter. 1928. "Chinese Colonization in Manchuria." Pt. 2, "Settlement Zones and Economic Effects." *Far Eastern Review* 24:296–303.

Yu Zhengxie. [1833] 1965. *Guisi leigao* (Classified drafts of the thirtieth year). Taipei: Shijie Shuju.

Yuanli zhenzhi (Gazetteer of Yuanli Township). 2002. Ed. Wang Zhenxun. Miaoli County: Yuanlizhen Gongsuo.

Yuanli zhi (Annals of Yuanli). 1897. Ed. Cai Zhenfeng. TW 48.

Yung, Judy. 1995. *Unbound Feet: A Social History of Chinese Women in San Francisco*. Berkeley: University of California Press.

Zeng Qingxian. 2007. "Wang Bu he 'Yin'an suoyu'" (Wang Bu and "Trivial thoughts in Yin An"). *Fujian Shida Fuqing fenxiao xuebao* (Journal of Fuqing Branch of Fujian Normal University) 1:37–39.

Zhang, Ying. 2017. *Confucian Image Politics: Masculine Morality in Seventeenth-Century China*. Seattle: University of Washington Press.

Zhang Jiasheng. 1999. *Manzu wenhua shi* (A history of Manchu culture). Shenyang: Liaoning Minzu Chubanshe.

Zhang Qizhuo. 1984. *Manzu zai Xiuyan* (Manchus in Xiuyan). Shenyang: Liaoning Renmin Chubanshe.

Zhang Qu. [1738] 1990. *Yuedong wenjian lu* (Things seen and heard in Guangdong). Guangzhou: Guangdong Gaodeng Jiaoyu Chubanshe.

Zhang Ruohua. 2014. *Sancun jinlian yiqiannian* (One thousand years of the three-inch golden lotus). Jinan: Shandong Huabao Chubanshe.

Zhang Shiwen. [1936] 2009. *Dingxian nongcun gongye diaocha* (A survey of rural industry in Ding County). Minguo shiliao congkan, jingji gongye, 581. Zhengzhou: Daxiang Chubanshe.

Zhang Shuwen. 2008. "Rizhi shiqi Taiwan jiechanzu yundong zhi yanjiu" (A study of the anti-footbinding movement in Taiwan during the Japanese colonial period). Master's thesis, Guoli Yunlin Keji Daxue (National Yunlin University of Science and Technology).

Zhao Yi. [Ca. 1790] 1957. *Gaiyu congkao* (Miscellaneous investigations during retirement). Shanghai: Shangwu Yinshuguan.

Zhongguo minzu renkou ziliao (1990 nian renkou pucha shuju) (Tabulation on China's ethnic groups from the 1990 census). 1994. Beijing: Zhongguo Tongji Chubanshe.

Zhou Hong. 2005. *Manzu funü shenghuo yu minsu wenhua yanjiu* (Researches on the lives and folk culture of Manchu women). Beijing: Zhongguo Shehuikexue Chubanshe.

Zhou Jianxin and Zhang Haihua. 2015. *Kejia fushi de yishu renleixue yanjiu* (Anthropological researches on the art of Hakka dress). Beijing: Zhongguo Shehuikexue Chubanshe.

Zito, Angela. 2007. "Secularizing the Pain of Footbinding in China: Missionary and Medical Stagings of the Universal Body." *Journal of the American Academy of Religion* 75.1: 1–24.

Index

bound feet (*continued*)
75, 81–82, 99–100; as prerequisite to
respectability, 66–68, 95, 119, 165; pride
in, 28, 29, 54, 60–61, 66, 68, 92, 96–98,
166; released, 39–40, 42–43, 53–59,
67–68, 166, 173–75; sexual attractiveness
of, 3, 61, 98, 166; shame in, 37, 167, 173;
shape of, 82*fig.*; styles of, 66, 79–82, 169,
170. *See also* beauty; ethnic marker;
footbinding; women's feet
boundary maintenance, 12–13, 75, 91,
162–63, 211n81. *See also* ethnic marker
Boxer rebellion, 29, 114
bride-price, 62, 64, 97–98, 175, 192n3
brides, 62, 66–67, 69. *See also* marriage
Brown, Melissa, 116, 117, 190n43, 211n74

C

Canton, 100, 162, 171
census taking, 38–39, 114. *See also* footbinding, census data on; police
Chahar: census, 114–15; footbinding in,
115, 116; immigration to, 121–22; lack
of cotton handicrafts, 121–22, 143, 154;
Mongols in, 122
Chaozhou, 9, 42, 43, 66, 81, 90, 93–94,
96, 100, 188n1. *See also* Hakka; Hoklo;
Teochiu
Chen Shengxi, 25
Chihli. *See* Hebei; Zhili
child labor, 119–20. *See also* female labor in
agriculture; handicraft hypothesis
Chou Sheng-fang, 148
Christie, Dugald, 155
cities. *See* urban-rural differences
civil service exam, 8, 16–18, 48–49, 213n20.
See also class; literati
civilian population: in Beijing, 28, 150–52;
in China proper, 12–15, 17, 19–23, 144,
183n12; in Liaoning, 144, 150, 153–54,
155–57, 160, 162. *See also* banners;
bannerwomen
Cixi. *See* Empress Dowager Cixi

class: differences in footbinding, 5, 81–82,
93, 95, 96, 99, 107–9, 128, 168–72; poor
women and maid servants, 60, 93, 96,
196n42, 197n44; upward mobility, 5,
48–49; working, 29, 68. *See also* literati;
mercantile culture; status
cloth. *See* cotton textile handicrafts
Cohen, Myron, 102
communal strife, 75, 84
Communist Party, 174–76
concubines, 61, 97, 124, 192n3. *See also*
courtesans
conformist pressure: favoring footbinding, 4, 9, 47, 76, 83–84, 95–98, 109–10,
167–70; favoring natural feet, 92, 155,
160; overriding economic loss, 112,
118–20; weakened, 76, 83, 89, 92–93, 95,
152. *See also* footbinding, as hegemonic;
ridicule
Confucian views of footbinding, 3, 17–18,
27, 164; modesty and morality, 98, 167
conspicuous consumption, 3, 5, 49, 99, 109,
169–70. *See also* class; literati; mercantile culture; status
conspicuous morality, 49, 191n60
cotton: as crop, 100, 121–22, 123, 125–26,
138–39, 204n115; picking, 119, 171
cotton textile handicrafts, 118; and changes
in production of, 125–30; footbinding,
5, 131–41, 201n26; imports of, 121–3. *See
also* female labor in handicrafts; handicraft hypothesis
courtesans, 3, 4, 24–26. *See also* concubines
crops, 8, 121, 122; dry vs. wet, 99–107. *See
also* cotton
cross-cultural influence, 75–78, 83, 87–95,
163, 165
cucumber feet, 66, 80, 169. *See also*
bound feet

D

Dajia mats, 123–24
daotiao, 145

daughters. *See* fathers; mothers

Davidson, James, 123

demonstration effect, 89–95, 196n34

Denham, Captain Frank, 47

Ding county, Hebei, 116–17, 151–52; agriculture, 100–101; cloth production, 122, 127, 128; footbinding in, 47, 116–17; yarn production, 139

Ding Yizhuang, 156

divorcées, 67–68

Dong Rong, 25

Doolittle, Justus, 109, 112, 197n44

Dudgeon, John, 150, 151

Dutch East India Company, 33

E

Ebrey, Patricia, 5, 181n3

eight-legged essay, 16–18

elites. *See* class; literati; mercantile culture; status

Empress Dowager Cixi, platform shoes of, 146; anti-footbinding edict, 174

erotic attraction of bound feet, 3, 61, 98, 166

ethnic conflict, 75, 84, 161

ethnic group formation. *See* boundary maintenance; ethnic marker

ethnic groups. *See* bannerwomen; Fujianese; Guangdongese; Hakka; Hoklo; Manchus; Mongols; plains aborigines; Teochiu

ethnic marker: bound feet as, 10, 12, 23–26, 27–28, 91, 161, 163; and ethnic identity, 8–9, 28–29, 91, 164–65, 181n3, 183n14; and group competition, 75, 122, 161, 163, 164–65; natural feet as, 12, 30. *See also* boundary maintenance; queue

ethnographic accounts. *See* footbinding, accounts of

exams. *See* civil service exam

F

family budgets: contribution to, from field labor, 64, 90–92, 98, 99, 103;

contribution to, from handicrafts, 113, 118–20, 125–28, 132; and footbinding, 53, 168–69

fashion: as arbitrary, 4, 119, 164; exclusivity, 169–70; force of convention, 9, 50, 118, 156, 170, 193n14. *See also* beauty; conformist pressure; footbinding, as hegemonic; status

fathers: and daughters, 15, 27, 37; provenance, 41, 90; status concerns of, 66–67, 69, 97–98. *See also* bride-price; family budgets; footbinding, male attitudes toward

feet. *See* women's feet

female agency, 167, 188n99. *See also* Qing anti-footbinding policies, resistance to; self-binding by young women

female labor in agriculture, 50, 90–92, 99–109, 112; girls, 118–20; Hakka, 50, 89–90, 101–2, 120; as reason to release bindings, 37, 68, 166. *See also* family budgets

female labor in handicrafts, 113–20; in Chahar, 121–22; Hakka, 124; in Hebei, 125–31, 131–40; in Jiangbei, 124–25; in Liaoning, 121–22; in Taiwan, 122–24. *See also* cotton textile handicrafts; handicraft hypothesis

female writers on footbinding. *See* footbinding, accounts of

Feng Erkang, 22

Fengtian. *See* Liaoning

Fielde, Adele, 81, 93, 96, 109, 111, 168, 194n22

fields: dry vs. wet, 99–107; owner-operated, 107–9

Fong, H.D., 131

footbinding: age at, 16, 45–46, 78–83, 104–5, 111–12, 194n10; costs of, 90–92, 99, 119–20, 168–72; decline of, 142, 172–76; generational differences in, 45–47, 55–56, 58, 112, 116–17, 129–30, 173; historical origins and spread of, 4–6, 10, 12–13, 47–50, 118, 166, 168–72; measures of prevalence, 39–40, 116, 130–31; severity of, 79–83, 170. *See also* bound feet; marriage footbinding, accounts of: anecdotal, 6, 32, 117; ethnographic, 6–7, 167; female writers, 26–27; interviews, 7, 66, 117, 130, 164, 166–67; Liaoning, 156; Sichuan, 30, 61, 68, 117, 130, 166; Taiwan, 53–54, 66, 80–81, 96–97, 165–67. *See also* Confucian views of footbinding; Fielde; Little; Macgowan

footbinding, as hegemonic, 4, 9, 95–98, 120, 160, 171; elite role as key to, 49, 89, 142, 155, 161–63, 173; undermined by banner presence, 9, 153, 163, 171; undermined by Hakka presence, 9, 76, 83, 89, 91, 93, 171. *See also* conformist pressure

footbinding, census data on, 6–7; Beijing, 114–15, 151, 208n39; Chahar, 114–15; China, 113–15, 199n4, 200n5; Hebei, 114–15; Jinan, 199n4, 209n51; Liaoning, 114–15, 156–57; Qingdao, 199n4; Taiwan, 32, 34–35, 38–40; Tianjin, 114–15

footbinding, male attitudes toward, 66–67, 92, 97–98; family budget concerns, 90–91; status concerns, 36–37, 66–67, 69. *See also* bride-price; family budgets; fathers; grooms

footbinding, prevalence in China: Beijing, 115, 150–52; Chahar, 115; Ding county, 116; Hebei, 115, 133–42; Jiangbei, 100; Jiangnan, 27, 100; Liaoning, 115, 156–60; Tianjin, 115. *See also* north-south differences; rural-urban differences; *and entries for each jurisdiction*

footbinding, prevalence in Taiwan, 41, 55; by age, 46, 55, 57, 79; by agricultural regime, 103–7; by class, 81–82; by ethnic group, 41, 73–74; by handicrafts, 122–24; by marital status, 63; by prefecture, 58, 70–83, 103–5; by townships, 83–89, 105–12; urban vs. rural, 109–12

footbinding, spatial variation. *See* footbinding, prevalence in China; footbinding, prevalence in Taiwan; north-south differences; rural-urban differences

footwear for bound feet, 66, 80–82, 162, 170, 187n76, 213n23. *See also* gait; platform shoes

Fu-ge, 150, 151

Fujian: cotton handicrafts in, 122; footbinding in, 40, 109, 190n32; history of, 8, 48–49; migrants from, 8, 33, 40. *See also* Fuzhou; Quanzhou; Xiamen area; Zhangzhou

Fujianese: as provenance category in Taiwan census, 39–42. *See also* Hoklo

Fukuzawa Yukichi, 35

Fuzhou, 109, 171

G

gait, 145, 147–48, 207n25, 207n28

Gamble, Sidney, 116, 127

Gao Hongxing, 27, 205n2

Gaoyang, Hebei, 122, 127–8, 133, 135, 137, 140–41

Gates, Hill, 116, 117

Gathered Fragrances, 162

girls' labor. *See* child labor; female labor in agriculture; handicraft hypothesis

Gotō Shimpei, 34

grasscloth, 123

Gray, John Henry, 3

grooms, 62, 66–67, 69. *See also* marriage

Gu Cheng, 25

Guangdong: footbinding in, 100, 172, 192n3, 197n44, 213n20; migrants from, 8, 33, 40, 42

Guangdongese: as provenance category in Taiwan census, 39–42, 43–44, 70. *See also* Chaozhou; Hakka; Teochiu

Guangzhou (Canton), 100, 162, 171

Guanyin, 96, 196n43

H

hair and dress regulations: banner, 144–45, 162; Japan, 35; Qing, 10–12, 13, 14, 23–25.

Ko, Dorothy, 5, 22, 188n99
Kodama, Gentarō, 34

L

labor discipline hypothesis, 119–20. *See also* female labor in handicrafts; handicraft hypothesis
large-footed. *See* natural-footed women
Lattimore, Owen, 150, 161
Leong, Sow-Theng, 22, 185n49, 192n67
letting out feet. *See* bound feet, released
Levy, Howard, 22, 96, 97, 165, 166, 211n2
Li Feng, 137
Li Yu, 26, 27, 207n25
Liang Qichao, 29, 174, 185n49
Liaoning: banner population in, 144, 153–55, 157–59; census taking, 114–15, 156–57; footbinding in, 115, 144, 157–60; immigration to, 8, 152–55; lack of cotton handicrafts, 121–22, 143, 154; natural feet in, 153–56; police, 157; prestige hierarchy, 154–55, 160
light labor hypothesis, 118–20. *See also* female labor in handicrafts; handicraft hypothesis
Lin Xiantang, 52, 58
literati: as elite strata practicing footbinding, 5, 8, 17, 18, 24, 27, 48–49, 154, 174, 181n3; writing by, 17, 27, 28, 32, 164. *See also* civil service exam; class; mercantile culture
Little, Mrs. Archibald, 81, 162
Liu Cheng-yuan, 101
Liu Rushi, 24–26
Lockhart, William, 150, 151
looms: gender and use of, 127; types of, 126–27. *See also* cotton textile handicrafts

M

Macartney, George, 147, 149
Macgowan, Rev. John, 96, 97

Mackay, George Leslie, 123
Mackie, Gerry, 181n2, 193n14
MacKinnon, Stephen, 114
maidservants. *See* class
male attitudes toward footbinding. *See* footbinding, male attitudes toward
Manchuria: cranes, 146; economy, 121–22; immigration to, 152–55; natural feet in, 152–56, 161–62. *See also* Liaoning
Manchus: banners, 5, 12; conquest of China, 10; martial skills, 11–12, 14; nativism, 17; in the northeast, 122, 154; platform shoes, 145–49, 151; as term referring to bannermen, 153; women's culture, 149–50. *See also* banners; bannerwomen; Beijing; Liaoning; Qing anti-footbinding policies
Mann, Susan, 188n99
manzi, 151, 153
Mao Zhibin, 183n23, 184n38
marriage: age at, 46, 62–64; cross-ethnic, 89–90, 156; footbinding as advantage to, 57, 60, 62–64, 165–66; hypergamy, 61–62, 193n5; major, 65; minor, 65–66; uxorilocal, 65; wedding, 66–67, 69. *See also* bride-price
mats, handcrafted, 123–24, 128
mechanization, of cotton textile production, 125–31
Meiji reforms, 34–35
mercantile culture, 5, 27, 31, 49, 50, 124, 171, 191n60. *See also* class; conspicuous consumption; literati
Michie, Alexander, 153
migration: to Chahar, 121–22; to east coast of Taiwan, 87; to Hebei, 182n16; to the northeast, 8, 152–55, 159; to Taiwan, 8, 33, 45
Ming dynasty: collapse of, 10, 13; precedents, 11, 14, 17, 23; spread of footbinding during, 5, 10, 48–49, 118, 201n26
Ming loyalism, 5, 10, 12–13, 23–26, 27–28, 29
minor marriage. *See* marriage
missionaries, 29, 167

Mongols: in banners, 12, 154; contact with Chinese, 122, 156, 161, 163

mother-daughter relationships, 48, 98, 197n51

mothers: binding daughters' feet, 27, 37, 54, 56, 68, 97, 117, 120; criteria for sons' brides, 60–61, 62; foster, status concerns of, 65–66, 69; provenance of, 41, 90. *See also* marriage; mother-daughter relationships

mothers-in-law, 175; status concerns, 56. *See also* marriage; mothers

Mukden (Shenyang), 153, 155–56

N

Nagao Ryūzō, 22

Nanjing government. *See* Republican government

nationalism and footbinding: anti-Qing, 10, 29; Republican, 24, 29, 173–74. *See also* anti-Manchu sentiment and footbinding

Nationalist Party, 174. *See also* Republican government

natural feet: pride in, 50, 146; as Qing ethnic marker, 12, 30. *See also* natural-footed women

natural-footed women: derisive names for, 96; identity as Han, 28–29; as "never-bound," 40. *See also* bannerwomen; class; Hakka; ridicule

northeast. *See* Manchuria

Northern Expedition, 113, 175

north-south differences: in agriculture, 8, 99–100; in binding, 3, 5, 27–28, 47, 99–101; within Taiwan, 101–7. *See also* footbinding, prevalence in China; footbinding, prevalence in Taiwan; rural-urban differences

Nurhaci, 11, 14

O

Oboi regents, 17, 18, 30

opium smoking, Taiwan, 35–36, 39

outlier townships, 86–89, 90, 106–9

owners vs. tenants, 107–9, 154, 172

P

patriarchy, 4, 45, 48, 76, 98, 168, 172

Patriotic Women of Taiwan, 53

Penghu, 101

photography, 145–46, 206n11

picul (unit of weight), 139

plains aborigines, 33, 39, 40–42, 70; absence of footbinding, 44–45; cross-cultural influences, 76, 87, 91, 190n43; rush mat weaving, 124

platform shoes, 145–49, 151, 154, 156, 162, 207n28; Japanese, 206n15; Korean, 206n15; Mongolian, 145

police: Beijing, 114–15, 151; Hebei, 114–15; Liaoning, 157; Taiwan, 38; Tianjin, 115. *See also* footbinding, census data on

poor women. *See* class

prestige. *See* status

prevalence of footbinding. *See* footbinding, measures of prevalence; footbinding, prevalence in China; footbinding, prevalence in Taiwan

Prince Qing, 114

Princess Duoluo Ganzhu, 146

Pu Songling, 26–27

Pu-Qua, 147

Putnam Weale, B. L., 154–55

Q

Qian Qianyi, 24, 27

Qian Yong, 13, 19–21, 27, 30, 173

Qianlong emperor, 147

Qing anti-footbinding policies: post-conquest, 13–23, 144–45, 174; pre-conquest, 5, 10–12; resistance to, 10, 12–13, 16, 23, 24–26, 27, 30–31, 188n99. *See also* queue

Qing dynasty: conquest, 10; origins, 11; spread of footbinding in, 5, 10, 12–13,

Steere, Joseph, 101

stigma: of bound feet, 36, 167; of natural feet, 9, 89, 96, 169–70, 173; of plains aborigines, 45. *See also* ridicule, shame

straw handicrafts, 128, 130, 132, 135

Strong, Anna Louise, 175

Struve, Lynn, 184nn37, 39

Sun Zhixie, 23–26

Suzhou, 27, 109–10, 171

Swatow, 43, 81, 93–94, 96, 109

T

Taibei prefecture, 58, 103, 110–11

Tainan prefecture, 37, 42–43, 52

Taipei Natural Foot Society, 36, 42, 58

Taiping rebellion, 29

Taiwan: handicrafts, 123–24; historical background, 8, 33–37, 47–50, 51–54; immigration to, 8, 33; interviews in, 53–54, 66, 80–81, 96–97, 165–67; lack of cotton handicrafts, 122–23. *See also* anti-footbinding, Taiwan; female labor in agriculture; footbinding, prevalence in Taiwan; Hakka; Hoklo; marriage

Taiwan Assimilation Society, 52–53

Taiwan Daily News, 53

Taiwan Household Register Database, 65, 90

Taizhong prefecture, 52, 58

Tan Qian, 24, 25

Tao Zongyi, 5, 213n15

"Tartar," 147, 149, 150–51, 207n18. *See also* bannerwomen, Manchus

Teochiu, 33, 42, 43, 93. *See also* Chaozhou; Hoklo

textiles. *See* cotton textile handicrafts; female labor in handicrafts

three degenerate practices, 35–36, 39, 189n11. *See also* Han customs

three-inch golden lotus, 80

Tianjin: census taking, 114–15; factory yarn from, 127, 137; footbinding in, 115, 142; police, 114–15

tonsure. *See* queue

Tujia, 211n74

U

unbinding. *See* bound feet, released

urban-rural differences: in decline of footbinding, 142, 173–76; in footbinding prevalence, 109–12, 171–72

uxorilocal marriage. *See* marriage

W

Wang Bu, 15, 18–21, 30

Wang Duanshu, 27

Wang Shizhen, 16–21

Wang Xi, 15–18, 20, 23, 30, 184n40

Wang Yongjiang, 157

warlord era, 113, 157

warps, using machine-spun yarn, 123, 126–27, 204n110. *See also* cotton textile handicrafts; female labor in handicrafts; wefts

wealth. *See* class; conspicuous consumption; mercantile culture

weaving. *See* Baodi; cotton textile handicrafts; female labor in handicrafts; Gaoyang

wedding, 62, 66–67, 69. *See also* marriage

wefts, using hand-spun yarn, 126–27, 128–29. *See also* cotton textile handicrafts, female labor in handicrafts; warps

widows, 67–68; chastity of, 49; suicides by, 49, 191n60

Williamson, Alexander, 153, 160

Wolf, Arthur P., 66

women's culture, 167, 169, 188n99

women's feet: bowed, 81, 145; cucumber, 66, 80, 169; currently bound, 39, 115–16, 130; *daotiao*, 145; ever-bound, 40, 130; released, 39, 42–43, 54–59; willow branch, 145. *See also* bound feet; natural feet; natural-footed women

work. *See* female labor in agriculture; female labor in handicrafts
Wuhan, 175

X

Xiamen area, 40, 96
Xie Qian, 23
Xu Ke, 25, 156
Xu Shichang, 157, 209n58
Xu Xuzeng, 50, 192n67

Y

Yalu river zone, 158–60
Yan Xishan, 214n31
Yangzhou, 27, 109, 110, 124, 143, 171
yarn. *See* cotton textile handicrafts; female labor in handicrafts; warps; wefts

Ye Mengzhu, 18, 21, 22, 49, 184n42
Yilan prefecture, 52, 58, 110–11
Young, C. Walter, 159
Yu Huai, 26, 27
Yu Zhengxie, 13, 19–22, 30
Yuan Mei, 26, 207n25
Yuan Shikai, 114–15
Yunnan, 102, 211n74

Z

Zhang Qu, 172, 197n44
Zhangjiakou (Kalgan), 161
Zhangzhou, 33, 49, 122; as sub-ethnic group in Taiwan, 73, 75
Zhao Yi, 5, 19–22, 27
Zheng regime, 33
Zhili (Chihli), 114, 153, 155, 200nn7,13. *See also* Hebei